Confession and Psychoanalysis

CHRISTIAN ARABIC TEXTS IN TRANSLATION

SERIES EDITOR
Stephen J. Davis (Yale University)

Advisory Board
Jimmy Daccache (Yale University)
Mark Swanson (Lutheran School of Theology)
Alexander Treiger (Dalhousie University)

Christian Arabic Texts in Translation (CATT) is a series dedicated to making Christian Arabic works available in English translation. Publications include works of biblical interpretation and commentary, treatises engaging with theological and ethical issues vital to Christian–Muslim encounters, as well as saints' lives, sermons, histories, and philosophical and scientific literature produced by Arabic-speaking Christians living in the medieval Islamicate world. Each accurate and accessible translation is presented with a concise, lucid, and engaging introduction to the historical context, authorship, and literary content of the work and selected critical notes providing resources for further study (biblical citations, bibliographical references, linguistic clarifications, etc.). These translations make it possible for Christian Arabic texts to be introduced to college, seminary, and graduate school curricula.

Confession and Psychoanalysis

Spiro Jabbour

Translated by Aaron Frederick Eldridge

FORDHAM UNIVERSITY PRESS
New York • 2026

Fordham University Press also publishes its books in a variety of electronic formats. Some content that appears in print may not be available in electronic books.

Visit us online at www.fordhampress.com.

For EU safety/GPSR concerns: Mare Nostrum Group B.V., Mauritskade 21D, 1091 GC Amsterdam, The Netherlands, gpsr@mare-nostrum.co.uk

Library of Congress Cataloging-in-Publication Data available online at https://catalog.loc.gov.

Printed in the United States of America

28 27 26   5 4 3 2 1

First edition

To his excellency, our venerable master and monastic Patriarch Yuḥannā the Tenth; I present to him this monastic book that stages an encounter between the monastic inheritance and the contemporary psychological sciences, seeking his approval, blessings, and his apostolic invocation, that this book may be of benefit to readers and a pure service to the Church.

Dayr al-Ḥarf
The Feast of the Repose of the Theotokos, 2013
His humble son, Deacon Spiro Jabbour

O my brethren, there should not be among you many teachers, knowing that we acquire by this a more severe judgement, for indeed we all stumble exceedingly. Anyone who does not stumble in speech is a perfect man, likewise capable of ordering his whole body with a bridle.

The Apostle James[1]

Woe to him who writes these elegies! For I am a victim of what I describe, and I have not the meagerest sigh of regret. Woe to me, I am he who writes while I weep bitterly, yet I have not begun the work of repentance. Woe to me, I am he who says the truth yet I do not do good. Woe to me, I am he who praises good and does evil.

Anba Isaiah[2]

If monks are found whose evil habits still command them, yet they are able to teach others, even if by mere speech, then let them teach. Perhaps they will be ashamed one day of their sayings, and begin to implement what they say . . . [3]

But woe to us, we wretches! We have left the path of the Holy Fathers, and for this reason we are bereft of all spiritual work.

Maximos the Confessor[4]

The beginning of salvation for every human is, rather, to condemn himself.

Evagrios[5]

Call yourself wretch. Say before God at all times: I am dust and clay, all sediment . . .

Evagrios[6]

1. 1 James 3:1–2.

2. Discourse 29:76, 85–87. [See Chryssavgis and Penkett's English translation, *Abba Isaiah of Scetis Ascetic Discourses*, 241–242.—Trans.]

3. Unattributed.—Trans.

4. *On the Ascetic Life*, 1.26. [See Sherwood's English translation, *The Ascetic Life*, 117.—Trans.]

5. *PG* 79, 1249 C.

6. Cited in Hausherr, *Les leçons d'un contemplatif* [Lessons from a contemplative], 111–112. See also Jabbour, *al-Tajalliyāt fī dustūr al-īmān* [Disclosures in the Constitution of Faith].

Contents

A Note on the Translation — *ix*

List of Abbreviations — *xiii*

Translator's Introduction — *xv*

The Eulogy of Metropolitan Ephraim Kyriakos for the Funeral of Spiro Jabbour — *xliii*

Author's Preface to the First Edition — *xlv*

Author's Preface to the Second Edition — *liii*

1 The Remembrance of Death — 1

2 The Child Is a Person — 8

3 Confession in the New Testament — 10
Confession in church usage, 18

4 Confession in Psychoanalysis — 21

5 The Sense of Guilt — 29
1. Ambivalence, 33 • 2. Ambivalence of the spirit and the body, 55 • 3. The sense of guilt, 58 • 4. The sense of guilt and the spiritual life, 62

6 The Confession of Transgressions 65
How do we confess? 71 • How does the spiritual elder guide the monastic? 75 • Of what kind is this war? 83

7 The Essence of Monastic Confession 94
The Hesychasts, 119

8 The Question of Psychosomatic Medicine, Philosophically Considered 121

9 Reiteration 130
Confession for churches in the world, 135 • Confession and repentance, 137 • Confession and communion, 137 • The prayer of absolution, 138 • Objection, 140 • Confession at the Monastery of the Holy Spirit, 142

10 Repentance and Joy 147
Excursus, 149 • Supplication, 150

11 A Historical-Geographical Fragment 152
1. The Current of Pseudo-Dionysius, 154
2. The Current of Makarios, 156

Glossary *159*

Works Cited *163*

Index *177*

A Note on the Translation

This translation of Jabbour's *Confession and Psychoanalysis* has sought to be useful to both scholars and new readers. At times quite aphoristically, the text explores the distinct terrains of Orthodox Christian asceticism, Freudian psychoanalysis, Islamic theology, and broader Arabic literature, philosophy, and poetics. For this reason—especially given the fact that the references to the languages of Islamic tradition and psychoanalysis largely appear in the conceptual grammar of the text, not in its explicit citations—I have undertaken extensive annotations to guide the reader.

Arabic words and names have been transliterated into the Latin alphabet according to the *International Journal of Middle East Studies* (*IJMES*) system; full diacritical marks have been maintained except where an established English transliteration already exists (e.g., Ahmed Shawqi, Suhrawardi, halal). Moreover, this translation occasionally retains the original Arabic terms in the text, provided that doing so is not highly disruptive to the reader—for example, the term *ṣūfī*. Where Jabbour translates Greek writings into Arabic, predominantly those of Maximos the Confessor and Gregory Palamas, a literal translation of his Arabic rendition has been maintained, although the original Greek text was consulted. Likewise, the numerous citations of the Old Testament, the Psalter, Epistles, and the four Gospels have been translated from the Arabic text rather than standardized according to one of the many existing English translations. This was done, in part, because Jabbour moves between multiple Arabic translations of these texts and often tracks their specific word choice—something that would be impossible to reflect in translation if one resorted to a standard English translation. When referencing the Psalms, Jabbour almost always uses the Septuagint numbering (LXX), which is used in the Orthodox Church. My notes likewise maintain the Septuagint numbering of the Psalter.

Finally, a great deal of effort has gone into completing Jabbour's many and, at times, fragmentary bibliographic citations. This has not always been entirely successful and has required the extrapolation of references. The list of his own writings, in particular, is far more extensive than the works cited here, but many of them are out of print. Jabbour's in-text references, moreover, have been moved to footnotes wherever possible, and their formatting has been standardized and corrected.

I am extremely grateful to the many people who made this translation possible. First, to Archimandrite Youssef ʿAbdullah, Father Ibrahim Sarruj, Raymond and Jamil Younes, and the monks of Mār Georgios. I am also exceedingly grateful to Stephen J. Davis for his patient editorial guidance, to the editorial board of the Christian Arabic Texts in Translation series (Mark Swanson, Alexander Treiger, and Jimmy Daccache), to Omnia El Shakry for her exceptionally encouraging and gracious comments, to the many friends and colleagues with whom I consulted in the course of producing this translation, especially Basit K. Iqbal and Daria Eldridge, and to Stefania Pandolfo, without whom the desire for such a project of translation would never have found its footing.

On Method

This work employs a method of translation and exegesis that derives from attending to the "grammar of concepts," a notion elaborated by Wittgenstein in his later writings and lectures.[1] The insight hit upon by this notion of grammar—here understood expansively as denoting the *material articulations* that become threaded together—is that a concept does not rely on the stipulation of a definition for its coherence. That is, a definition does not impart meaning to a concept. Moreover, insofar as "grammar" is what coheres a concept, it is bound up in the practices of life and the social relations that determine it. This condition of being threaded together means that concepts are constitutively open to their outside, the "family resemblances" that shift into other conceptual spaces of articulation

1. See his *Philosophical Investigations* and *The Blue and Brown Books.*

(practices and ways of speaking). The imbrication of grammars and practices implies that it is, as Talal Asad writes, "analogical reasoning (as opposed to deductive logic) that facilitates extensions of meaning."[2]

This translation and its annotations engage in such a practice of analogical reasoning, one which is occasioned by the textual practice of Jabbour himself, who set out to think psychoanalysis and Orthodox monastic confession together. This work of 'thinking together' is grammatical; it is articulated in the material gathering of these concepts, in the specific and concrete imbrication of their articulations. Jabbour's original Arabic text draws out resonances across multiple grammars—Freudian psychoanalysis, Orthodox Christianity, Islam, Sufism, Arab poetics, and French literature—without first establishing definitions that would delimit the possibility of their comparison. Their resonances, and insofar as they already have concrete meanings that are creatively worked upon and transformed, precede their definitions.

Working across grammars, then, is a work of what is in Greek *logos* or in Arabic *nuṭq*, a mode of thinking that is both a determinative mode of speech (*naṭaqa*) and a gathering together (*legein*). This gathering is, at once, a threading together and a growing outward; it is both a work of inside (the flourishing of a tradition, a concept) and outside (as a practice of alterity). Translation participates in this analogical work; its possibility is given in the grammatical resonances that striate languages and traditions as they are concretized into discrete articulations. "Translation is a mode [*eine Form*]," Walter Benjamin writes in his aphoristic rumination on the work of translation.[3] Tracing out the resonances of the original text's various conceptual grammars, which are, by necessity, the material traces of the original's "afterlife," has a transformative effect on the language of translation precisely because the translation's text *figures* the grammars of the original. The fragments of the concrete grammars in the original are thus inherently open to creative expansion precisely because they are outgrowths of various forms of life. *Ghayḍ min fayḍ*, "but a drop in the ocean," is a phrase that Jabbour uses often in this text.

This might be theologically speculated upon through the language of Maximos the Confessor, one of Jabbour's most important interlocutors, in the following way: every *logos* participates, as a harmonization of multiple

2. "Thinking about Religion through Wittgenstein," 406.
3. "Die Aufgabe des Übersetzers [The Task of the Translator]."

singularities, in the divine *Logos.* Translation manifests what Benjamin calls the "inner relationship between languages." The weaving together of a translation and its original is a practice that takes place in relation to an alterity that discloses a creative and divine source; an ocean without shore. Benjamin ends his essay on translation with what he takes to be the exemplary image of translation's work: "the interlinear version of the Holy Scriptures." This translation has been undertaken as an attempt toward such an analogical and interlinear work.

Abbreviations

SC Sources Chrétiennes

SE *The Standard Edition of the Complete Psychological Works of Sigmund Freud*, ed. James Strachey. 24 volumes. London: Hogarth Press, 1953–1974

PG *Patrologiae Cursus Completus, Series Graeca*, ed. Jacques-Paul Migne. 161 volumes. Paris: Imprimerie Catholique, 1857–1866

Translator's Introduction

Spiro Jurji Jabbour was born in Muzayraa, in the Syrian province of al-Lādhiqīyya (Latakia), in 1923, on the feast of Spyridon the Wonderworker, for whom he was named. Like the fourth-century bishop, Jabbour would become known for his fiery orations, gaining a reputation as a trenchant and outspoken agitator as well as a prolific writer. He studied law in Damascus before the Second World War and became an active and early member of the *Rūm*[1] Orthodox Christian revivalist organization, *ḥarakat al-shabība al-urthūdhuksiyya* ("the Orthodox Youth Movement"); he went to Paris from the beginning of 1959 to the end of 1961 where he briefly studied theology at St. Sergius Orthodox Theological Institute and then humanities at the Sorbonne. He became a deacon of the Antiochian Orthodox Church in 1972 at the Monastery of Mār Girgis in the village of al-Mishtāya, Syria.

Jabbour worked for a time as a lawyer in the Rūm Antiochian Orthodox religious court. After a brief period at the Monastery of Mār Georgios (St. George) in Dayr al-Ḥarf, Lebanon, Jabbour left to return to Syria—at the time undergoing a reactionary restoration of private property relations and the establishment of a comprehensive surveillance state under Hafez

1. This term refers to the Chalcedonian Orthodox churches in the Arabic-speaking world. The term derives from the Arabic designation for "Roman" and refers to an association with the Byzantine Empire, many of the inhabitants and rulers of which were co-religionists of those following the Orthodox Patriarchates of Antioch and Jerusalem.

al-Assad[2]—near the beginning of Lebanon's decade-and-a-half-long war (1975–1990). According to one source, and perhaps due to his regular confrontations with church leadership, Jabbour was deported from Syria over twenty times and imprisoned seven. He stayed in Homs for several years, during which he wrote many pieces, including the present volume, which was originally published around 1990, possibly in that city; a second edition was published in 2014 by the Diocese of Akkar and its Dependencies.

He returned to the Monastery of Mār Georgios in 1995. Following another dispute with church leaders, Jabbour was laicized and stripped of his diaconal status. He then went north to Tripoli and stayed at the Monastery of Ruqād al-Sayyida (Dormition of the Theotokos) in the village of Bkiftīn. He later returned for the final time to Mār Georgios, where he completed his life in ascetic struggle until his repose in 2018.

I did not have the benefit of meeting Abouna Spiro; he died not long before I first came to Dayr al-Ḥarf and its monastery. At that time, so soon after his passing, he was often invoked by the monastics there and especially by Shaykh Youssef ('Abdullāh), now head of the monastery, who gave me his blessing and permission to undertake this translation.

Confession and Psychoanalysis (*al-I'tirāf wa-l-taḥlīl al-nafsī*) was, according to the text, composed in Homs in 1983. It is one of numerous writings that Jabbour produced throughout his long life: theological treatises, a study of Arabic semiotics, studies in church law, scriptural exegesis, short stories, a play, hagiographies, and translations of the Gospels of John and Matthew from Greek into Arabic. *Confession and Psychoanalysis* is not, however, a strictly theological treatise or a textual exegesis, although it includes elements of both. Instead, it must be squarely placed in the (typically monastic) genealogy of spiritual guidance (*irshād*), an interlocution between a disciple and a spiritual elder (*shaykh*). This is noted in the text itself; Jabbour was queried by a woman from Homs concerning confession (*i'tirāf*), the result of which is this text.

This genre of writing, notable for the ascetic guidance provided by the various authors quoted in this book—Isaac the Syrian, Maximos the Confessor, and Gregory Palamas, to name a few—has as its principal site a dialogue between the disciple and the elder. The production of this text is thus only an artifact of that encounter, in the same way that an oral excursus in the salon of a monastery, wherein a crowd gathers to listen to

2. See Batatu, *Syria's Peasantry*, and Wedeen, *Ambiguities of Domination*.

the words of an elder answering a query put to him by a seeker, might subsequently circulate as written "sayings." In this way, the singularity of the exchange between two persons, which today may circulate not only in print but also in audio and video recordings, would expand into the multiplicity of a wider audience. Even while its inception was in a specific context of dialogue, *Confession and Psychoanalysis* was, in Jabbour's words, an "attempt to illumine the growing number of those holding to spiritual endeavors, men and women monastics, and cultivated readers."[3]

This audience and the concrete interventions of the text, as the author attests, concern the entangled histories of Antiochian Orthodox Christian revival and the return of monasticism to a colonial and postcolonial Mashriq. The former is marked by the establishment of the Orthodox Youth Movement (often known by the French acronym "MJO," Mouvement de Jeunesse Orthodoxe) in 1942, an organization that Jabbour joined in its infancy while he was living in coastal Syria. The movement was founded by a number of university students in Beirut with the intention of renewing the institutional and spiritual life of their church, the Orthodox Patriarchate of Antioch, whose historical jurisdiction is largely in Syria and Lebanon. This movement, whose activities continue to this day, was originally patterned after *L'Action catholique*, and its membership was involved in anti- and postcolonial struggles that included protesting the French occupation of Syria and Lebanon, working with organized labor, and supporting the Palestinian struggle after the Nakba.[4] Indeed, Jabbour was a lifelong and outspoken advocate of the Palestinian cause.

A main impetus of the MJO's endeavors included making new political claims on and revitalizing Orthodox church institutions. While the former appeared in the increased democratization of decision-making within ecclesial structures, the latter had a more lasting effect in reforming educational curricula and training clergy, culminating in the establishment of a center for theological learning at Balamand Monastery in the mid-1960s.

3. Jabbour, preface to the first edition of *Confession and Psychoanalysis.*

4. For an anthology of the MJO's writings, see *Anṭākiyya tatajaddad*; Ḥaydar, *Tarjamāt qiyāmiyya*. Georges Khodr, one of the architects of the revival movement and now retired Archbishop of Mount Lebanon, has contributed numerous pieces to the Lebanese newspaper *An-Nahar*. See also his writings on Jerusalem, *al-Quds*, and his aphoristic autobiography, *Law ḥakaytu masrā al-ṭufūla* along with Nuha Jurayj's English translation, *The Ways of Childhood.*

The resulting bourgeois emphases on liturgy, youth education, and clerical training departed from the more radical claims that the movement had made on church authority, the latter's relation to broader social and political struggles, as well as modern experiments in collective monastic life. The bureaucratization of church authority in 1972, with the ratification of a new synodal constitution—but also the collapse of political pan-Arabism, the Israeli occupation of what remained of Palestine post-1967, Syria's social and economic retrenchment, and the beginning of Lebanon's destructive and multifaceted war—contributed to the collapse of certain political horizons of struggle. At the same time, these struggles produced, as a counterpoint, a movement toward monasticism, effected as the withdrawal to and re-inhabitation of derelict Orthodox monasteries in Lebanon and Syria. Members of the MJO, a group of women who would eventually settle at the Monastery of Mār Yaʿqūb (St. Jacob) in northern Lebanon, were the first to make a concerted effort to restart communal monastic life in the 1940s. Following them was a group of men who would take up residence at Mār Georgios in Dayr al-Ḥarf,[5] the monastery that served as Jabbour's home community.

Efforts to establish monastic communities in Lebanon grew during the war[6] and they have further burgeoned in the last three decades. These monastic sites have become major communal centers at the same time that they host a collective gesture of radical reorientation, one that shifts the coordinates of human struggle in the world as being under the penumbra of a divine trial.[7] This torsion in the project of postcolonial renewal, intensified by the reactionary collapse of Arab revolutionary social projects,[8] is marked by the question of incapacity that it poses for human endeavors and that is taken up by these monastic collectives.

As *Confession and Psychoanalysis* shows, the question of incapacity is manifest in the topography shared by psychoanalysis and a monastic science of the soul. Both sciences mark the emergence of a disturbing truth,

5. For more on this monastery and its community, see Kassatly, *La communauté monastique de Deir el Harf.*

6. See Metropolitan Ephraim Kyriakos's remarkable account of his founding the monastery of the Archangel Michael during Lebanon's war, "Visite de Mgr Ephrem de Tripoli à l'Institut Saint-Serge."

7. See Eldridge and Iqbal, "A Tropics of Estrangement."

8. Bardawil, *Revolution and Disenchantment.*

the problem of what Jabbour calls, in this text and elsewhere, the *muzayyaf*, the "counterfeit." Both psychoanalysis and monasticism point to a constitutive groundlessness that runs through personal and collective life, which is at once the historical aftermath of cultural life and an ontological gap. The problem presented by the counterfeit traditions and identities of the present, what Jabbour calls "counterfeit Christianity" and "counterfeit struggle," is not easily resolved, but demands an ethical engagement. Jabbour finds such an engagement in both ascetic practice and psychoanalysis.[9]

It is for this reason that *Confession and Psychoanalysis* cites the Orthodox "monastic inheritance" and its "procedure," in the forms of confession and spiritual interlocution, as the critical path lately opened for the "revivalist youth" in Lebanon and Syria.[10] Insofar as this ascetic and psychoanalytic science, staged through speech, allows for the problem of the counterfeit to manifest, it marks a struggle to seek God at the very site of cultural loss. This mode articulates another means of attending to the collapse of social life and cultural devastation; it pivots on, rather than abandons, the terms of failed social struggle and its disorientating effect.

Jabbour's writing finds an ally in his contemporary, the critic and artist Jalal Toufic, who draws on the variegated histories of disasters in the traditions of Islam, Christianity, and Judaism, the Nakba, and the wars in Iraq and Lebanon, to outline the counterfeit as a problem of the double, one that follows what Toufic calls "the surpassing disaster." In this disaster, the double threatens to surreptitiously replace the traditional resources of cultural and social life with its counterfeited simulacra. The danger, as *Confession and Psychoanalysis* also attests, is between those who recognize

9. In his second seminar, *The Ego in Freud's Theory and the Technique of Psychoanalysis*, Lacan demarcates egoism from a problem of self-love:

> In La Rochefoucauld, what is scandalous is not so much that for him self-love is the basis of all human behaviour, but rather that it is deceiving, inauthentic. There is a hedonism specific to the ego, and which is precisely what lures us, that is, which at one and the same time frustrates us of our immediate pleasure and of the satisfactions which we can draw from our superiority with respect to this pleasure. (10)

As Lacan explains, the torsion of a moralist tradition is effected by the introduction of a "so-called perspective of truth into the observation of moral conduct and mores . . . you are deluded, no doubt, but the truth lies elsewhere" (10).

10. Jabbour, *Confession and Psychoanalysis*, 136.

the surpassing disaster and the unavailability of tradition, and those who "as a cheap reaction, are advocating a return to tradition without noticing that it has been withdrawn."[11] In Toufic's description of the problematic of the counterfeit, which draws on Freud's own thoughts on the double and uncanny,[12] there is a splitting insofar as what "*was materially present* . . . [is] unavailable to perception except through a resurrection"; "what is materially still there is immaterially withdrawn as a consequence of a surpassing disaster (that was seemingly averted)."[13] As Jabbour avers in the present text, recognizing this withdrawal is the beginning of struggle.

In this way, *Confession and Psychoanalysis* participates in as it demarcates a particular historical conjuncture in contemporary Arab Orthodox tradition, one in which the terms of postcolonial revival, both of Antiochian Orthodoxy and social struggle in the Mashriq, are modulated within the loss of certain horizons of action and forms of life. The archive of the text is constituted, principally, by the scriptures—the Psalter, the Septuagint, and the Gospels—and the Greek writings of Orthodox Christian monastics, compiled in part from the *Philokalia*, the masterwork by Nikodimos the Athonite and Makarios of Corinth, into which Orthodox Christian ascetic writings from the fourth to the fifteenth century were gathered into a single collection. Maximos the Confessor, the seventh-century Byzantine scholar and martyr, and Gregory Palamas, the fourteenth-century monk and apologist, are central authorities in the text. The latter was responsible for codifying the forms of Orthodox asceticism practiced on Mount Athos, which had come to be grouped together and labelled as "hesychasm" (meaning "stillness" in Greek). The ascetic practice of the hesychasts and their claims to witness the uncreated and divine light of God later became subjected to intense criticism by modern Roman Catholic scholars like Irénée Hausherr and Martin Jugie. Both are named in this text,[14] along with some of Palamas's main contemporary Orthodox defenders, John Meyendorff and Vladi-

11. Toufic, *The Withdrawal of Tradition Past a Surpassing Disaster*, 29. See also Omnia El Shakry's engagement with Toufic in "The Work of Illness in the Aftermath of a 'Surpassing Disaster'."

12. See Freud, "The Uncanny" (1919), *SE* 17:218–256.

13. Toufic, *The Withdrawal of Tradition Past a Surpassing Disaster*, 25.

14. See Hausherr, *La méthode d'oraison hésychaste*, as well as Jugie, "Palamas, Grégoire" and "Palamite (controverse)," 1735–1818; Jugie, *Theologia dogmatica Christianorum Orientalium*.

mir Lossky.[15] These debates, however, are only noted in passing by Jabbour, who routinely sidesteps the trap of academic theology in order to emphasize the need to engage in ascetic struggle and its science of the soul.

It is in the context of this struggle that Jabbour explicates Freud's formulation of the unconscious, its effects, and the psychoanalytic therapy—the "talking cure"—that it compels. For Jabbour, the modern concept of the unconscious reiterates the problem of the counterfeit and the infidelity of the soul/psyche. As Freud writes in his text on jokes:

> These opponents of the unconscious . . . had never realized the idea that the unconscious is something which we really do not know, but which we are obliged by compelling inferences to supply; they had understood it as being something capable of becoming conscious but which was not being thought of at the moment, which did not occupy "the focal point of attention" . . . I have also formed an impression that fundamental emotional resistances stand in the way of accepting "the unconscious," and that these are based on the fact that no one wants to get to know his unconscious and that the most convenient plan is to deny its possibility altogether.[16]

The unconscious not only marks a gap, an "unknown," but an unknowing that is, at once, constitutive of human life and repressed.

Throughout his text Jabbour draws from both of what are known as Freud's two topographies: the first is his initial formulation of the preconscious, conscious, and unconscious systems; the second subsequently developed into the now popularly known concepts of the Ich, Es, and Über-ich (ego, id, super-ego; or, more literally, I, it, and above-I).[17] Jabbour utilizes Freud's studies of ego-formation as well as his investigations

15. See Norman Russell's succinct account of the terms of this debate and its history in *Gregory Palamas and the Making of Palamism in the Modern Age*, especially his first chapter, "Martin Jugie and the Invention of Palamism," 45–74. The debates around so-called "Palamism" and hesychastic practice have grown considerably in recent decades. See, for example, Bradshaw, *Aristotle East and West*; the four-volume special issue series "St. Gregory Palamas" in *Analogia*; and, in Arabic, Isṭfān, *Aʿmidat al-īmān al-urthūdhuksī* [Pillars of the Orthodox faith].

16. *Jokes and their Relation to the Unconscious* (1905), *SE* 8:162.

17. See Freud, "The Unconscious" (1915), *SE* 14:159–215; "The Ego and the Id" (1923), *SE* 19:1–66.

into the preponderance of the unconscious in the pathologies of daily life. In much the same way that *Confession and Psychoanalysis* places theology in a secondary relation to ascetic struggle, psychoanalytic theory is offered here only insofar as its concepts illuminate particular problematics in monastic and ascetic practice; unlike the monastic literature that constitutes the initial side of this encounter, only one work of Freud, *Beyond the Pleasure Principle,* is explicitly cited.

Despite this, Jabbour's reading of Freud appears to be extensive. His knowledge of psychoanalysis was drawn from Arabic, French, and English translations of Freud (he did not, it seems, read German), as well as from the writings of other analysts, such as Ernest Jones, Edward Glover, and Oskar Pfister. In one of his two contributions to the 1967 volume *L'ambivalence dans la culture arabe,* an article entitled "L'interprétation psychanalytique des *ad'dad*" (The psychoanalytic interpretation of contronyms),[18] Jabbour cites a French compilation of Freud's essays (*Essais de psychanalyse* [Essays on psychoanalysis]).[19] This collection included several works that resonate with the text at hand: *Beyond the Pleasure Principle,* "The Ego and the Id," "Group Psychology and the Analysis of the Ego," and "Thoughts for the Times on War and Death."[20] Along with other critical writings of Freud,[21] Jabbour also cites in its French translation, Otto Fenichel's seminal *The Psychoanalytic Theory of Neuroses,* and Roland Dalbiez's *La méthode psychanalytique et la doctrine freudienne* (The

18. In Arabic, the terms for "ambivalence" and "contronym share the root *ḍ-d-d.*

19. Jabbour does not provide a complete citation, but it is likely the 1927 French translation of Samuel Jankélévitch.

20. See the English translations of these texts in the *Standard Edition* as follows: *Beyond the Pleasure Principle* (1920), *SE* 18:1–64; "The Ego and the Id" (1923), *SE* 19:1–66; "Group Psychology and the Analysis of the Ego" (1921), *SE* 18:65–144; "Thoughts for the Times on War and Death" (1925), *SE* 14:275–300.

21. Among them, a French translation of Freud's 1913 writing "Totem and Taboo" (*SE* 13:1–165), *Introductory Lectures on Psycho-analysis* (*SE* 15 and 16), and the compiled volume, *Essais de psychanalyse appliquée* (Essays on applied psychoanalysis), which includes some of Freud's writings between 1906 and 1923 including, importantly, his 1910 essay, "The Antithetical Meaning of Primary Words" (*SE* 11:153–162).

psychoanalytic method and freudian doctrine). The main theme of his brief essay is the influence of German linguist Karl Abel in Freud's foundational text, *The Interpretation of Dreams.*[22]

There is also the strong possibility that Jabbour attended the seminars of Jacques Lacan while in Paris, although there is no citation of him (or any other French psychoanalyst) in *Confession and Psychoanalysis.* At the time, Jabbour was studying in Paris (1959–1961), Lacan was delivering his seminars on psychoanalysis at the Saint-Anne Hospital.[23] The specific seminars he delivered over these two academic years, however, may offer hints of such an encounter: Seminar VII, *L'éthique de la psychanalyse* (*The Ethics of Psychoanalysis*) in 1959–1960; and Seminar VIII, *Le transfert* (*Transference*) in 1960–1961. The latter seminar centered on Lacan's understanding of the transference, the key concept in psychoanalysis for understanding the role of interlocution during therapy and the one most rigorously treated by Jabbour in this book. The former seminar raised an expansive question regarding the destructive drive (*Trieb*), asking what a psychoanalytic ethics might be under its shadow and "beyond" the Aristotelian ethics of the good. In doing so, Lacan invoked the European mystical tradition as well as Islamic sources, namely Ibn al-ʿArabī, who is directly referenced in the seminar via the writing of Henri Corbin,[24] and who is possibly, if anonymously, invoked in this volume.

Confession and Psychoanalysis is divided into ten chapters of highly variable length, with an additional, "fragmentary" geographical-historical summary at its conclusion. The book opens with the remembrance of

22. See Freud's engagement with Abel in *The Interpretation of Dreams* (1900), *SE* 4:318; his lecture "Dream-Work" in *Introductory Lectures on Psycho-Analysis* (1915–1916), *SE* 15:170–183; and the aforementioned essay, "The Antithetical Meaning of Primal Words" (1910), *SE* 11:153–162.

23. This was directly before Lacan's break with the Société française de psychanalyse and his subsequent movement to the École normale supérieure, concomitant with the establishment of the École freudienne de Paris.

24. See Lacan, "Courtly Love as Anamorphosis," the eleventh chapter of *The Ethics of Psychoanalysis.* Lacan references the work of Henri Corbin, *L'Imagination créatrice dans le soufisme d'Ibn' Arabi.* See also Ralph Manheim's translation, *Alone with the Alone: Creative Imagination in the Sufism of Ibn Arabi*, and Marc De Kesel's helpful commentary on Lacan's seminar, *Eros and Ethics.*

death and its intimate relationship to birth. The "leap" that is the human's expansive capacities for individual growth and civilization, Jabbour argues, is the same potentiality that enables the annihilatory development of nuclear weapons. The "atom" at the heart of both these processes is, in fact, the same—at once the incipient chemical force of nuclear explosion and the human in the womb. The text's opening pages align Jabbour with Freud's "speculative" formulation of the drive (*Trieb*), toward death and toward life, in *Beyond the Pleasure Principle* and also his "Thoughts for the Times on War and Death." "It would be keeping with the times," Freud writes, "to alter [the old saying]: *Si vis vitam, para mortem.* If you want to endure life, prepare yourself for death."[25] The remembrance of death, which in Jabbour's text strikingly precedes his remarks on the infant and birth, echoes Freud's theorization of a regressive drive toward the "inorganic," that is, a life that is always already in the arc of its being-for-death.

It is with this scene in mind that the text turns in the third and fourth chapters to define three different iterations of *iʿtirāf*, confession: in the New Testament, in the history of Orthodox Christian tradition, and in Freudian psychoanalysis. For Jabbour, these are the archives of courageous speech found in asceticism, social-historical struggle, and psychotherapy, respectively. These disparate archives are united by the concept of confession as an encounter with truth through interlocution and so are closely tied to martyrdom (*shahāda*) as a lived form of witnessing to that truth and a brave steadfastness (*ṣumūd*) in the face of oppression; each poses the question of collective and individual transformation in the relationship to the practice of dialogic speech and bravery. The first archive, ascetic confession, begins with citations of repentance in the Gospels and Epistles but moves to a remarkable enumeration of great ascetic penitents: Maximos the Confessor, Isaac the Bishop of Nineveh, Symeon the New Theologian, Imām al-Ghazālī, and Ibn al-ʿIbrī (Bar ʿEbroyo). The inclusion of both al-Ghazālī, the prolific eleventh-century Muslim scholar, and Ibn al-ʿIbrī, the thirteenth-century Syriac Orthodox bishop and polymath, is striking. The invoked imbrication of the (non-Chalcedonian) Syriac Orthodox Christian and Islamic traditions with Jabbour's Orthodoxy is intensified where he explains the intent of Isaac of Nineveh's words by references to the Arabic "*ṣūfī*" (that is, mystic) concepts of divine union (*ittiḥād*) and witnessing (*mushāhada*) which have their respective Greek Christian ana-

25. "Thoughts for the Times on War and Death," *SE* 14:300.

logues in *henōsis* and *theoria*.[26] The second archive of confession, speaking truth in the struggle against political oppression, is marked by a brief retelling of Maximos the Confessor's martyrdom and death through exile at the hands of the Byzantine emperor and church authorities. The third archive draws on Freud to explain confession in the practice of psychoanalytic therapy as a response to the formation of repression qua symptomatic obstacles. What unites all three archives of confession is the "bravery" needed to enunciate one's witness to divine truth, to the reality of human transgression. The act of confession, Jabbour writes, bravely overturns one's narcissistic relation to the self and its libidinal economy of self-love.

The fifth and longest chapter concerns the conscious sense of guilt and wrongdoing. Guilt—which in Freud's theory emerges in the demand placed on the "I" by the "above-the-I" (that is, the superego)—is tethered to a fundamental and intensely contradictory ambivalence (*taḍādd*)[27] at the threshold of the unconscious, and thus to repression. Guilt, at the site of the unconscious, is an "unknown-known."[28] As Freud notes in a 1907 essay: "We may say that the sufferer from compulsions and prohibitions behaves as if he were dominated by a sense of guilt, of which, however, he knows nothing, so that we must call it an unconscious sense of guilt, in spite of the apparent contradiction in terms."[29] The sense of guilt signals the inherent ambivalence of the drive, toward both life and death at once, manifesting in human action and social relations. Language is shown in the text to be a manifestation of such ambivalence,[30] something Jabbour

26. This grammatical resonance was pointed out by Alexander Treiger in his comments on this introduction.

27. This Arabic term is glossed multiple times by Jabbour with the French, *ambivalence*, but it does not connote ambiguity or uncertainty as it sometimes does in English. Instead, this term implies an existing contradiction and overdetermination—the simultaneous and actual condition of love and hate, for example.

28. Pandolfo, *Knot of the Soul*, 17.

29. Freud, "Obsessive Actions and Religious Practices," *SE* 9:123. In his translator's footnote to this text, James Strachey mentions that the German term for the "sense of guilt" is *Schuldbewusstsein*, literally "consciousness of guilt" (ftn. 1, 123). This corresponds precisely to the Arabic term *shuʿūr bi-l-dhanb*, which also invokes consciousness and awareness as much as feeling.

30. In this, Jabbour agrees with Lacan's assessment that "it is the signifier that is repressed" (Lacan, "In Memory of Ernest Jones: On His Theory of Symbolism," 598).

relates to his earlier work on contronyms and his study of Ibn al-Anbārī's *Kitāb al-aḍdād* (Book of contronyms).[31] This actually existing overdetermination, the chapter concludes, "is a true reality from which there is no escape."[32] As such, the sense of guilt signals the necessity of grappling with the drive and the unknown-known of the unconscious. Rather than constituting another form of narcissistic relation to the self, the sense of guilt is transposed into an orectic confrontation with the Real (*al-ḥaqq*); it is what makes possible an inversion, a "leap toward God."[33]

The sixth chapter turns to the means of grappling with this ambivalence, which, for Jabbour, is militant spiritual struggle (*jihād al-nafs*). Critical to this form of struggle and exemplified by monasticism is the realization—both a coming to awareness and an activity—of the ambivalent and "counterfeit" condition that cuts across collective and individual life (a space which, as what is *neither* individual *nor* collective, is also that of the unconscious). This condition is likewise demarcated by the theological concept of evil: "I am a void," Jabbour writes, "or rather I approach a void, because a void is the loss of existence, and the loss of existence is not evil."[34] This realization, then, implies a risk; it leads either to the melancholic and suicidal "black bile" or to a blessed struggle on the terrain of the psyche, one lived through the disciplined forms of fasting, keeping vigil, and continual prayer, all under guidance from a spiritual shaykh.[35] The chapter, while making a strong distinction between the intense ascetic activities of the monastics and the condition of traumatized psychiatric patients, brings the therapeutic shifts effected within each into a resonance. Specifically, both processes are effected through the force of a transference, between the shaykh and disciple on the one hand, and between the analyst and analysand on the other.

31. For more on al-Anbārī see Brockelmann, "al-Anbāri, Abū Bakr."
32. Jabbour, *Confession and Psychoanalysis*, 62.
33. Jabbour, *Confession and Psychoanalysis*, 48.
34. Jabbour, *Confession and Psychoanalysis*, 71.
35. Jabbour's description follows closely that of Islamic Sufism, and indeed *Confession and Psychoanalysis* cites one Muslim saying in the sixth chapter. El Shakry's treatment of the writings of Abū al-Wafā al-Ghunaymī al-Taftāzānī in the second chapter of *The Arabic Freud* draws out the same resonance between Sufism and psychoanalysis. See also Mian, "Genres of Desire," for an excellent rendering of the transference in Deobandī Islamic practices.

The seventh chapter deals explicitly with Freud's concept of transference (*Übertragung*), translated into Arabic as *taḥwīl*—a term that implies a transformation or a change in one's condition (*ḥāl*). Jabbour follows Freud's expansive concept of transference, which is concerned with the investment of libidinal energies into new objects (cathexes), and its intensification in the therapeutic relationship between analyst and analysand, or monastic guide and disciple. As Freud writes, "this transference is *ambivalent*: it comprises positive (affectionate) as well as negative (hostile) attitudes towards the analyst."[36] This is because, as he notes in *Beyond the Pleasure Principle*, "in the unconscious cathexes can easily be completely transferred, displaced, and condensed,"[37] a point solidified in his early study of dreams. The procedure of transference, Jabbour argues, is the very essence of monastic confession and ascetic watchfulness. Here, Jabbour reads Freud's topography of the psyche through the writings of Gregory Palamas and Maximos, in which the lower energies of the soul, the unconscious, are redirected toward God. Anger and love, when viewed in the light of ambivalence, are two vectors of the same instinctual drive (*gharīza*),[38] opening up the possibility of illumination, or in psychoanalytic terms, sublimation. "Sublimation itself is transference,"[39] Jabbour concludes. To overcome anger is not to repress it, but to direct its fury toward the divine as the known unknown.

Transferring the aim of the drive is, at once, a stilling of the passions and their enkindling toward God, which Jabbour reads through the hesychastic practice of the coordination of the breath, posture, and the recitation of the "prayer of the heart," also known as the Jesus Prayer. This leads to his commentary on psychosomatic medicine that comprises the eighth chapter. Jabbour argues that for the hesychasts, the *nafs* (soul/psyche) and the body are not properly differentiated; the passible aspects

36. "An Outline of Psycho-Analysis" (1938), *SE* 23:175. This also marks a strong contrast with Jung, who viewed psychic energy as continuous and uniform rather than overdetermined.

37. *Beyond the Pleasure Principle, SE* 18:40.

38. This term has important connotations in Arabic and Islamic writings. As Alexander Treiger shows, for al-Ghazālī, the term *gharīza* denotes an "intrinsic feature AH." This concept was influenced by the Sufi teacher al-Ḥārith al-Muḥāsibī (d. 234 AH), who is mentioned in al-Ghazālī's *Munqidh min al-ḍalāl* (Deliverance from error). See Treiger, *Inspired Knowledge in Islamic Thought*, 19.

39. Jabbour, *Confession and Psychoanalysis*, 111.

of the psyche (the affects of rage and craving) act as mediators between lower and higher elements, in part because they constitute the regulatory function of the nervous system and the breath. The redirection of the aim of these energies is, in turn, organized around the heart—which in hesychasm is both a site of plentitude and a vacuole, described by Jabbour as an "amplitude" or "capaciousness" (*saʿa*). For this reason, the heart is the site of the "transference of self-love into divine desire."[40]

The ninth chapter recapitulates the major theses of the book, the most important of which is that the lower soul/psyche—that is, the body—is not extinguished in repression but redirected in pursuit of divine disclosure. This redirection is a risk-laden procedure that requires guidance and care. Here, Jabbour again marks a distinction between psychoanalytic patients suffering from neurosis and the monastics engaged in spiritual warfare. The former requires a reduction in the supervisory force of the "above-the-I" (the superego), the interdiction of the moral law; the latter intensifies it as a "spiritual" conscience of total "watchfulness." This practice, common to Islamic and Eastern Christian asceticism, is called in Arabic *murāqaba* or *yaqaẓa*. In Greek, the term is *nēpsis*: the writings and sayings gathered in the *Philokalia* are often referred to as those of the "neptic" or "watchful" Fathers. Through the concept of watchfulness, Jabbour brings his reader to the heart of the ascetic procedure—a mode of life not easily captured in the typical language used to describe asceticism and monasticism, that of either cultivation or renunciation:

> Whither does the monastic arrive at the hands of his elder? He ends up implementing the words of Paul: for the monastic, food and its lack become equivalent, as do drink and its lack, possession and its lack, marriage and its lack. These are no longer positive and negative elements, but, more precisely, their being and nonbeing are equivalent, because the monastic lives as one who possesses and is not a possessor, as one who eats and is not an eater. Add to this the holiness of spirit and body, as well as a faith, love, and sure hope that are no longer deficient. That is, the monastic truly departs from his own being to become in God.[41]

40. Jabbour, *Confession and Psychoanalysis*, 128.

41. Jabbour, *Confession and Psychoanalysis*, 132. Elsewhere in this chapter Jabbour quotes Paul's Epistle to the Galatians, "For I by the law have died to the law

This form of life, whereby the passible parts of the psyche are stilled, is what the monastic writers describe as dispassion (Gr. *apatheia*; Ar. *ʿadamal-hawā*), and its chief mark is tears, the "common activity" of the body and psyche—what one can call, however paradoxically, an *undifferentiated* movement[42]—as what belongs to neither the body nor the mind. It is also the supersensory, the spiritual sense spoken of by Gregory Palamas when he describes with what faculty the hesychast monks witness the uncreated light.

Jabbour expands upon this undifferentiated movement in his brief tenth chapter, which focuses on the coincidence of lamentation and joy. The death of Christ and his resurrection exemplify their inversion: "the penitent crucifies his psyche in sorrow with Christ, being regretful, remorseful, mournful and melancholic, lamenting and weeping; yet his sadness turns into joy."[43] The chapter closes with a digression on the insufficiency of Kantian anthropology for grasping an exceptional relationship to what is beyond the pleasure principle and so the moral law of the good. Jabbour, evoking John Climacus's own account in *The Ladder* of the monastic site that was called "The Prison,"[44] notes that both evildoers and ascetics ("Sufis" and "mystics") exemplify this exceptional form; the ambivalent force that drives great evil can be overturned into that which sanctifies.

Confession and Psychoanalysis closes with a "Historical-Geographical Fragment," one that enumerates the inheritance of Arab Orthodox Christianity in the Eastern Mediterranean through key ascetic movements and writers. At the same time, Jabbour finds himself lamenting, "What remains in our lives of this inheritance? Ignorance that we are of this inheritance remains." Jabbour concludes with a note that the current struggle is nothing but a preparation for a future restoration that comes from the mercy of God alone.

---

in order to live for God. With Christ I was crucified so it is not I who live but rather Christ lives in me, and if I am now in the body, then my faith is in the Son of God Who loved me and gave Himself for me" (Galatians 2:19–20).

42. Compare Freud's comment: "In the present discussion, moreover, I am only putting forward a hypothesis; I have no proof to offer. It seems a plausible view that this displaceable and indifferent energy, which is undoubtedly active both in the ego and in the id, proceeds from the narcissistic store of libido—that it is desexualized Eros." "The Ego and the Id," *SE* 19:45.

43. Jabbour, *Confession and Psychoanalysis*, 149.

44. See the fifth "rung" of *The Ladder of Divine Ascent.*

Psychoanalysis, Eastern Christianity, Islam

Confession and Psychoanalysis stages what Jabbour calls an encounter (*muqābala*) between the practices of Orthodox Christian asceticism and Freudian psychoanalysis. They find their common resonances in a practice of therapeutic interlocution, a material struggle for truth articulated through the grammar of the psyche—in Arabic, *nafs*.[45] This term, much like its Greek counterpart *psychē*, connotes both the soul and psyche as well as the self.[46] *ʿIlm al-nafs*, at once a 'psychology' and a 'knowledge of the soul,' finds its bearing in the text as a specific mode of scientific speculation held in common by psychoanalysis (*al-taḥlīl al-nafsī*) and ascetic struggle (*jihād al-nafs*). Arsenius Mikhail, in the glossary to his translation of Medieval Coptic guides to the Eucharist,[47] points out that the Arabic word for absolution (the prayers said at the end of confession) is also often rendered in Arabic as *taḥlīl*. This term, which comes from the same root as the verb *ḥalla* ("to loose, untie") is used to translate "analysis" in "psychoanalysis." The phrase *al-taḥlīl al-nafsī*, then, implies not only an analysis of the psyche but an unfettering of the soul. The encounter in question, between psyche and soul, serves to catalyze Jabbour's inquiry—his desire to grapple with an ambivalence and historical groundlessness that cuts across the collective and individual life of the soul, but that also serves as a stage for drawing near to God.

Insofar as the text is organized around a set of material practices—namely, the psychoanalytic "talking cure" and monastic confession between a disciple and elder—it belies a reading practice that would merely

45. There are two related terms to *nafs*: *shakhṣ* (person or character) and *dhāt* (one's being or the self). *Nafs* implies not only breath but a reflexive condition (one's relationship to one's self, taken as a subject of action). *Shakhṣ*, person, is closer to a sense of character and, especially for Jabbour, has a deep, intersubjective, qualitative aspect—one's personhood is always in relation to another. *Dhāt* is the self taken as an object of action; it is analogous to the German *Dasein*, existence but literally being-there, insofar as it also works as a demonstrative pronoun.

46. This follows Bruno Bettelheim's argument that Freud's use of the German term *Seele* is poorly rendered in the Standard Edition translation as "mind," as it also implies "soul." See Bettelheim, *Freud and Man's Soul*.

47. Mikhail, *Guides to the Eucharist in Medieval Egypt*.

see a comparison of theology with modern, secular philosophy.[48] *Confession and Psychoanalysis*, as Jabbour himself notes, is organized around the practical question of the psyche and the struggle for knowledge of it. It reads psychoanalysis and the ascetic science of the soul in relation to a shared object, the unconscious, and thus troubles the modern and constitutive separation between the secular and the religious.[49] Jabbour's text can thus be read alongside other contemporary studies of psychoanalytic practice that have stringently challenged the assumption that a universal and secular subject is the necessary object of psychoanalysis—that is, where attachments or practices deemed "religious" are simply pathologies of the psyche to be undone through therapy.[50] The kind of encounter exemplified in *Confession and Psychoanalysis*, as the editors of the 2018 special issue of *Psychoanalysis and History* argue, cannot be conceived through a "preconceived mold" wherein the "theoretical world" of the Euro-Atlantic is supplemented by the "empirical world" of the so-called Global South. Rather, they read this conjuncture as "alchemical," one that "entails a working through of psychoanalysis *otherwise*."[51]

48. There has been an increasing attention to the resonances between Orthodox Christianity and psychoanalysis, but one that often takes the form of comparison and apologetics. See, for example, Delli and Thermos, eds., *Soul and Psyche as a Surprise*; and Waitz and Tisdale, *Lacanian Psychoanalysis and Eastern Orthodox Christian Anthropology in Dialogue*. The most adjacent effort to Jabbour's is that of Costi Bendaly (1926–2013), an Orthodox writer and scholar from Tripoli who knew Jabbour and was an active member in the MJO: see Bendaly, *Images parentales et attitudes religieuses* (Parental images and religious attitudes). Like Jabbour, Nikolaos Loudovikos has written on psychoanalysis through the work of Maximos the Confessor. See Loudovikos, *Psykanalysē kai Orthodoxē theologia* (Psychoanalysis and Orthodox theology).

49. For more on the development of the modern concepts of the secular and the religious see Asad, *Genealogies of Religion*. Asad also offers some incisive comments about Freud's theories in the second chapter of his book *Formations of the Secular*.

50. See, for example, Khanna, *Dark Continents*; Kapila, "The 'Godless' Freud and His Indian Friends"; Soyubol, "Turkey Psychoanalyzed, Psychoanalysis Turkified."

51. El Shakry, Pursley, and McKusick, "Introduction," in "Psychoanalysis and the Middle East: Discourses and Encounters," special issue, *Psychoanalysis and History*. On anthropological studies of this alchemical relation between psycho-

Scholarship on the colonial and postcolonial friction between psychoanalysis and the religious and medical traditions of the Middle East has rightly turned on the place of Islamic practices in this conjuncture—the question of Muslim subjectivity in psychoanalytic therapy,[52] as well as the role of European colonial interventions in the remaking (or extinguishment) of vernacular Islamic therapies.[53] Within the conscription of Islamic practices into Western Christian (now secular) modernity, globalized European Christianity operates as a kind of "vanishing mediator"[54] between Islam and psychoanalysis, turning the latter into what Alberto Toscano describes as a "secular clinic."[55] Importantly, *Confession and Psychoanalysis* performs a break with Europe, a space of what Jabbour calls "counterfeit Christianity," that the Gospel was "incapable of instructing."[56] It is, moreover, "the Christian," Jabbour notes, who has perpetrated over the "last five centuries, the most dreadful wars and the basest kinds of eradication."[57] In this, the Arab

---

analysis and sites in the Global South see Ewing, *Arguing Sainthood*; Odabaei, "Modernity from Elsewhere"; and Hauter, "Reconstructing the Community, Reconstructing the Image."

52. See the writings of Fethi Benslama, in particular, *La psychanalyse à l'épreuve de l'Islam* and Robert Bononno's translation, *Psychoanalysis and the Challenge of Islam*.

53. See Safouan, *Pourquoi le monde arabe n'est pas libre* and, in translation, *Why Are the Arabs Not Free?*.

54. Fredric Jameson writes, concerning the function of Protestantism in Max Weber's sociology of rationalization: "For what happens here is essentially that once Protestantism has accomplished the task of allowing a rationalization of innerworldly life to take place, it has no further reason for being and disappears from the historical scene. It is thus in the strictest sense of the word a catalytic agent which permits an exchange of energies between two otherwise mutually exclusive terms." "The Vanishing Mediator," 78.

55. Alberto Toscano argues that the "idea of transforming psychoanalysis into a secular clinic aimed at diagnosing the phantasmatic impasses that prevent 'Arabs' or 'Muslims' from becoming the properly pathological subjects of modernity (rather than fanatics stuck between crumbling tradition and fear of 'Westoxification') leaves itself open to the accusation that psychoanalysis might constitute yet another stage in that cunning of Christianity which has often taken the name of 'secularism'." Toscano, *Fanaticism*, 165–166, quoted in El Shakry, *Arabic Freud*, 10.

56. Jabbour, *Confession and Psychoanalysis*, 4.

57. Jabbour, *Confession and Psychoanalysis*, 4.

and Orthodox Christian tradition from which the text is written cannot be assimilated to the (post)colonial adventures of Europe's "Christendom," not just because it espouses an intimate relationship to the Islamic traditions of the Arabic-speaking world but also because it represents another site of colonial transformation. It thus demands from its English reader an attunement to this difference, to the particular way this text folds, and is folded into, the Arabic archives of Islam and psychoanalysis.

The Arabic Freud, Omnia El Shakry's essential study documenting the reception and translation of Freud's texts into Arabic in postwar Egypt, demonstrates that the entanglement between Islam and psychoanalysis occurs at the very moment of Freud's translation into Arabic. El Shakry recounts how the psychology professor Yusuf Murad introduced the term *al-lā-shuʿūr* as a translation of Freud's concept of *das Unbewusste,* the unconscious. The term chosen by Murad, used in Arabic translations from then on and also by Jabbour, originates with Ibn al-ʿArabī (sixth–seventh century AH; twelfth–thirteenth century AD). Murad adopted *al-lā-shuʿūr* from Ibn al-ʿArabī's work *Fuṣūṣ al-ḥikam* (*The Ringstones of Wisdom*), a meditation on the different essential forms of wisdom attained by each of the prophets, from Adam to Muhammad. Beginning with Murad's creative usage of an Islamic Sufi text, El Shakry historically tracks the alchemical resonances—those unexpected and creative linkages, extensions of thought and practice—between Islam and psychoanalysis forged in Arabic translation.

Stefania Pandolfo's magisterial ethnography of madness, *Knot of the Soul,* tracks this same resonance in the contemporary life of psychotherapy in Morocco. Tracing the experience of madness as it striates the postcolonial psychiatric hospital and the Muslim space of the Qurʾānic cure (the *ruqya*), Pandolfo works in the fecund space of a "family resemblance" between psychoanalytic and Islamic traditions, one that "digs its roots into the intercultural exchanges around the thought of the trace of the intermediate realm of imagination (*Mundus imaginalis/ ʿālam al-mithāl*)."[58] Taking this resemblance seriously, Pandolfo argues, means in part "admitting a subject whose freedom and finitude, responsibility and praxis are articulated in relation to God, and who is simultaneously ethically active in relation to others in a community."[59]

These authors trace out an important historical and ethnographic reading practice, one that is attentive to the transformative effects of transla-

58. Pandolfo, *Knot of the Soul,* 11.
59. Pandolfo, *Knot of the Soul,* 11.

tion and archival resonance. By deferring the mere comparison and thus fixing of one archive against another, these authors allow for the productive work of resemblance to manifest—the work of the imaginal as such. Such a method of reading is appropriate for Jabbour's text. *Confession and Psychoanalysis* does not offer much justification for bringing together its two archives (Orthodox Christianity and psychoanalysis). Instead, it works from a pressing question—the unconscious, the cure of the soul—wherein the immanent reverberations of these archives gain force.

This reading practice is crucial for understanding *Confession and Psychoanalysis*, not only because Jabbour's text is itself one of the "unexpected interlocutors"[60] of the psychoanalytic archive but also because of the role of Islam. The text displays a subtle fluency in Islamic grammars that readers may find remarkable. Indeed, it is hardly possible to understand the contours of Jabbour's argument without knowledge of concepts and practices that are also pivotal within many Islamic traditions of the Middle East. Just as with psychoanalysis, the aim of *Confession and Psychoanalysis* is not to stage a dialogue with Islam, although the text includes some explicit Islamic references: listing Abū Ḥāmid al-Ghazālī among the righteous Orthodox Christian ascetics and scholars and referencing "Muslim Sufi" forms of spiritual guidance under an elder. These references are clearly shifts between the inside of a tradition (the authority of Orthodox Christianity) and its outside; but to focus on them exclusively would bely the unmarked resonances with Islam that suffuse the grammar of the text, what is in effect a common vocabulary spoken across these traditions: *irshād* (spiritual guidance), *sujūd* (prostrating in worship), *jihād* (struggle), *zuhd/nusk* (asceticism), *murāqaba* (watchfulness), *kufr* (infidelity or unfaithfulness to God), *dunyā* (this life), *dhikr* (remembrance [of God and death]), *nafs* (the psyche), *rūḥ* (spirit), and the ninety-nine "beautiful names" (*asmā' ḥusnā*) of God that constitute the divine attributes and at least a dozen of which appear in this text.

The most remarkable site of this imbrication comes in the form of Jabbour's employment of the term *khalīlī*, a nisba adjective,[61] that he develops to translate the Greek term *mystikos* in Maximos's writings. *Khalīl*, as a noun, denotes an intimate friend and is used as the epithet for the Prophet Ibrāhīm

60. El Shakry, Pursley, McKuick, "Introduction," 270.
61. That is, an adjective of belonging.

(Abraham), *khalīl allāh*, an "intimate" or "true friend of God."[62] This language is found in the Arabic text of Isaiah 41:8 ("You O Israel, are my servant, O Jacob, whom I have chosen, the seed of Ibrāhīm my friend [*khalīlī*]"), as well as in the Qur'ān and various hadith sayings attributed to the Prophet Muhammad. Accordingly, Sūrat Nisā' (4:125) reads, "And who is better in religion than he who delivers his face to God, doing what is good, and following the creed [*milla*] of Ibrāhīm with right inclination? God took Ibrāhīm as an intimate [*khalīl*]."[63] Jabbour's striking adjectival and adverbial usage of the term *khalīlī* is a way of invoking the specific creed or way of Ibrāhīm invoked by the Qur'ān and in the later Sufi commentaries.

The most influential of the latter is Ibn al-'Arabī's *Fuṣūṣ al-ḥikam*. This text, the reader will recall, is the source of Yusuf Murad's term for translating the Freudian unconscious into Arabic, *al-lā-shu'ūr*, and is drawn specifically from the episode recounting Ibrāhīm's vision to sacrifice his son Isḥāq (Isaac). The previous chapter in Ibn al-'Arabī's text, treating Ibrāhīm's divine attribute of rapturous love (*ḥikma muhayyamiyya*), begins: "He was called *al-khalīl*, an intimate, because he was inundated [*takhallal*] and he encompassed all that by which the Divine in Himself is described. The poet has said: You have inundated [*takhallalta*] the course of my spirit, and by this *al-khalīl* was called an intimate."[64] Ibn al-'Arabī likewise emphasizes the fact that "the Truth [*al-ḥaqq*] inundated the being of Ibrahīm's form."[65] *Al-Ḥaqq*, "the Truth" or "the Real," and one of the divine names of God in Islam, manifests in the form of Ibrāhīm, and indeed in the forms of creation (*al-makhlūq*): "[D]o you not see that the creation is manifest with the attributes of the Real from their first to last, and each of them has a truth,

62. *Al-Qāmūs al-muḥīṭ*, the ninth century (AH) dictionary of al-Fayrūzabādī, notes the reference to Ibrahīm and adds: "[your intimate] *khalīluka*: your heart [*qalbuka*], or your nose"; the *Arabic-English Lexicon* of Edward Lane also notes that *khalīl* denotes the "heart" for Ibn al-'Arabī. It also indicates that *khalīl* can connote an interval or a gap; it can also refer to the movement around the perimeter, something that is piercing (e.g., a sword) or something that is pierced.

63. Qur'ān, Sūrat Nisā' 4:125. See also Renard, "Images of Abraham in the Writings of Jalāl Ad-Dīn Rūmī."

64. Ibn al-'Arabī, *Fuṣūṣ al-ḥikam*, 80.

65. Ibn al-'Arabī, *Fuṣūṣ al-ḥikam*, 80.

just as the attributes of passing things are truth of the Truth?"[66] The Sufi lexicon of ʿAbd al-Razzāq al-Kāshānī, a follower of Ibn al-ʿArabī, describes "*al-khulla*"—the intimacy that Ibrāhīm has with God—as one in which "the servant materialized the attributes of the Truth [*al-ḥaqq*] whereby the Truth inundates [*yatakhallal*] him, and he is not emptied of what has manifest upon him of His attributes. Thus the servant becomes a mirror for the Truth."[67] Elsewhere, in his commentary on *Fuṣūṣ al-ḥikam,* al-Kāshānī describes this inundation as that of dye coloring the essence (*jawhar*) of a material, or of water inundating a tuft of wool.[68]

Jabbour is likely drawing on this genealogy in his creative use of the adjective *khalīlī*. Indeed, elsewhere in his corpus of writings, the terminological shift he employs from "ṣūfī" and "mystic" to *khalīlī*—which in *Confession and Psychoanalysis* is only done through translation and without explication for his readers—is explicitly discussed: "[I]n our book *al-Muzayyafūn* [*The Counterfeits*]," Jabbour writes, "we made use of the term *al-mukhālala*, rather than the term *al-taṣawwuf* [sufism], because divine blessing inundates us [*tatakhallal*] and abides in our whole creaturely being. The term *'al-taṣawwuf'* does not lead to this implication."[69] *Al-mukhālala*, he notes in yet another writing, describes both Ibrāhīm's coming to be completely in God and his participation in the life of the Trinity: "[W]e say that the Hypostases [*aqānīm*] indwell, each in the others. This is the absolute depth of this inundating intimacy [*al-mukhālala*],[70] unlimited, indescribable, and ineffable."[71]

66. Ibn al-ʿArabī, *Fuṣūṣ al-ḥikam*, 80–81.

67. al-Kāshānī, *Iṣṭilāḥāt al-ṣūfiyya*, 179. See also Treiger, "Al-Ghazālī's 'Mirror Christology.'"

68. See this commentary on the Ibrāhīm chapter in al-Kāshānī, *Sharḥ al-qashānī ʿalā fuṣūṣ al-ḥikam.*

69. Jabbour, *Rūḥāniyyat al-kanīsa al-urthūdhuksiyya*, ftn. 25.

70. This is likely a reference to the Greek patristic concept of *perikhōrēsis*, referencing the co-inhering *cum* "circling" of both the Trinity in itself and the divine and human natures in Christ. See also ʿAjam Rafīq's *Mawsūʿat muṣṭalaḥāt al-taṣawwuf al-islāmī* [Encyclopedia of the lexicon of Islamic sufism] and its entry "*akhillāʾ*," the plural of *khalīl*: "*al-mukhālala* is not true except between God and his servant, being the station of union" (24).

71. Jabbour, *al-Tajalliyyāt fī dustūr al-īmān*, ftn. 38. As Andrew Louth also notes, "the doctrine of the Trinity reveals God as unknowable, not so much beyond our powers of comprehension as unknowable in Himself." *The Origins of*

It is, moreover, crucial that *khalīlī* is employed precisely as a rearticulation of the concept of the "mystical"—folded between the Greek and Latin term *mystikos/mysticus*, as well as the Arabic term *ṣūfī*—for Jabbour's contemporary reader.[72] It marks the insufficiency and opacity of the received concept at the level of practice and bespeaks the counterfeit inheritance of what we term "the mystical."[73] This incapacity, as Jabbour's text attests, impels a shift in language in order to demarcate what has been lost.[74] As with the problem of the counterfeit, the articulation of loss is

the Christian Mystical Tradition, 162. Likewise, Jabbour appears to be pursuing an adequate concept of *mystikos* as conceived in Vladimir Lossky's *Essai sur la théologie mystique de l'Église d'Orient* (in translation, *The Mystical Theology of the Eastern Church*). As Lossky, whom Jabbour cites approvingly, argues, *mystikos* denotes a life in God which, quite unlike the individual biographies of Western mystics, "remains hidden from the eyes of all." Lossky, *The Mystical Theology of the Eastern Church*, 20–21. See also Arida, "Hearing, Receiving and Entering TO ΜΥΣΤΗΡΙΟΝ/ΤΑ ΜΥΣΤΗΡΙΑ: Patristic Insights Unveiling the Crux Interpretum (Isaiah 6:9–10) of the Sower Parable."

72. The term appears four times in this text, once as an adverb (for *mystikōs*), twice as an adjective (for *mystikos*) and finally as a noun. It is accompanied by the parenthetical glosses of two terms: the Arabic term "ṣūfī" and the French term "mystique." The first, second and fourth times occur in the quotation and translation of Maximos the Confessor's Greek writings: "Jesus was born in a bodily birth, 'overcoming by it the power of our condemnation and restoring as *khalīlī* (*ṣūfī*), birth in the spirit.'" "Christ is ever born in the *khalīliyya* manner (*ṣūfī*, mystic) from the soul"; "In the life of the *khalīliyyūn* of God (that is, the Sufis, the mystics), withdrawing from the material is well-known"; and, finally, "the *khalīlī* water, mystic (*ṣūfī*)."

73. "I will end with this so as not to exhaust the Arab reader, as they have not yet practiced *ṣūfī* theology and its marvelous texts." Jabbour, *Rūḥāniyyat al-kanīsa al-urthūdhuksiyya*, n.p.

74. The effect of translating *mystikos* through an enigmatic term is all the more striking given the conventional use of the Arabic term *sirr* for the Greek *mysterion*, both referring to the hidden "secret" unveiled in divine disclosure in liturgical and ascetic practices. *Sirr*—a concept shared in Islamic Sufism—has an adjectival form, *sirrī*, which is conventionally found in contemporary Arab Orthodox tradition as the translation of the adjective *mystikos*, that which corresponds to the noun *mysterion*. While the grammatical correspondence between *mysterion* and *mystikos* is maintained in the Arabic translation of *sirr* and *sirrī* respectively, the use of a relatively opaque term, *khalīlī*, for *mystikos* introduces a division between the adjectival and nominal forms. Interpolating this distinction

necessary before any renewal is possible. It is, in the language of Jabbour's Christian interlocutors, the initial recognition of the vacuity of oneself, the distance of the creature from a life in God, that incites the struggle to repent, transform, and realize divine disclosure.

This ethical risk is what compels spiritual struggle as a striving for transformation or transference (*taḥwīl*), the conceptual keystone of *Confession and Psychoanalysis.* Through the concept of transference, Jabbour combines a psychoanalytic notion of the redirection of the drive with Orthodox Christian ascetic teaching on the integration of the human, body, soul, and spirit in *theōsis* (the inundation of the creature by its Creator). The stress that Jabbour places on the necessity of the body, including the affects of anger and desire, for this transformation reaffirms—following the teachings of Gregory Palamas and Maximos, as well as, anonymously, al-Kāshānī and Ibn al-ʿArabī[75]—the possibility of the uncreated God man-

---

retreads the split that marks the late-medieval developments in the Latin West and the subsequent emergence of *la mystique*, or "mystics," in the sixteenth and seventeenth centuries and from which the contemporary term "mysticism" eventually derives. Andrew Louth likewise remarks that the split emerging between *mystikos* and *mysterion* is marked in medieval Latin translation; where the latter was translated as *sacramentum*, the former is only rendered as *mysticus,* marking another space from which "mystic" operations could be launched centuries later. The translator of de Certeau's *The Mystic Fable*, Michael B. Smith, importantly notes that *la mystique* that is the object of De Certeau's study cannot be rendered as mysticism (*le mysticisme*); Smith decided to render *la mystique* as "mystics," paralleling the English formations of the terms "metaphysics" and "optics." See Smith's Translator's Note to de Certeau, *The Mystic Fable*, vol. 1; and Louth, *The Origins of the Christian Mystical Tradition*. See also de Certeau, *The Mystic Fable,* vol. 1, especially 84–85 and 104.

75. The Freud translator Yusuf Murad, as El Shakry notes, grew up in the *Rūm* Orthodox tradition of Jabbour (*Arabic Freud*, 28). These mutual inflections moreover mark the continuing imbrication of grammars across Eastern Christian ascetic and Islamic *ṣūfī* traditions. For historical examples, see Treiger, "Mutual Influences and Borrowings"; al-Shābushtī, *The Book of Monasteries*, translated by Hilary Kilpatrick; Bowman, "Refuge in the Bosoms of the Mountains" and *Christian Monastic Life in Early Islam*; Tannous, *The Making of the Medieval Middle East;* Grehan, *Twilight of the Saints*; Ibn Abī al-Dunyā, *al-Muntiqā min kitāb al-ruhbān*; and *Christian-Muslim Relations: A Bibliographical History*, edited by David Thomas.

ifesting in, or more precisely *as*, the forms of creation. This is the possibility of *tajallī*, the transfiguration of God's self-disclosure.

It is crucial, moreover, that this process of transfiguration occurs as a function of address. "It seems impossible to me," Lacan noted in his seminar on transference, "to eliminate from the phenomenon of transference the fact that it manifests itself in a relationship with someone to whom one speaks."[76] As Lacan would argue, this address is located during analysis at the locus of the analyst. In Jabbour's case, this locus is the spiritual guide, but, like the analyst, the guide is merely the site of that speech—the aim of the address is oriented elsewhere.[77] Hence, Jabbour writes the "reclusive ascetics" are "blessed with a sense of great dread-awe in the presence of God,"[78] that impels a form of address that is bodily. It takes the form of *sujūd*, the act of humbly prostrating oneself before God.

The work of transformation outlined by Jabbour is a kind of struggle with the soul and its capacity for evil and self-destruction that has no end save in death. For Jabbour, Freud's discovery of the unconscious and its relationship to repression corroborates the teachings of the ascetic science of the soul. As a force of making-unconscious, repression does not extinguish the drive. It only suppresses its ideational form as a signifier, and thus it yields "minor virtue."[79] The interdictions of the moral law are thus necessary but crucially insufficient. It is precisely the forgetting of the other side of the law (its vacuity that compels evil and self-destruction) that stymies the transference of the powers of the soul, that is, grappling with the re-coordination of the drive.

76. Lacan, *Transference*, 175. For more on transference, see Laplanche and Pontalis, *The Language of Psycho-analysis*.

77. These practices at the margins of modernity turn around a question, keenly glossed by Michel de Certeau, as "what *remains* of the spoken word"? This space of interlocution in which the divine may be disclosed is not a bald mysticism (an object of social science) but a form of life. It is telling, then, that the so-called "lover's bubble" in Hieronymus Bosch's Garden of Earthly Delights, featured on the cover of *The Mystic Fable*, is described as both the site of interlocution (e.g., the psychoanalytic session, spiritual guidance) and the "monastery." See Certeau, *The Mystic Fable*, 12–13 and ftn. 13, p. 305.

78. Jabbour, *Confession and Psychoanalysis*, 125.

79. Jabbour, *Confession and Psychoanalysis*, 74.

This re-coordination aims at a site beyond the economy of the moral good: "The utmost aim of existence is nothing but this life in the Trinity,"[80] Jabbour writes. This way of proceeding and of being, as seen in the development of *khalīlī* as the adequate concept of "ṣūfī,"[81] is the "true ethics" of Orthodox Christianity:

> In Freud's theory, reaction formations (*formations réactionnelles*), are moral reactions that repress the instincts. Meekness represses anger, for example. Therefore, in Orthodoxy, the true ethics are of a *ṣūfī* nature. Within them, meekness is a new *ṣūfī* acquisition based on the transference of anger into love, gentleness, and sympathy toward the existence of the other as a Christ disclosed before me.[82]

This transformation effected through "total watchfulness" emerges through grappling with the ambivalent space of the heart—the site and possibility of both evil and divine manifestation. As such, Jabbour insists that struggling with evil (of the soul and the neighbor) is also a struggle for this total transfiguration, wherein the creature is entirely riven, inundated, by its divine Creator.

Hence, *Confession and Psychoanalysis* performs, at once, an inversion and intensification of Freud's science on the unconscious, and the accompanying procedures of interpretation and therapeutic speech. Following his ascetic and monastic interlocutors, Jabbour shows the waking world to be somnolent. Rousing the waking soul in *yaqaẓa* (watchfulness) thus mirrors Freud's own therapeutic dream-work and talking cure through

80. Jabbour, preface to the first edition of *Confession and Psychoanalysis*.

81. Even where the text could resort to a standard plural noun for *khalīl*, whether *akhillā'* or *khullān allāh* ("the intimates/friends of God"), the text reads: *khalīliyyūn allāh*, "those of God's who follow in the path of *al-khalīl*." The term is formed out of what is termed in Arabic a *nisba* adjective, the part of language that denotes a kind of belonging. The grammatical form *nisba* is related to *nasab*, the social "tie," and its counter form of *ḥasab*, the "account." As Stefania Pandolfo writes, tracing the dynamics of these forms in the life of a Moroccan village, "*nasab* is the valley of articulation, the forming of form"; where *ḥasab* belongs to the "foundational order" (the positive affirmation of one's lineage, the rules of poetry, the "order of the law"), *nasab* belongs to the "interstitial order," the "empty space . . . between two terms of a binary system." Pandolfo, *Impasse of the Angels*, 118.

82. Jabbour, *Confession and Psychoanalysis*, 100.

the monastic practices of keeping vigil while depriving oneself of sleep (a practice often deemphasized in contemporary studies on Christian asceticism) and in spiritual guidance; the "other scene" of the unconscious, as the site of the self's falling away, is encountered in the waking world itself.[83] This mode of life—in which the self has subsided in the waking world—is what Orthodox tradition also describes as "madness for Christ."

By this, Jabbour draws out a mode of relating to the hollowing out of his Orthodox tradition within the broader frame of cultural devastation and dispossession in the postcolonial Mashriq. Grappling with the evil of the drive and the groundlessness of human life at the level of the unconscious is a risk, one that Jabbour describes as "melancholia"—the ascetic's conscious awareness of the heart is expanded, but so too is the awareness of its intimate evil. This total watchfulness that leads to dispassion is not a dissipation of the affective drives of the psyche. Instead, it is a sorrowful joy, whereby the drive of self-love, likewise present in the material existence of social relations, no longer attains its satisfaction. In this, *Confession and Psychoanalysis* asks what an ethical relationship to the unconscious might mean. Psychoanalytic science and spiritual struggle become a shared site wherein, at once, the constitutive emptiness of the world and the self is disclosed and where a desire to be united with the uncreated—that which is not the world, neither the body nor the soul—and to subsist completely therein is enkindled. Jabbour's work is written out of such a desire—to quote the words of Metropolitan Ephraim Kyriakos in his eulogy for Jabbour, which I have translated and appended below, the desire of a "Holy Madman for Christ."

83. For an Islamic itinerary of this encounter, see al-Ghazālī, *On Vigilance and Self Examination*.

The Eulogy of Metropolitan Ephraim Kyriakos for the Funeral of Spiro Jabbour

In the name of the Father and of the Son and of the Holy Spirit, Amen.

Deacon Spiro Jabbour, a unique [divine] sign. The Church embraced him, while the world did not. He boarded the ship of the Orthodox Youth Movement early, yet at the same time, he never left the matter of earthly affairs.

He was a keen lawyer, which impelled him at times to analyze the complex ruses of politicians, exposing him to the criticism of many. Undoubtedly, he was a great theologian who knew the Holy Scripture very well, the New Testament in particular. Even at the end of his life, he never lost his remarkable memory; he knew and could lay out the history of credal doctrine to the day, month, and year, naming its place and time. At the same time, he was capable of plunging into spiritual and psychological topics.

Whence came this scientific knowledge of his, one molded by ascetic insight? He was close with monastic men, and he served monastic women. He especially found contentment at this ancient monastery, the Monastery of Mar Jirjis, al-Ḥarf. He was in a long and profound relationship with his late Archimandrite and Father Elias Murqus of eternal memory. It was he who embraced him at his most difficult times. Deacon Spiro Jabbour was a marvel. God alone knows the secret of it. He ardently loved the Antiochian Church, and he exemplified and embodied its critical, political, and credal history, but also its ascetic history. He would take solace in the prayer of the monks, participating in their prostrations. This is what gave him abject humility. It gave him a deep poverty, an awesome simplicity in life. He knew how to speak to the young and old, to men and women. He was always ready to offer an answer to people's questions. A mobile encyclopedia. At the same time, he lived as a stranger on this earth, following the example of his Master. He did not know the taste of luxury, and so he did not taste corruption.

He lived as a pauper—in need of Christ first, but also in need of the nourishment of those around him—and as a scholar, transmitting the teaching, exhorting, and ever prepared; whoever asked found him ready to answer. This was his strength. This was his daily strength. He was nourished by the Divine Word and by others being nourished by it. He knew the Holy Scripture by heart, by chapter and verse. He knew the Holy Fathers. He read, poring over texts day and night. His intellectual and spiritual struggle persisted. To his last breath, he made use of a magnifying glass to read words as well as abstruse letters. He was an ardent lover of the Lord and his Orthodox Church. Here, I make bold, I say and I bear witness that he is one of the Holy Madmen for the sake of Christ. His name is inscribed in the book of life. He struggled unto blood. He gave blood and received spirit. He took the Kingdom by force while he was on earth. People looked upon him as one dispossessed, hiding silently in the cellars of the monastery, as a stranger among his compatriots. Yet upon being approached, he was radiant, expounding on his knowledge that was at once broad and precise. I would witness him on many occasions beside the Holy Father Elias Murqus. The latter is silent. He gives the whole role of discoursing, exhorting, and interpreting to Spiro. One is silent, praying, ruminating in his heart. The other is preaching, eloquent and bold in his speech and exhortations. Now he has departed us in body, and along with him, these great men have departed us. I wonder, what will become of us? We who need them urgently in these difficult times?

It consoles our hearts that Deacon Spiro and his spiritual contemporaries, who are known to you all, left us many treasures: their writings and sermons, their thinking and courage, their divine speculations, and their enkindling by the Divine Word, by their love for the Lord and the Church. All of this urges us not to falter in our hope, so that the flame of the Lord might remain burning in our souls until our last breath. Amen.

Preface to the First Edition

The night of the mystical supper, the Apostle Philip asked Jesus, "O Lord, show us the Father and we will be satisfied." Jesus answered him: "whoever sees me has seen the Father . . . otherwise trust for the sake of these works."[1]

Pentecost had not yet inundated Philip so as to know by experience life in the Holy Spirit. This Spirit that descended upon him baptized him and so carved out a dwelling for Jesus within him, or, more precisely, He caused Jesus to be born in him; that this very Spirit had come to subsist in him as a brilliant light. How could one, having Jesus and the Holy Spirit dwelling within him, not see in them both the Father, who begot the beloved Son Jesus and emanated the Holy Spirit without their separation from Him? In Jesus and the Holy Spirit, we announce the Father, the Light,[2] by His Light residing within us.

The utmost aim of being is nothing but this life in the Trinity, that we then behold the heavenly Father just as Paul taught.

This book is an attempt to illumine the growing number of those holding to spiritual endeavors, men and women monastics, and cultivated readers, that perhaps they and I will tear away the thick veil of transgression which—just as Diadochos of Photiki and others have said—veils the

1. John 14:8–9, 11 (Jesuit and Pauline Revised).

2. The term used here is *al-Nūr*, one of the ninety-nine names of God contemplated in Islam.—Trans.

brilliance of the divine light residing within us.[3] Truly, God eviscerated evil utterly so that we might have communion with one another and with the Father and His son Jesus Christ, for we reach the fullness of joy together.[4]

This book realizes something of the twin desires of two venerable scholars: first, the desire of the late scholar Father Irénée Hausherr for a study combining the history of spirituality and the science of the psyche,[5] and second, the desire of Bishop Kallistos Ware, the Orthodox Englishman who hoped that we would make use of the contemporary psychological sciences just as the Holy Fathers used the science of the psyche current in their time.

I was told that a Greek carried out a study and composed a book on this matter, but it did not satisfy the monks of Mount Athos. Undoubtedly, the work is truly quite difficult. The time has not yet come for research that can satisfy all its truth, for the science of fetal psychology has not taken any definitive steps forward since 1975, after which the first book was published in 1981,[6] although it did not entirely fill the gap.

Diadochos of Photiki refers to the condition of the young child in the womb as a life of leisure and pleasure. The English schools and others' study of children has arrived at this great issue, even if there remains incompleteness and obscurity. It may be nearly impossible to elucidate all the obscurities in the development of the originary elements of the child's psychology; perhaps the impossibility remains as God wills.

3. Jesus does not forget the cold cup of water that we offer the other. The beloved daughter Rulā Aḥsān Naḥḥās (of Homs) asked after the subject of "confession," and it was later turned into this book. Her aunt Victoria Jabbour wholeheartedly encouraged it, and so it was published.

4. 1 John 1:3–4.

5. *Nafs*, a term that implies psyche, self, and soul.—Trans.

6. See our volume *Qird am Insān?* [Ape or human?]. I asked a professor of anthropology at the Lebanese University in Tripoli about the status of anthropology in Paris. She answered that every professor studies and writes according to his caprice. So there is no French anthropology. In *Qird am Insān?* I criticized Nutin, the lead researcher in personality. Our personalist line is deeper and more powerful.

We still need theology and metaphysics in the work of interpretation,[7] even if psychoanalysts have made great strides in the science of analyzing temperament (*caractérologie psychanalytique*). In light of theology and the Christian ascetic writings, however, the matter requires a completely new cast. I only touch upon it here incidentally. The matter needs sizable volumes of an equally high ascetic and scientific character, and this presents a significant difficulty for the Arabic reader.

This book is nothing but a research framework; I have wrung my soul into it with great fervor, so that it may come as some benefit, albeit limited, to the Arabic reader. On another point, the material is not well trodden. The Swiss minister Pfister, a friend and one of the great pursuers of this issue, tried, in two of his writings, to illustrate the positive aspects of psychoanalysis for use in Christian pedagogy.[8] Many of the Christians in the West wrote on this, even though Carl Jung, a schismatic who renounced Freud, caught the eye of Christians and monopolized their attention, almost more than any other.[9] Surely, the West remains Aristotelian-rationalist in theology, scholarship, and research.

Since 1947, the book *The Ladder to God*[10] has penetrated my being, and then, at the beginning of the 1950s, Cassian and other ascetic writers in-

7. *Tafsīr*, a term that implies both scriptural exegesis and interpretation.—Trans.

8. A reference to Oskar Pfister, an associate and interlocutor of Freud's. For the two books possibility alluded to here, see Pfister, *Das Christentum und die Angst* (translated by W. H. Johnston in 1948 as *Christianity and Fear*) and *Die psychnalytische Methode* (The psychoanalytic method). Pfister carried on a lively correspondence with Freud (see Freud, *Sigmund Freud, Oskar Pfister: Briefwechsel*), a translated English compilation of which can be found in *Psychoanalysis and Faith*.—Trans.

9. Jabbour's strong rebuff of Jung in favor of Freud is notable, and likely derives from Jabbour's insistence that ambivalence (polarity) is a structural contradiction of the life of the soul. Moreover, and given his citation of Edward Glover, it also points to a reading of the latter's text: *Freud or Jung*.—Trans.

10. *Al-Sullam ilā allāh*, the Arabic title of John Climacus's *The Ladder of Divine Ascent*, composed in AD 600. The text details the different stages of spiritual ascent to God, which resolves with the attainment of quiescence (stillness, the namesake of hesychasm) and *apatheia* (dispassion, in Arabic *ʿadam al-hawā*). For an English translation of John Climacus's text, see Lazarus Moore's translation, *The Ladder of Divine Ascent*.—Trans.

undated it. And when I was compelled at the end of 1952 to diagnose the condition of a man presented to me by his companions, I found myself driven to diagnose a mental illness. Immersed in those books, I noted the possibility of making use of them by integrating them with the writings of the ascetics. Since that time, this issue has been my sought-after objective.

I found the new Freudians and their analytic technique the most profound and capable of diving into the depths, provided one is free of some of their conceptions.

Our ascetic literature—from the first Desert Fathers and the writings of Evagrios and Cassian, the ascetic school of Gaza and of Sinai (John Climacus and his inheritance) and their great contemporaries, Maximos the Confessor and Isaac of Nineveh, up to Gregory Palamas and the monks of Mount Athos—has not acquired all the scientific technique that appears with Freud and after him. Their research was ascetic-*ṣūfī*-ethical-pedagogical.[11]

Psychoanalysis is a contemporary medicine of the psyche; it has plunged into the labyrinths of dreams, the unconscious, childhood, and an analysis of the development of psychological illnesses in early childhood, and so created for itself a scientific framework for broad research. Still, psychoanalysis is a very rough apparatus and fraught with dangers. It may cause one to be afflicted by misinterpretation and deviate toward explaining the human's states by what is most base in him. Hence, if one does not possess sufficient intellectual faculties, having a strong logical sense and sound judgment, one will interpose a great distortion into the field of his perception, after which control over the situation will be quite difficult for him.

I am not a blind Freudian; my dependence on the ascetics is by length greater. I have only ripped out of psychoanalysis what I may, integrating it

11. This term and its related words—not only *ṣūfī*, the adjective used here, but also *mutaṣawwif* (a practitioner of Sufism), and *al-taṣawwuf* (Sufism)—are used throughout Jabbour's text to indicate something adjacent to but not synonymous with, the terms "mystic" and "mystical" (he often glosses his use of *ṣūfī* with the French term *mystique*). Jabbour uses an additional and innovative term, *khalīlī*, when translating Maximos' Greek term *mystikos*. See the Translator's Introduction.—Trans.

into my general cultural milieu, and exercising precise critique with equanimity, even-handedness, and control.

There is also extensive progress being made in psychosomatic medicine. Its advancement will help solidify information on the reciprocal relations between the psyche and the body and increase our knowledge about the mechanisms of the body's neurological regulation,[12] in order to turn the spirit toward the Holy Trinity. This has no relation to Yoga or the like. Our practice is a spiritual practice, not a bodily one; its foundational basis is pure prayer unto union[13] with God. Hence, the more the unrest of the body's wishes and its movements diminishes (through wisdom and lucidity), the more our spiritual fervor increases in prayer, if we are people of divine ardor.[14]

If this book is pleasing to the monastics of Mount Athos and those following in the footsteps of Father Hausherr, like Father Spidlik,[15] then steps toward a method continue. Father Ephraim Kyriakos can offer Mount Athos a glimpse of the book. It will be within Father Spidlik's capacity to familiarize himself with its content, at which time it will be incumbent on

12. This subject is suitable for the training of mature persons, not for theoretical pedantry and unserious, premature publication. It is specific to those who have made considerable headway, and it carries massive risks for novices. Those things that are psychological, pedagogical, ascetic, and *ṣūfī* are very delicate. May God aid me in discerning between those things of asceticism [*nuskiyyāt*] and those of sufism [*ṣūfiyyāt*] (*mystique*), and rescue my intelligence from delusion, lest I commit obscene errors. I relied on observation and was economical in the application of scientific knowledge before considering the situation; that is, I never relied on random theories. In truth, I was a psychoanalyst, watching and intervening with subtlety, and this approach was successful.

13. *Ittiḥād*, with the Greek analogue *henōsis*, is also a critical concept in Islamic debates on the manner of God's relationship to humans. It is found in both *ṣūfī* writings on the nature of the creature's possible union with God and in marking distinctions between Islam and Christianity concerning divine incarnation. See Nicholson and Anawati, "Ittiḥād."—Trans.

14. *Al-ʿishq al-ilāhī*, a form of desirous love. *ʿIshq* is also used to describe the rapturous longing of lovers and so an insatiability in one's passional desire: hence, its importance in being redirected toward the divine.—Trans.

15. Likely, a reference to Tomáš Josef Špidlík, a Jesuit and scholar of Eastern Christianity.—Trans.

me to shift to writing in French.[16] The material is toilsome and may take volumes, and not in Arabic; no one reads the volumes, and no one funds them. I am not scorning anyone, but I also have an interest in history. I have noticed that the Turkish nation in its two iterations, Seljuk and Ottoman, was an enemy of science, culture, and civilization; it demolished them all in our East, emptying us of all spiritual, cultural, and personal depth and spreading superficiality, feeble-mindedness, and vapidity.

What is the spread of the worship of money, opinions, foods, foolish hobbies, and clothes but a trace of the effects of the inner evacuation of all deep faith—of a life that is profound, personal, and authentic. Our faith is a rudimentary one, not one civilized or deep.[17]

At the close of this introduction, I advise men and women monastics and those interested in spiritual guidance neither to become impatient in studying this book frequently, nor to despair immediately at its occasional obscurity. Its benefits will not manifest for a time until one becomes intimately familiar with it.

My request to God is that He enkindle in all readers a spirit like the Apostle Philip, in his solicitation for a vision of the heavenly Father. May

16. However, the condition of my eyesight since 1984 and age do not support my usual degree of effort.

17. I ventured, with difficulty, a study of "the faith" of the Bedouins. How difficult discussions were with them! Their religiosity is superficial, approaching our own superficiality. Some of them are driven by unease to gather their strength, with manliness and bravery, to seek refuge at the Monastery of Mar Girgis, Humayrā', and others, with compassion, sympathy, and gentleness. These outbursts are often fleeting emotional outbursts. The basis of the Bedouin tribal mode is a "group-feeling" [*'aṣabiyya*, see Ibn Khaldun, *Muqaddima*] for kin and a hatred of non-kin. Within it, there manifests a kind of schizophrenic split between the feelings of love and hatred, but it does not reach a point of separation. These two sentiments are present and coexist. They flare up in crises and certain circumstances but are relatively subdued otherwise. For some, the paradigm is inverted: he treats the other very kindly and he honors them, whereas with kin, he commits malicious deeds. We will see the causes for this in the section titled "ambivalence" [see chapter 5]; moreover, I would like to note, as an aside, that the loss of objectivity, impartiality, and neutrality resulting from passion is one of the fruits of this. It is said, "the blight of one's vision is passion," passion [*hawā*] here being this excessive emotional feeling.

God make each one of us equal to the Apostle Philip and to him who acquainted us with him, that is, John the Evangelist.

Of course, some may find it strange that I venture to address precise scientific subjects like psychoanalysis and psychosomatic medicine since I have, principally, been a lawyer since February 10, 1947.

The perfect response is in the letter of my friend,[18] Doctor Pierre Marty, founder of the first hospital in the world for psychosomatic medicine, which also houses the Institute of Psychosomatic Medicine in Paris.

I publish his letter as it is, without translation, so as not to lose its aroma. In it, he recognizes the depth of my analysis of psychosomatic illnesses and urges a copy of the book to be sent to him quickly once it is published. In Paris, I had already written a linguistic research paper and another on psychoanalysis, which were published at the Sorbonne in 1960, in collaboration with several university professors. An extensive volume was published in 1967, in which twenty-five authors participated, entitled *L'Ambivalence Dans la Culture Arabe.*

I ask that this book meet with a good outcome. May God be glorified.

August 14, 1990

18. This letter was appended to the second edition of this book in both French and Arabic translation. In it, Dr. Marty expresses his enthusiasm for Jabbour's text and asks that he send him a copy.—Trans.

Preface to the Second Edition

Sister Carol Kamāl ʿAbūd was very kind as she recited this book in my hearing to correct printing errors and review it; she deserves all my thanks. I hope that the second edition finds circulation, so that spiritual understanding may penetrate our hearts in order to realize a shining spiritual awakening through the leadership of our master, the highly esteemed monastic Patriarch Yūḥannā.

I have included with my book *Confession and Psychoanalysis* the booklet *Monastic Confession,*[1] which is supported by the witness of the Fathers.

August 25, 2013

The Feast of Apostles Bartholomew and Titus

O Holy Trinity,

I do not know how I, who am ignorant, dare write about the confession of offenses. For what I feel of my iniquities and my transgressive state may not even equate to five one hundredths, the rest of which I know nothing.

How can he who asks to be a little disciple be appointed a teacher!

1. *Al-Iʿtirāf al-ruhbānī.* This second writing, a fictional narrative composed by Jabbour about repentance, is not included in this translation.—Trans.

I rely on You, O Holy Trinity, for You are the Light that enlightens my darkness.

By Your light, I am able to know You, at once, as radiant brightness. You are the Light, and Your trace upon me is the Light; my vision of You is made perfect in the Light that exerts itself upon me.

I ask the Father, the Light, to send down the Holy Spirit, the Light, a light for my soul, so that I witness the Father, the Light, in glory.[2]

Yea, O Holy Trinity, the Father and the Son and the Holy Spirit. You are my creator, You are my savior, You are my light. I fell and You saved me, I was darkened and You enlightened me, I denied Your benefactions and You covered over my denial with the plenitude of Your gentleness and condescension.

Perfume my mind and thought with Your divine oils, and pour out Your blessing upon my heart, that my tongue may articulate righteous speech, and that my pen may inscribe salvific teachings for the glory of Your Name and for the good of the faithful. My concern is confined to You, making me obedient to Your hands, subject to Your sign.

Accept this dedication in the blood of Christ and make me to be a sacrifice by the blessing of the Holy Spirit upon Your heavenly altar, that You alone be all in all within this book, one donated to Your heavenly tithe and Your chosen church, ransomed by the blameless blood of Jesus Christ. Your love for Your church (which is the body of Christ) is a herald, for You enthrall Your beloveds by her love.

Make distant and far from me all evil powers, that Your blessing may remain my loyal guide in all that I say and do. Teach me as You will, that I be just as You will, and I will be an infidel to the world, to myself, and be for You in my entirety. For indeed, no righteous thing dwells within me, only Your saving blessing.

I have no hope in my own soul, but rather You are my hope, my rock, my refuge, my sanctuary, my light, my salvation. You are everything to me; we illude ourselves that we are something, and the truth is that we are less than nothing. Whereas by Your grace, O Trinity, raise me up from the stinking garbage pit to Your glory in heaven. Make my heart and my tongue a wine pressed from thanks, praise, glorifying Your mighty majesty, so that I may present to You the prayer rope without fatigue or weari-

2. 2 Corinthians 4:6.

ness, in the time of night and the divisions of the day, O Compassionate and Gracious One!

The good graces of parents visited on their children are never forgotten. For from January 11, 1944, you came to your heavenly rest, my dear mother, who lived as the very dearest under the wing of the noblest, most compassionate guardians, generous of soul and hand: my two grandparents, Sallūm and Maryam. Remember them, along with my father, stalwart in loyalty, heart, and constancy, Jīrjī, in Your heavenly kingdom with the righteous and the upright. Accept this book as a pure oblation on Your heavenly altar, around which are their spirits and those of their departed kin,[3] within whom the brilliant light of Your great glory shines.

3. Among them are Nāyif, Salīm, and Bahjat.

Confession and Psychoanalysis

CHAPTER

1

The Remembrance of Death

Upon the earth, the human alone turns his sight[1] toward the heavens, toward God, contemplating this strange existence and searching for his place and fate within it. From the third year of life, children stump their families with philosophical questions about the origin of the existence and causes of things. Causation is an inseparable part of our ways of thinking. We see death as a scythe, reaping people, and so we wonder at our fate after the decomposition of our bodies and their transformation into dust in bouts of stomach-turning rot. Youth and the freshness of the young have deceived us. The intensification of power and the strength of purpose in the prime of youth inflates a demonic self-importance, and so we imagine ourselves capable of everything. We collide with reality and lose something of this conviction, but then we reclaim it at the beginning of young adulthood, at times with exceptional delusion and often accompanied by general ignorance.

The truth is that disease and old age are coming to annihilate the fortitude of our bodies. For neither bodily strength, nor wealth, rank, knowledge, nor anything else in the world can save us from the extinguishment of our bodies' power through death. Our earthen body is bound to lose its power, its beauty, and to become a repulsive and odious cadaver.

1. *Baṣar*, the form of external sight that is explicitly contrasted with *baṣīra*, insight or inner vision.—Trans.

Our bodies would tremble before the remembrance of death[2] if it occurred to our minds with daily regularity, just as we pose to ourselves the question of our daily nourishment. The remembrance of death is the food of the spirit that extinguishes our gluttony and greed. As long as our life ends in death, death is the basic problem of our existence. Either our life is like that of insects and mice, or it is of another, peculiar quality. If it is of the former kind, then we are typical animals like any number that now live, without any great distinction. We would be ewes in a herd; whether this herd dies or lives is all the same.

In that case, the slaughter of a sheep and a human is equivalent, as long as both of them are animals, ending in death with no hope or expectation.

Being becomes meaningless inanity and the intellect becomes hellfire for the human. It would be better for us to be mindless, with no understanding, if our end is that of insects.

However, we are not insects, and we do not die as mice; otherwise, we would be the most intensely miserable things in existence, and the animal would be happier than us by a thousandfold. Whereas the animal is without fate and does not make a fate for its own being,[3] the human possesses a fate, forging it amid hardships and bitter struggle. Fortunately for us, we are mortal creatures who use the remembrance of death as a sword upon our necks, so as to renounce the earth, all its pleasures and its wealth. Death is the nemesis of our desires, passions, and wishes.

We cannot exert control over our passions by mere intellectual inducement, as they are not checked save through violence. The violence

2. *Dhikr al-mawt*, the remembrance of death. The remembrance of death is the sixth "rung" of John Climacus's aforementioned ascetic treatise, *The Ladder of Divine Ascent*. For more on its importance in *The Ladder* and in Greek asceticism, see Zecher, *The Role of Death in the Ladder of Divine Ascent*. It is likewise a subject that has been written extensively on in Islamic spiritual discipline and treated concertedly in the writings of al-Ghazālī, whom Jabbour cites in this text. See the fortieth chapter of al-Ghazālī's magnum opus *Iḥyāʾ ʿulūm al-dīn* [The revival of the religious sciences], titled *Kitāb dhikr al-mawt wa ma baʿdahu* [The remembrance of death and what follows it]. See also an English translation by Timothy Winter (ʿAbd al-Ḥakīm Murād), *The Remembrance of Death and the Afterlife*.—Trans.

3. *Dhāt*, which could also be translated as "self." See ftn. 45 in the Translator's Introduction.—Trans.

that cures them is found in being cowed by death, renunciation, and strict asceticism.

The remembrance of death makes philosophers out of us in our view of existence. The fetus in his mother's womb lives in relative pleasure, and the one in life remains, through the course of his lifetime, tied to his pleasures and longs for them. A class of people remains in this world whom we call "the wastrels";[4] these are people incapable of bridling the caprice of childhood and its later stages. Their end will be hell if they do not cauterize their wanton pride with asceticism, as pride of the body kills the spirit and causes ruin in the Hereafter. The remembrance of death terrifies "the wastrels," and so they hate hearing of it. The remembrance of death is a powerful check, restraining our capricious passions and keeping us from all the evil deeds of the earth. It is a great educator, for what person does not tremble at envisioning himself departing life!

Though death may frighten us, it is still a blessing from heaven[5] for a number of reasons:

1. No one hopes to live past one hundred years, living at the expense of one's offspring at a time when loyalty has diminished and children are no longer devoted to their parents, for in what way are they devoted to those who come before them?
2. One is subjected to feeble-mindedness; everyone possessing an intellect prefers death to senility.
3. Some illnesses have a deadly effect, more violent than the blow of a sharp sword. We have known the pain of some of those afflicted by cancer where death is sweeter than its agony.
4. Discontent, ennui, and boredom; the dogged enemies of humanity. Children are discontented; so what of one who surpasses one hundred years in age?

4. *Al-baṭrānīn.* According to Yāsīn ʿAbd al-Raḥīm's colloquial Syrian dictionary, it denotes someone who is "indifferent, devoid of a sense of responsibility in order to fulfil all his desires." See "baṭrān" in *Mawsūʿat al-ʿāmmiyya al-sūriyya.*—Trans.

5. See my writings *Sirr al-tadbīr al-ilāhī* [*The Mystery of the Divine Economy*]; *al-Tajalliyāt fī dustūr al-imān* [*Disclosures in the Constitution of Faith*]. Gregory the Theologian said of death that it is a tool for the eradication of error in order that evil may not endure ceaselessly. He also said that this retribution has become love for humanity. This is the divine method of inflicting punishment (Sermon 45:8 [*PG* 36, 624]).

5. The most virtuous are not able to keep their spirits purified joined to the body indefinitely. For as long as the human is in the body, he remains estranged from God to some degree because the itch of transgression does not depart from him save through death; and so he desires—like the Apostle Paul—to be released and to be with the Lord.

6. If not for the fear of what awaits us after death, people would devour one another like fish, especially in our era. The tools of eradication and destruction are able to liquefy the earth and annihilate the human race, and no impediment will prevent people from inclining to these tools except the fear of Gehenna or annihilation.[6]

Indeed, the animals have become so ferocious that they are not worth mentioning. Complete, unlimited malice is the signature of today's lords of the atomic, hydrogen, and cobalt bombs. The only beasts left in the twentieth century are these bombs' inventors and users; their inventors do not deserve the title of "scientists"[7] but rather the title of monstrosities of a distorted humanity and the demon-possessed. Whoever boasts in them boasts in the instruments of the devil.

Thanks be to God for his good economy[8] that we are punished with death, as He established it as a nemesis to frighten our barbarous instincts and as a check deterring us from evils. Despite the existence of this nemesis, the Christian in this world is the one who has perpetrated, throughout the last five centuries, the most dreadful wars and the basest kinds of eradication. If the Gospel was incapable of instructing Europe, what would

6. *Fanā'*, a word that also is used extensively in Islamic Sufism to refer to one's annihilation in God through divine union and is always paired with a new and subsequent form of subsistence in God (*baqā'*).—Trans.

7. *'Ulamā'*, an expansive term meaning not only scientists but scholars and learned authorities.—Trans.

8. *Tadbīr*, the preferred translation in contemporary Arab Orthodox texts for the Greek term *oikonomia*. This term, from which the modern word "economy" derives, instead invokes here divine mercy in God's treatment of his creatures. It is the excessive term in the dyad of strictness (Gr. *akrevia*) and merciful leniency (*oikonomia*) that is central to spiritual guidance (Ar. *irshād*). Hence, it is used here to point to the mercy of death as a divine check and ultimate limit on the human capacity for evil.—Trans.

the situation be if death were nonexistent? Would not those counterfeit scientists have annihilated this world?

This first atom, this first seed which encompasses all the fractured potentialities in the human of today, confounds the understanding of science. How does this spiritual seed utilize the body and its senses to form the functions of the psyche, harmonizing and cohering into the "I" of the human? Or more precisely, from where does this "I"—that enfolds everything in the human without being able to be equated with any one thing within him—emerge? That is, the "I" is not the intellect, the affects, the will, or the body; on the contrary, the intellect, affects, will, and body are all subordinate to it, for we say: my intellect, my thought, my freedom, my affects, my will, my body, my hand, my head, my house, my shop . . .

Researchers were able to discover the existence of a sense[9] (*conscience*) possessed by the fetus in the sixth month; they were able to discover that psychological growth is related to the human environment that exists around the newborn child, and that early teaching is necessary. Otherwise, teaching the child later is a very difficult and unproductive matter, as we mentioned in our book, *Ape or Human?*[10]

Still, researchers were not able to identify the singular nature of the first atom—the first seed that grows and flourishes in the nurturing bosom of parents, family, and educators—nor how it departs from what is given in the senses to the extraordinary conceptual genesis that forged today's world, what preceded it, and what will follow it tomorrow.

This civilizational and cultural leap separates, radically and in a peculiar way, the world of the human from the world of the animal; it makes the animal one thing and the human another, completely different thing.

People say that it is the spirit that distinguishes the human from the animal, and by that they interpret every enigma of human existence. The incapacity to understand persists and is difficult to overcome. Still, the existence of the spirit in itself does not resolve all enigmas. Does the spirit exist as an element joined to the body? How does the former unite with the latter? How does the spirit work through the body and its mediation? How does it utilize the body?

9. *Shuʿūr*, feeling, awareness, or intuition, but also consciousness, as in the Arabic term used for the unconscious, *al-lā-shuʿūr*.—Trans.

10. [Jabbour, *Qird am insān?*]

Science is still incapable of solving these puzzles, and perhaps there will never come a day for the study of the first spiritual atom within the human.

In theology, we resolved the dilemma by saying that God created the person together; He ordered the body and the spirit within it as a unity, firm in nature while frail in character.

Transgression remains within the human according to his will. In terms of pedagogy, the human is in inner conflict between good and evil, although his person is one; his body and his spirit are united in a union that is not rent save by death.

Human nature is composed from the moment of creation and it exists in the person.[11] For my person is that which says "I, my hand, my head, my intellect, my thought, my freedom, my will, my affects . . ." Is it a phenomenon floating on the surface of my mental and bodily activity?

11. The use of *shakhṣ*, which might be translated as "individual" or "person," aligns Jabbour with the intellectual movement known as personalism, among the greatest exponents of which in twentieth-century Orthodox Christian tradition are Metropolitan John Zizioulas, Christos Yannaras, Dumitru Stăniloae, the aforementioned Metropolitan Kallistos Ware, and before them the Russian Orthodox writers Nicholas Berdyaev and Vladimir Lossky, both of whom are cited by Jabbour. In his *Sirr al-tadbīr al-ilāhī* [*The Mystery of the Divine Economy*], Jabbour writes: "From the general conceptual point of view, the Christian theological struggle was reflected by the idea of rescuing it from the philosophy of essences [*māhiyyāt*], and placing it within the framework of the concept of the person [*shakhṣ*]. When Thomas Aquinas and his successors followed in the footsteps of Aristotle, the West lost its way until existential philosophy came at the hands of Søren Kierkegaard, paving the way for the personalism advocated by the Russian immigrant Berdyaev and the French [Emmanuel] Mounier" (n.p.). This genealogy aside, the function of the term *shakhṣ* in this text is tied to the concept of *nafs*, which Jabbour will go on to describe as that which knots the spirit and the body. In that sense, the individual person qua *nafs* functions as an isthmus between the worlds of matter and spirit. Hence, the term *shakhṣ* should not be taken either as a "person" or "individual" in their moral iterations in English (bearers of rights or the capitalist individual of consumption and of production) but is closer to the notion of a relational "locus" (of communion) as Jabbour's interest with the "first atom" and its potentiality for transformation and destruction evinces. For a relevant genealogy of personalism and politics in Syria see Weiss, "Genealogies of Baʿthism."—Trans.

No. If that were the case, it would be the branch, and that activity would be the root.[12]

So, O Holy Trinity, Who has chastised us through death, do not allow the devil to divert our intellects from the remembrance of death, nor our hearts from trembling at the time of its recollection or the time of imagining the agony of the fire! We are a volcano simmering with iniquitous inclinations. The worm of iniquity is within us sleeplessly. Have compassion and incline unto us, and make us to be crucified day and night upon the pillar of the remembrance of death, that we may live the day and the night in trembling and fear of Your dread minbar—the minbar of Your just judgment.

Truly, souls are humbled by the remembrance of death. So then do not deprive us of this humility! O my soul! Death awaits you. Repent before it is too late, for you do not know when your master comes.

My Lord! Do not come to me while I am heedless of You, but draw me to You while I am a flame blazing with divine ardor for the light of Your splendid guise, not in the abatement of my love and yearning.

O my God, enkindle me by the divine fire, extinguish my laxity, idleness, negligence, and indifference. For indeed You are the Most Merciful;[13] rather, you are Mercy, Love, and Righteousness. To You be praise unto eternity. Amen!

12. This is an indirect refutation of the line of argument pursued by Hume and Kant regarding the transcendental apperception, in which the self is precisely a *phenomenal* appearance, derived from the transcendental unity of experience, grounded in the transcendental ego. Cf. Meister Eckhart's notion of *Grund* (ground) in Lossky, *Eckhart's Apophatic Theology* and Dubilet, *The Self-Emptying Subject.*—Trans.

13. *Arḥām al-rāḥimīn*, a term related to the divine name *al-raḥīm* [The Merciful], and which appears in the Qur'ān multiple times (7:151; 12:64; 12:92; 21:83). Its status as both hyperbolic and superlative also implies that it is a translation of *al-raḥmān* [The Most Merciful], the highest of the divine names in Islamic tradition apart from "God". Jabbour's use of it here is striking. For more, see Haddad, "Beautiful Names of Allah (al-Asmā' al-Ḥusnā)."—Trans.

CHAPTER 2

The Child Is a Person

Perhaps Catholic researchers found what they sought in the collective unconscious (*inconscient collectif*):[1] something that supports their belief in the importance of the Christian tradition[2] for preserving the Christian faith. However, this concept remains philosophical more than scientific. In theology, our teaching is built upon that which came from Holy Scripture concerning the creation of Adam and Eve according to the image of God and His likeness, their dwelling in paradise, as well as their fall and its effects on their offspring.

Adam was perfectly created from the first day, and he lived in blessed ease. However, his will stumbled by demonic allurement, and so he fell from that ease, deforming his creation. God drove him from paradise into the earth to live with Eve in misery, distress, pain, transgression, and ignorance. They knew each other and produced children who inherited from them their miserable condition. The end was death, a worn-out body's return to the dust, and the departure of the spirit to the world of the unknown.

Adam and Eve were innocent in paradise and followed in the light of the Lord, living in bliss. But after transgression, they came to live in desperation and toil. Their offspring came into existence in the latter reality. The fetus begins as an atom in the womb, then grows little by little over

1. That is, Carl Jung's psychoanalytic theory, to which, as Jabbour mentioned in the previous chapter, Western Christian writers were almost singularly attracted.—Trans.

2. *Taqlīd*, a word that also connotes "repetition" or "emulation."—Trans.

nine months, becoming a child and a perfect creation in body. We know that the child is an atom in the womb, and scientists have studied this atom. Yet, what is the atom from which the child's spirit begins?

The child's body resembles the body of higher animals; as for the child's senses, they are inferior to those of animals. How did things in the human come to all this brilliance of mind, to the point that he appears as a great creator according to the image of the most awesome Creator? All this obscurity in our knowledge is one of the effects of the fall of Adam and Eve,[3] and only the light of Tabor[4] ensures its dispersion. Its attainment does not rest on theoretical philosophizing, but on being established in pure prayer that guides love, in humility and gentleness, to the full stature of our Lord Jesus.[5] All this is from the fruits of the Holy Spirit dwelling within us. For however much the intellect is a leader, the Holy Spirit remains our true leader, untouched by error and weakness.

The Holy Spirit alone remains our leader toward the heavenly Father in Jesus Christ our Lord, to Him be glory.

3. If not for Adam's fall, we would not know ignorance. We would not acquire learning through hardships, nor would our will be duplicitous and divided, nor would indecision be the bane of many, nor would, nor would . . . how many of us hesitate in learning! How many among us are ignorant! Our gaze has turned absolutely to the superficial, the external, and peripheral, instead of to the profound (Basil [the Great]). We judge by what is manifest [*ẓāhir*]. We are taken in by what dazzles the eye. We see glory in the wrong places. We envy the rich for the glory of their funerals, while they are cadavers in gilded caskets—no one save God can know the fate of their spirits. Capital is, usually, an instrument of corruption. Rare are those rich persons who dedicate their wealth to God. If they do well, the love of appearance overtakes them. God has created all manner of things and affairs. It may be that a rich person is better than a poor person; God is the final judge [*dayyān*], and whatever we think just and right, our weakness, passions, and ignorance are agents of error. Haste is a slippery slope.

4. That is, the disclosure of the uncreated light that shone from Christ after his ascent upon Mount Tabor with Peter, James, and John. See Matthew 17:1–8, Mark 9:2–9, Luke 9:28–36, and 2 Peter 1:16–19.—Trans.

5. John Climacus did not advise being submerged in theological studies. The fullness of Jesus is perfected through pure prayer; all else aids in that. Study may be a mechanism for suppressing the passions but not for transforming them. It distracts us from the originary task: the free transference of our fervent desires to God.

CHAPTER

3

Confession in the New Testament

We learn from the Gospel that John the Baptist confessed people before baptizing them, and that his baptism was one of repentance. The apostles baptized before Pentecost, although the baptism after Pentecost differed from the baptism that took place before it.

Before Pentecost, the apostles' baptism was one of repentance, like that of John the Baptist, and therefore confession preceded it. After Pentecost, things were different. The Holy Spirit baptized the apostles on the day of Pentecost and made His dwelling within them eternally.

Before the descent of the Holy Spirit on Pentecost, the effects of the Holy Spirit were external, but on Pentecost, the Holy Spirit came to dwell within us.

The holy Gregory Palamas followed in the footsteps of the church Fathers in this and held the view that the Holy Spirit did not come to dwell within the disciples Peter, James, and John on the day of the Lord's Transfiguration [*al-tajallī*].[1] That is, that the effect of the Holy Spirit even on the day

1. The concept of *tajallī*, while most precisely articulated as divine disclosure, is used here to refer to Christ's revelation of his divine glory on Mount Tabor, an event that is celebrated in August within the Orthodox Church. It is commonly known in English as the Feast of Transfiguration—a Latin translation of the Greek *metamorphōsē*. However, the connotations of the Arabic term and its root derivations (*j-l-ū*) point less to a change in form and more to a work of burnishing, manifesting, and revealing. Indeed, *tajallī* is found in Islamic archives as well, especially the works of Ibn al-ʿArabī, where it is typically translated by contemporary commentators as "Theophany."—Trans.

of the Transfiguration was external, for the light came to them from outside just as it came to Moses.

The "I" [the ego] is more prominent than this activity of the spirit in the life of the human. The body works largely without the human's awareness of its *inconscient* work, and so he is rarely aware of the activity and functions of his inner body. Those ill with anxious whisperings[2] are afflicted by an excessive feeling of their inner bodily activity. However, they are mentally unwell and in need of a physician, as this excessive concern for the functions of their body has made them ill. The more a person's movements are folded into unknowing[3] (*inconscience*), the more fully those movements become operative. A skilled driver only supervises the movements of his hands and legs as needed; otherwise, he would become confused and crash. Blood courses through the veins of the human without his knowledge of it or a conscious sense of it, but if the whisperings seize him and oversee his movement, he is at risk of an obsessive disorder.

Memory can retrieve a given day's success or failure, but the necessities of life and successful work require this state of unknowing. And so, my own person continues to be the true actuality that lives alongside me without separation, while my susceptibility[4] remains what is strongest within me.[5]

2. *Waswās* (whispering). Its verbal form *waswasa* means to whisper or speak under one's breath—something that is present phonetically in the articulation of the word itself. It refers above all to the work of the *shayṭān* (the devil), whose trials and deceptions manifest as audible and insistent whispers. It is also broadly used to speak about neurotic obsession or excessive anxiety. See Rippin, "Waswas"; Chabbi, "Whisper"; MacDonald, "Ilhām." See also Freud, "Notes Upon a Case of Obsessional Neurosis" (1909), in vol. 10 of *The Standard Edition of the Complete Psychological Works of Sigmund Freud*, trans. and ed. James Strachey et al. (London: Hogarth Press, 1981; cited hereafter as *SE*), 151–318; Freud, "The uncanny" (1919), *SE* 17:217–256.—Trans.

3. *ʿAdam al-shuʿūr*, similar but not precisely equivalent to *al-lā-shuʿūr*, the unconscious.—Trans.

4. *Iḥsās*, implying a sensitivity that marks the constitutive exposure of affect, which in turn cuts across the typical division between subjective 'feeling' and objective 'sensation.' The symptom of one hearing 'whispers,' which occurs precisely at the point of indistinguishability between feeling and perception, evinces this.—Trans.

5. See also Freud "A Note Upon the 'Mystic Writing-Pad'" (1924), *SE* 19:227–232.—Trans.

Here is an important point. What is the hidden power in the child that causes him to take on the personalities and natures of the children in his environment while he is of meager comprehension? His identifications are something singular, and his uniqueness confounds any attempt to analyze the elements of his personality and nature as we might chemically analyze matter. The child is not a true facsimile.[6] Rather, this singularity distinguishes him from his family, however near his psychological formation may be to their own. He is a true human facsimile of his father and mother only while he is limited in his movements.

Although humans resemble[7] one another, there is a marvel in each one of them. Children are intellectually incapable, but they are formidable in the realm of affectivity. If we view this in terms of the conscious and the unconscious, consciousness is limited because the intellect is limited. So how does one access the child's unconscious while he is nearly incapable of speech and understanding?

The first year of life—after birth—is surrounded by mysteries and enigmas, but they are crucial for the fate of the human and his proper formation; the second year is closer to being understood. On the whole, the main lines of affective life are drawn in the first years. As long as we live, our affective life remains on the edges of obscurity. However great the intellectual faculty may become, the affective part remains significant in our personhood.

6. This line of thinking is possibly drawn from John of Damascus, who writes in his *Three Treatises on the Divine Images*: "the image of a human may give expression to the shape of the body, but it does not have the powers of the soul; for it does not live, nor does it think, or give utterance, or feel, or move its members. And a son, although the natural image of a father, has something different from him, for he is son and not father." (95) John goes on to describe the body as a veil of the soul; Jabbur's use of the psychological concept of "identification" (*taqammuṣ*) utilizes the same root form (*q-m-ṣ*) for clothing oneself.—Trans.

7. *Mutashābihūn*. This term implies not only similitude but poses the problem of alterity within the reproduction of 'the same'—the difference that appears as what is singular or unique in the pure "facsimile." *Mutashābihāt*, for example, is a technical term referring to points of obscurity in the Qur'ān, and the root *sh-b-h* is used as a grammatical equivalency for 'pseudo.' The problem of resemblance is distinct from that of the counterfeit. Whereas the former can be thought of as the difference within *any* reproduction, the latter points to the hidden inauthenticity that is effective on the level of appearance (see Translator's Introduction).—Trans.

People in whom intellection has grown exponentially large at the expense of the affects lose the taste of joy and the sense of personal repletion. They suffer, in short, from an existential void.

The affectively full person will be full in his character. If my heart overflows with love, my person has become full. If it lacks this, I am empty, vapid, and fatuous. Even if I were to gather together in my memory all knowledge and understanding, my person would be impoverished; it would be unsettled and miserable.

Malice is the enemy of God, because God is love.[8] Therefore the "I" and one's person are both tightly bound to the affective structure of the human and can never be equated with the intellect or thinking. The human is one, and the person is one.

We may see people who suppose that they have reached a degree of sufficiency, or that they uphold what is right and good, or that they are no longer in need of anything, or that they do not commit errors, or that they are righteous in their own eyes.

Repentance in the Gospel is contrary to all of this. The Apostle Paul considered himself the greatest of transgressors, and in his sayings, he strongly rebukes himself. Paul knows his divine fate as a militant apostle,[9] yet he also knows himself as a transgressor, the greatest of them, who has no measure except in what has been gifted him by Jesus.[10]

The one who is baptized repents, and confession precedes baptism. Confession is part of repentance, but it is not itself repentance. Repentance is more comprehensive than that. Confession is the avowal of transgressions, whereas repentance is a violent overturning of the past. I use here the word "violent" because in the nature of repentance there is a violence, not a laxity, against transgressions. There is no such thing as lax repentance.

Repentance is not only the sense of guilt[11] but the gathering of all the energies of the psyche to combat iniquity and acquire virtue. It is rare

8. 1 John 4:8

9. *Rasūl mujāhid*.—Trans.

10. 1 Timothy 1:15.

11. *Shuʿūr bi-al-dhanb*. This phrase, used often by Jabbour, could also be rendered as "feeling at fault." We have elected for the English word "sense" over "feeling" to keep the usage more proximate to both Freud's notion of a "sense of guilt" (*Schuldbewusstsein*) and the key dyad of the conscious (*al-shuʿūr*) and the unconscious (*al-lā-shuʿūr*), where *shuʿūr* connotes a sense of intuited knowledge.—Trans.

among Christians for a transgressor to exist who is not aware that he is a transgressor. Nevertheless, what is the portion of true penitents? God knows. Maximos the Confessor, Isaac the Bishop of Nineveh, the holy Symeon the New Theologian, Imam al-Ghazālī, and Ibn al-ʿIbrī [Bar ʿEbroyo] mourned the rarity of righteous people capable of upright prayer and even mourned over the state of their own souls. Maximos said, "Where do we find in the present generation a soul completely free from all thoughts and passions, one becoming worthy through pure, immaterial prayer?"[12]

Isaac likewise said, "It is rare that you find one among the multitude who has been counted worthy of pure prayer. Many were not counted worthy of pure prayer, only a few." Isaac continues with regard to the latter category, saying that it is rare for a single man to exist in each generation who has drawn near to knowledge of this blessing of God. What is intended by the end of this sentence is the highest spiritual state to which the Sufis[13] are joined: unity with God, divine witnessing.[14]

Isaac voiced in this same section his own incapacity, as he said:

> and especially transgressors such as us . . . by His (that is, God's) righteousness, He opened our blind heart to understand by contemplation of the divine scriptures and by the guidance of the venerable Fathers; and though I have not yet been accounted worthy to know by experience, through personal zeal, one thousandth of what I have written by my own hand—specifically in this small book that we

12. Maximos, *Four Hundred Texts on Love* 4.51.

13. *Al-mutaṣawwifūn*, and so equally "the mystics." This remarkable passage utilizes theological grammar that is also typical of Islamic Sufism—of gnosis (*maʿrifa*) and of unity with God (*ittiḥād*) in a divine witnessing (*mushāhada*)—to translate the "aim" (*maqṣūd*) of Isaac's words, which Jabbour notes is likewise drawn from Evagrios (and, one could add, Pseudo-Dionysius). The final term, *al-mushāhada al-ilāhī*, confound the localizability of witness in terms of subject and object. In this union, God is not an object of contemplation; this union is marked by a paradoxical (because non-phenomenological) experience of the very threshold between the contemplated and the contemplator breaking down.—Trans.

14. Isaac here was influenced by Evagrios in this expression, however, Isaac is of a sound view in all his sayings, unlike Evagrios, whom the fifth ecumenical council condemned.

> have hazarded—we have written it for the sake of the illumination and exhortation of our soul and those who encounter it. Perhaps (our souls) because of their desire, will be able to rouse and come nearer to pursuing (action).[15]

Pentecost is that which brought about us the Holy Spirit dwelling in the heart.[16] He baptizes us and seals Christ within us. He anoints us with chrism, and so He Himself is sealed within us. The bread and the wine are changed into the body of Jesus and His blood; hence, He changes us through them into the body of the Lord and His blood. It was not so before Pentecost; all the glory of Moses, and those like him, was an outer glory. As for our glory, it is an inner glory.

The holy Epiphanios says that Jesus, when He descended into hell, found all the Fathers, from Adam, Noah, and Abraham to John the Baptist. The Triodion[17] adds that Lazarus was also there before His resurrection.

What is repentance? The New Testament used, in the original Greek, the term *metanoia*, which means "conversion,"[18] the substitution and transposition of one condition for another.

15. Isḥāq [Isaac], *Nusukīyyāt*, chapter 22 [p. 85. See also, in English, Isaac the Syrian, *The Ascetical Homilies*—Trans.].

16. Palamas, *Défense des saints hésychastes*, 190–192, 574–575, and 710–712. Something similar was mentioned in the translation of the blessed Patriarch Ilyās [Muʿawaad] for an article that appeared in *al-Nashra al-Baṭrīarkiyya* [The Patriarchal newsletter], entitled "al-Ṣūra al-ilāhiyya fī al-insān ladā ghrīghūrīus bālāmās" [The divine image in the human being according to Gregory Palamas], December Issue 1973. I have put together an article for the esteemed periodical *al-Nūr* (1978) on the subject; Palamas cited Symeon the Translator [Metaphrast] in his explanation of the sermons of Pseudo-Makarios. See also Kallistos of Athos and Igantios Xanthopolous, "al-Mi'awiyya al-rūḥiyya" [*On the Life of Stillness and the Monastic State,* in *Philokalia* vol. 5] Chapter 5. ʿAdnān [Ṭarābulsī?] 1993 furthered the discussion in two books.

17. *Triodion* is a Greek term referring to a set of church books for the liturgical season preceding Pascha, and, more broadly, the time of the Great Fast, named so because of the triple ode canons that characterize the dawn prayer during this time.—Trans.

18. *Ihtidā*ʾ, a word that also implies the right guidance.—Trans.

The penitent—in a Christ-like manner—overthrows his being in a complete overturning. He passes from wallowing in iniquities to being adorned with the virtues. The Gospel gives us numerous examples of it, and the most striking to the soul is the proverb of the divisive son.[19] The Greek term [*asōtos*] means "profligate" or "squanderer," and, indeed, the son was a profligate. He had squandered the fortune of his father by committing offenses, even becoming the caretaker of swine, which are considered impure for the Jews. That is, he had taken up a profession loathsome to the Jews, through which he became a great sinner who had overstepped the Mosaic law. This human moved from the degradation of iniquity and squalor to the bosom of the heavenly Father.

The publican[20]—that is, the tax collector—shifted from an embezzling enemy of his community [*ummah*] to a remorseful penitent. The Apostle Paul turned from being the greatest oppressor of the church to her greatest servant. In the lives of the saints there are numerous stories of turning from great malefaction to great holiness; likewise, from great piety to great transgression and then becoming an even greater penitent.

In all of these cases, the penitent shifts from one condition to another that is completely counterposed. For example:

The murderer becomes merciful and tender, mourning over his transgressions. He does not grow cold; the stream of his tears does not cease.
The thief becomes the epitome of faithfulness, impartiality, and trust.
The fornicator comes to radiate integrity and purity.
The liar becomes the epitome of veracity.
The malicious becomes a flame of love, gentleness, and sympathy.
The arrogant, in manifold humility, becomes mere dust before all.
The miser becomes generous, spreading his wealth to the needy without measure, and so on.

19. *Al-ibn al-shāṭir*, referring to the parable of the prodigal son (Luke 15:11–24), which, in the Orthodox calendar, is read two Sundays before the start of the Great Fast. The Arabic translation does not refer to the son as a profligate but as *al-shāṭir*, that is, one who "divides" by taking his share of inheritance and breaking with his family. Colloquially, it is a term that is used to refer to someone who is clever or cunning.—Trans.

20. See Luke 18:9–14.—Trans.

All this is accompanied by intense regret, great lamentation, and abundant weeping over a loathsome past. The remembrance of past mistakes and transgressions remains as a wound that bores into the holy ones, increasing humility and zeal for acquiring the virtues.

When one supposes that he has attained something of the virtues or that he has atoned perfectly for his faults, he forfeits his struggle. When one feels sufficient, one falls from one's standing. Therefore, refined Christians lose the general capacity for struggle and progress once they feel that they are satisfied, that they have come far enough, that they are good friends, that they no longer lack anything, that they do not commit transgressions, or that they are righteous in their own eyes.

In the early church, the avowal of offenses occurred publicly and was connected to three offenses: 1) denying the Christian faith, 2) murder, and 3) sexual immorality.[21]

From there, things developed into making an acknowledgement before men of religion;[22] however, the monastics greatly developed these matters in the fourth century and arrived at a method of confession resembling contemporary psychoanalysis.[23]

The monastic is a human who has withdrawn from others, renounced wealth, possessions, and the world, and chosen virginity as a form of life; he has rallied around the authority of the head of the monastery and chosen a spiritual father from among the monastic elders. The monastic elder is one who practices spiritual struggle, battling cravings, wishes, passions, and the trials of the devil, and therefore he is skilled in this warfare. God granted him the gift of discernment, and so he became sagacious as one experienced in matters of the psyche and the tactics of the devil; he took hold of his passions and ordered them, and became filled with humility, meekness, graciousness, sympathy, and humanity.

21. *Zinā*.—Trans.

22. *Rijāl al-dīn*, a common term in the Mashriq for referring to the male heads of Christian, Muslim, and Druze communities—in this case it is a synonym for the clergy.—Trans.

23. See our book *Fī al-tawba* [On repentance], that looks at Symeon the New Theologian limiting the hearing of confession in his time (AD 949–1022) to monastics due to his clergy's lack of competence.

Confession in church usage

The church uses the term "confession" in the following ways:

—The avowal of the correct Christian faith. If the church doubts the health of the faith of one of the people, it requests an avowal of the proper faith to examine that person's faith and the extent to which it agrees with the Orthodox faith. Not all those who are in the record of Orthodox souls are, in fact, Orthodox. He who is Orthodox remains established in the Orthodox faith. We cannot be ignorant of the obscene deficiency in the instruction of the Orthodox regarding the principles of their faith, nor can we be ignorant of the miserliness of the Orthodox with regard to the purchase of, or expenditure on, religious writings. And if they purchase them, they do not read them—our discussion here is anxiously flitting between topics. They may spend millions on other subjects but will not part with a few piastres for a religious publication. They are a decomposing nation, just as salt dissolves into water; they are heedless of their condition and in a deep slumber.

—In times of oppression, people confronted oppressive rulers, their men, their mobs, by declaring that they are Christians, and refusing to return to idolatry. Among them were those who met death as martyrs, and those who encountered many kinds of torture without departing this life.

We have a holy confessor whom we greatly honor; on the one hand, he is a perfect theological and spiritual model of a monastic and ascetic, and, on the other, of a confessor, a champion of the faith and of the truth. It is the holy Maximos the Confessor, one of the glorious men of the seventh century. He is the rarest of greats in the history of the church. He took a stand in the eastern, western, and southern corners of the Byzantine Empire, threatened at that time by extensive fragmentation. He refused to confuse religious obligation and politics in the interest of the latter. At that time, the patriarchs of Constantinople, Alexandria, Antioch, and al-Quds [Jerusalem] followed the teaching of the one will,[24] while Rome was a sanctuary for Maximos and his followers. In the year 649, the martyr-pope

24. That is, the doctrine of Monothelitism, which argued that Christ had only one will rather than one human and one divine.—Trans.

Martinus convened a Lateran council and condemned the heretical innovation. Still, the winds blow not as ships desire.[25] The letter of the new Pope arrived in Constantinople without addressing these doctrinal issues. The Patriarch of Constantinople interpreted this as friendliness. Therefore, he was encouraged and came to the prison, visiting Maximos in his cell to show him this accession to the false coalition. This was on the feast of mid-Pentecost, the 18th of April, 658; even so, Maximos responded to the display in the tone of the martyrs.

The Patriarch of Constantinople said to him: "Of which church are you? Are you of the church of Constantinople? Of Rome? Of Antioch? Of Alexandria? Of Jerusalem? Look, they are all as one and their dioceses have united. So, if you are of the universal Church, you too join with us, fearing that you will suffer what you did not regard because of your persistence in a foreign and unfamiliar path."

Maximos answered him: "The God of all acclaimed Peter blessed because he confessed Him with an apposite confession;[26] He (that is, the Divine Jesus) has shown us that the catholic (the universal) church is, rather, a sound confession and salvation is through her herself. Still, at least allow me to learn the confession upon which the unity of all the churches rests, for I am not opposed when it is sound . . ."

It was then said to him: "The Emperor and the Patriarch have decided that a charge will be laid against you, on advice from the Pope, if you do not submit, and that you will endure a death prescribed by them."

He answered: "May what God has appointed in me before all ages find its end in me, as I offer up to Him His glory, which He knew before the ages."[27]

In the year 662, the relations between Rome and Constantinople had entered a chapter of perfect alliance and stability. Therefore, the adversaries of Maximos dared to convene their Monothelite Council, "preaching the one will," in Constantinople. Maximos was summoned from prison, he and his disciples were tried, and a sentence was issued against them: flogging, the tongue ripped out, the right hand severed, and exile to the Caucasus in present-day Georgia. The trip overburdened Maximos, who

25. *Al-riyāḥ tajrī bimā lā tashtahī al-sufun*, a paraphrase of a verse written by the Abbasid era poet al-Mutanabbī, whom Jabbour will cite later in this text.—Trans.

26. Matthew 16:18.

27. See John 17:5.—Trans.

was a man of eighty-two, and he gave up his spirit to God on August 13, 662, after having fulfilled, like his master Jesus, the true martyrdom of his time.[28] The command of the dissembling devils did not last, and they fell. The holy Pope Agatho emerged as the successor to the Orthodox martyr Maximos.[29]

The sixth ecumenical council was convened and Maximos's victory at it was a most magnificent one. His name was immortalized, and his adversaries bore the ignominy of history. If not for Maximos, they would have deformed the faith and distorted the doctrine. Indeed, he is a man of divine providence at a decisive interval of general and specific history. He refused all compromises, for compromising in the faith is a great iniquity. The truth does not accept compromises. The truth is all perfect and does not accept partition, neither bargaining nor adjustment. Either you accept the truth in its completeness, or you are not a man of truth. No partition in the truth, no patchwork, no embellishment. Indeed, it is perfectly one, without deficiency.

28. See *PG* 90, 132 A–133 A and 169 C–173 D.

29. Maximos was from Khisfīn in the Golan. [Khisfīn was a Palestinian village of Muslims and Christians who were driven into part of Syria by Israeli forces in 1967. The village remained occupied from then on and became the site of an illegal Israeli settlement called Haspin in 1978.—Trans.] He is not from Constantinople, as had been previously supposed. He is a pearl that we add to the glory of the bygone Antiochian See. Maximos is a marvel of our history in every domain.

CHAPTER

4

Confession in Psychoanalysis

Freud, the one who discovered psychoanalysis, grew up in a Catholic country, and he was not aware of the trajectory of these issues for the Orthodox. In 1782, Nikodemos the Athonite (that is, a monk of Mount Athos in Greece) published a book, the *Philokalia*, a collection of sayings on prayer selected from thirty-five Fathers of the church over ten centuries—from the fourth century to the eighteenth. In 1793, Paisii Velichkovskii published a translation of it in the Slavonic language, and it had the greatest impact in Russia. We read something of the impact of this translation in the book, *A Russian Pilgrim on the Paths of the Lord*.[1] The *Philokalia* penetrated the life of monastics in Russia, and there was a brilliant monastic and spiritual renaissance in the nineteenth century.[2] The Optina Monastery emerged through its radiant monks as a spiritual citadel and a lighthouse for the cultural greats. Brilliant spiritual writers emerged, among them Ignatius Brianchaninov and Theophan the Recluse, the latter being

1. *Sā'iḥ rūsī ʿalā durūb al-rabb.* This book, *Otkrovennye rasskazy strannika dukhovnomu svoemu ottsu* [Candid stories of a pilgrim to his spiritual father]—known in its English translations as *The Way of a Pilgrim*, or *The Pilgrim's Tale* (see Pentovsky [ed.], *The Pilgrim's Tale*)—is a Russian story of a mendicant pilgrim learning to recite the Jesus Prayer. It was published in the late nineteenth century and was presented to the monks of Mount Athos at that time.—Trans.

2. Paisii also had a considerable impact in Romania. He was a leader of renewal both there and in Russia. Theophan the Recluse translated the *Philokalia* into Russian and expanded its reach.

the translator of the *Philokalia* into Russian and the one who brought the Russians' writing to maturity.

Freud did not know Russian, and he was of Jewish origin. So, he only knew the Catholic confession of transgressions, which is tantamount to a mechanical enumeration. A council of Swiss Catholic bishops criticized this in 1963, calling for a greater focus on repentance rather than on the mechanical enumeration of transgressions.

Freud drew a comparison between his method in psychoanalysis and the confession of transgressions to give himself claim, preference, and distinction. In psychoanalysis, one reclines on the divan, and the analyst sits behind him in such a manner that he does not see the face of the analyst, lest he be affected by what he surmises of the analyst's bearing, emotions, and reactions.

Analysts rely on a method called "the free association of concepts," which requires one to divulge all that wanders into one's mind to the analyst without hesitation, shame, planning, framing, omission, oversight, or preamble. One recounts thoughts just as they arrive, without omission, verification, or censorship. Of course, this situation is the ideal; it never happens in reality with such ease. The patient's complexity is still an obstacle because he is afflicted by a neurosis (*psychonévrose*), and the basis of neurosis is a deep conflict between ambivalent forces.[3]

This conflict is established in childhood, between the child's inclinations and his initial environment. The "I" of the patient was not strong enough to resolve the conflict positively because it was small and limited. Instead of developing his capacities toward what was best for his age's development, he followed the path of repression. Repression causes one's energies to recede into the unconscious, and seeds, for some, a conflict that results in the symptoms of a neurosis. Ethicists use the term "conscience," whereas analysts use three technical research terms: "it," "the I," and "above the I."[4] In truth, the human's person is as far removed as can be from all

3. For more on the relationship between neurosis and free association, see Freud, *From the History of an Infantile Neurosis* (1918), *SE* 17:1–124.—Trans.

4. This refers to Freud's so-called second topography, which is ubiquitously translated into English via the Latin terms *id*, *ego*, and *superego*. However, this translation practice obscures the immediate linguistic register of this terminology. The Arabic translation employed here by Jabbour maintains the immediate meaning of Freud's terminology—*Das Es, Ich, Über-Ich*, are translated as *huwa*

partition but, the exigencies of scientific research require, at times, research terminology, as the inner conflict in the human fragments it. There is no doubt that forgetting plays a role in life, that our psychological life does not enjoy complete presence, and that our memory does not manifest to us in a single facet, but rather manifests all the history of our life at once.

In the fourth century, monastics spread out in groups of ten, with each elder leading ten monks. The monastic was exceedingly attached to his elder, and so he confessed to him every notion that wandered within his breast, and he did so without delay. At that time, the obedience demanded was a perfect obedience. The monastic contends with diverse species of the passions, wishes, and cravings and he begins as one naive in the arts of war; therefore, he needs a guide to lead and direct him.

What is the throughline of these three types of attestation? Indeed, it is bravery. Paul taught us that no one says that Jesus is Lord except by the Holy Spirit.[5] The acquisition of the Holy Spirit is bravery, and speaking by Him[6] before the minbar of the church is bravery, because He is a testimony[7] to Jesus. All testimony is a kind of bravery, a martyrdom, and a blameless oblation[8] to God.

The Holy Scripture regards Jesus's avowal before Pilate and likewise before Caiaphas as bravery. The avowal of Maximos the Confessor was accompanied by a bitter worldly struggle, resulting in prison, trial, the severing

("he" or "it"), *al-ana* ("the I"), and *fawq al-ana* ("above the I"). The final term ("the superego" or "above the I" is the site of conscience (in Arabic, *ḍamīr*) and the interdiction of the law. As such, this translation maintains the clear linguistic register of Freud's topography—where the first-person pronoun marks the reflexive construction of the self ("I speak"), insufficient without the third person that marks its libidinal investment ("I want it"). As Freud, in his most famous statement on this relationship, wrote: "Wo Es war, soll Ich werden," "Where *it* was, there *I* will be." *New Introductory Lectures on Psycho-Analysis* (1933), *SE* 22:80 (emphasis added).—Trans.

5. 1 Corinthians 12:3.

6. *Nuṭq*, a reference to the Nicene creed, wherein the Holy Spirit is said to be He who "speaks by the prophets," *al-nāṭiq bi-l-anbiyā*ʾ.—Trans.

7. *Shahada*, a term, as in the Greek *martyria*, that carries the meaning of witness, testimony, and martyrdom.—Trans.

8. *Qurbān*, also the eucharistic offering.—Trans.

of the tongue and the right hand, and the hardship of exile when he was eighty-two.

The avowal of transgressions, then, is bravery. Paul taught us: "If we condemned ourselves, we would not be condemned."[9]

The court of conscience is a terrible court, which precedes the hearing before the minbar of the Lord Jesus.[10] The hearing before the priest is one before a representative of Jesus. There is nothing more difficult than saying with humility, honesty, and perfect submissiveness: "I am a great sinner."

Our egoism, pride, self-amazement, our confidence in ourselves, our knowledge, our righteousness, and our virtue, as well as the sense of our own stature and nobility; all this impedes our capacity for knowledge of our souls and an avowal of their evil before the other. Every human is eager to appear superior to others, and thus jealousy and envy are constantly at work.

In childhood, the affection of the family and their esteem are our psyche's daily bread. The esteem of people remains an urgent need and our "essential" bread[11] into adulthood. People desire with all their hearts to gain the esteem and approval of others. A scornful word may lead one to ruin. A sense of vanishing[12] embitters one, and then one is struck, at times,

9. 1 Corinthians 11:31.

10. It is worth mentioning that this "court of conscience" cannot be thought of as synonymous to the court of reason, which grounds Kant's concept of conscience, even though they parallel one another. For Jabbour, conscience invokes a problem of the heteronomy of the divine law, the unconscious, and thus the *lack* of the subject's autonomy. For a discussion of this see El Shakry, *The Arabic Freud*, 59.—Trans.

11. *Khubz jawharī*, the "essential bread" invoked in the Lord's Prayer (from the Greek term *epiousios*, almost universally mistranslated into English as "daily bread").—Trans.

12. *Shuʿūr bi-l-talāshī*, likely a translation of the Greek term *aphanisis* (fading or disappearance) that was developed in psychoanalytic theory by Ernest Jones and Jacques Lacan. In a 1927 essay, Ernest Jones coins *aphanisis* as the broader force at work in Freud's theory of castration and the basis of all neuroses: *aphanisis* is the "main blow of total extinction . . . the total, and of course permanent, extinction of the capacity (including opportunity) for sexual enjoyment" (135). Lacan in his eighth seminar on transference, develops Jones's term beyond the extinguishment of sexuality toward the broader fading of desire, one that resonates more with Jabbour's remarks in the text (further evidence that Jabbour

by bouts of nervous breakdown. A scornful word may also impel acts of injury or, perhaps, murder. The human's confidence in himself and his nobility are inseparable from his egoism.

Then there is shame. We are ashamed of ourselves; we are ashamed to face the priest and others, lest we appear weak and erring. How many people are puffed up and haughty! Perfectly rousing a conscious sense of guilt is nearly impossible, save for the holy ascetics and those like them. The sense of guilt throws some into a swoon. It is never an easy matter to discover that the human is scum and refuse, a mass of abhorrent passions stripped bare of all human value.[13] This is an exemplary state to which the holy ones arrive at the close of a bitter struggle.

Indeed, whoever confesses his condition humbly and submissively murders his egoism and puts to death all the aforementioned disgraces. He approaches his psyche as a martyr, and this is something that requires rare bravery.

Daily life shows us people wrapped up in pride, unable to bear a passing remark; how would they be if we censured them with deep criticism? Is not the one who confesses his transgressions perfectly and humbly brave and a martyr?

Gregory Palamas said that God "created everything in beauty."[14] This is clearest with regard to the creation of the human. God has indeed created

---

may have attended this seminar). Lacan notes that, in *aphanisis*, "the subject designates himself here in the evacuated object. It is, so to speak, the starting point of an *aphanisis* of desire. It is entirely based upon the effect of the Other's demand—the Other makes the decision. The root of the neurotic's dependence clearly lies here. . . . It depends so much on the Other's demand that what the neurotic demands of the Other is his neurotic demand for love, is that he be allowed to do something." Lacan *Transference*, 216.—Trans.

13. Note Lacan's words in his seminar on transference just before speaking of *aphanisis* (see previous footnote): "Furthermore, we are not surprised to see that idealists, enamored of the theme of a hominization of the cosmos or, as they are forced to express themselves in our times, of the planet, neglect that one of the manifest stages, since the beginning of time, of the hominization of the planet is that the human animal turns the planet into a garbage dump" (216).—Trans.

14. Sermon 52:1 in *Tou en hagiois patros hemōn Grēgoriou*, 120–130. Meyendorff notes that this sermon was delivered sometime between 1347 and 1359 and that it is different from Sermon 53, which is a treatise written by Palamas in 1335, found on pages 131–180 of the aforementioned collection. See Meyendorff,

all things by His divine command, but when it came to the human, God molded him with His own two hands. How beautiful is this image! God molded the human with His fingertips. The sculptor molds with a delicate artistry; the draftsman communes with his quill. God participated in the work of the human's creation with an aesthetic sense, masterful and indescribable; He sketched for Himself a singular image of the human that is unparalleled by other creatures, because this earthen corpse is one molded with divine touch[15] and a beautiful, divine artistic sensitivity, to be a residence for the Spirit and an image of God. God created the human as a person according to His image and His likeness and arranged within the human's person a spirit and body, devising them both in a blessed creativity. Gregory the Theologian said that the human is "a masterpiece from the hand of God."[16]

And yet, O dire misfortune, the human did not preserve his nobility; he plunged from it and fell. He forfeited eternity, fell into corruption, death, and decay. The human was fashioned for incorruption, but became corrupt, capable of decomposition, dissolution, and deterioration, entering into weakness and enervation.

Adam and Eve craved the forbidden fruit. It was first sweet to their eyes, then they tasted it and it was sweet to their lips. The worm of corruption, dissolution, and decomposition came upon the human race. Covetous desire was the gateway to iniquity and destruction; because of pleasures, the gates of blasphemy and dissolution were knocked upon. The devil breathed his spirit of false theosis into the pair and hence pulled them outside the orbit of God.

God was the axis of their lives, and then each one became an axis for themself. They retreated from God, turned in upon themselves, seeking a delusional and false self-interest, and so each of the two ardently loved themself instead of ardently loving God.

Introduction á l'étude de Grégoire Palamas, 390–393; Gregory Palamas "Homélie sur la Présentation de la Vierge," 22–23.

15. *Dhawq*, taste, also implying firsthand experience. The concept of *dhawq* is used in Islamic Sufism to refer to an intimate knowledge of God in divine union.—Trans.

16. Sermon 45:12 [*PG* 36, 624]; and see also sermon 7 [*PG* 35, 755]. Maximos writes much on this subject. Paul himself said that the woman is the glory of the man and the man the glory of God (1 Corinthians 11:7).

What comes from the archive of psychoanalysis confirms that the greatest part of those things preserved for the patient of his feelings and impressions are outside the scene of conscious awareness, hidden in deep basements; in this, the human appears as if he is composed of a number of floors and apartments.[17]

During free association therapy (in a state of lying down, relaxation, and the relative disappearance of psychological censure), the repressed floats to the surface bit by bit.[18] The physician responds with great forbearance; he encourages the patient and weakens the latter's stringent resolve toward self-censorship, encouraging him to release gradually. What the patient grasps of the analyst's forbearance encourages him to release. The ambit of awareness into which the repressions enter expands, and then the human "I" incorporates them into itself. Whenever the realm of the "I" widens to account for repressions, the patient moves toward safe shores.

Repressions do not stop at the "it" [the id]; the "above-the-I" [the superego] works unconsciously, and part of the "I" itself is unconscious.[19] What analysts call defense mechanisms work unconsciously on the whole, yet analysis stills[20] these mechanisms piece by piece.

17. This analogy echoes Freud's own comparison of the unconscious to Rome, the "Eternal City," in *Civilization and Its Discontent*: "Let us, by a flight of imagination, suppose that Rome is not a human habitation but a psychical entity with a similarly long and copious past—an entity, that is to say, in which nothing that has once come into existence will have passed away and all the earlier phases of development continue to exist alongside the latest one" (32).—Trans.

18. Freud likewise comments: "consciousness is the surface of the mental apparatus; that is, we have ascribed it as a function to a system which is spatially the first one reached from the external world—and spatially not only in the functional sense but, on this occasion, also in the sense of anatomical dissection" and "the ego is first and foremost a bodily ego; it is not merely a surface entity, but is itself the projection of a surface." *The Ego and the Id* (1923), *SE* 19:1–66, 19, and 26.—Trans.

19. As Freud notes: "We have come upon something in the ego itself which is also unconscious, which behaves exactly like the repressed—that is, which produces powerful effects without itself being conscious and which requires special work before it can be made conscious." *The Ego and the Id* (1923), *SE* 19:19.—Trans.

20. *Yuhadda'*, this word in both its verbal form *hada'* and as a noun *hudū'* connotes calm, stillness, or tranquility. It is also the word from which the Arabic term *hudū'iyya*—a translation of the Greek term *hesychia*—derives. Jabbour's

Consequently, the conflict that chokes the patient's person and constricts the scene of his "I" is broken down, piece by piece, to be replaced with harmony.

What we might call, in ethical terms, the "conscience" of the patient is afflicted by mercilessness and constriction, because he has retained the conscience of the child; it has not become that of an adult.[21] The "aggression instinct"[22] engulfs him, and then he begins to assault his own being interiorly. That is, he comes to orient his aggressivity against himself instead of orienting it to the external world or in actions. For these patients, the sense of guilt plays an enormous role, and this requires a specific chapter; words about it are somewhat incomprehensible for those who do not deal in these issues.

---

use of it here signals the way the techniques of psychoanalysis work toward the monastic aim of attaining divine stillness.—Trans.

21. That is, following Freud, the regression of the "I" (ego) into an earlier phase of its development.—Trans.

22. *Gharīza al-ʿudwān*, a drive or instinct toward enmity or aggression, invokes Freud's well-known formulation of the death drive (*Todestrieb*). Jabbour's formulation here appears in keeping with Freud's argument in *Civilization and Its Discontents*, in particular the final chapter.—Trans.

CHAPTER

5

The Sense of Guilt

Theologically, we learn that Adam and Eve committed an offense, so God drove them out of Paradise to live out a spiritual death of transgression until this results in their bodily death with the separation of the spirit from the body. We learn, likewise, that corruption, death, and decay befell the human because of transgression that, through reproduction, was transferred to the seed of Adam and Eve.

Without a doubt, our vitality is an enduring gift for us, yet its value is very relative. Our body—wonderful, strange, and beautiful—enjoys but a temporary splendor, because it bears in itself the propensity for deterioration in illness, old age, death, and a return to the dust. If we had not witnessed the cadaverous corpses of the dead transformed into a handful of dust, we would be incapable of imagining that our body, a living, beautiful, and wondrous workmanship, is capable of being worn out.

In the opening of the book of Genesis, there is a wonderful image of creation and the human. Whenever God created something, He saw it as "good." An aesthetic sense[1] is very apparent in the first chapter of the book of Genesis.

1. *Al-mafhūm al-jamālī*.—Trans.

After transgression, the human focused on himself and became filled with self-love[2] and egoism,[3] infested with cravings (the cravings of the eye, of the ear, of the lips, in sum, the cravings of the body); arrogant pride became an inseparable part of his egoism.

The body was greatly weakened and cleaved to the external world in order to live. Food, drink, garments, and all else came to be for the body. One of the misfortunes of our reality after transgression is that bodily needs are now deeply connected to pleasure. Our digestive system, for example, is not a receptacle for food alone but a source of delight and of various sensations. The art of cooking is an ardent love of humankind, and a god for many. Cravings do not know moderation and do not cease at the limit of sufficiency, and so they garner insatiable covetousness and voracity. Covetousness is a ferocious and devouring fire; if the human body had the capacity for its ambitions, it would swallow the whole universe.

2. In my book, *Fī al-tawba* [On repentance], I had translated a term on which Maximos the Confessor focused heavily using the term *athara* [self-love]. The Apostle Paul used the term "*philautos*" (2 Timothy 3:2); the [Roman Catholic] Pauline translation translates it as "*'abīdan li-l-athara* [a servant of self-love]". A certain person composed an article in the Kuwaiti journal *al-'Arabiyya* on the distinction between *athara* and *anāniyya* [egoism], which noted: "*athir* is masculine and *athira* is feminine, the gerund [*maṣdar*] is *athara*, meaning a love of oneself while being uncaring of others, the gerund *al-athara*, is opposed to *al-īthār* [a word meaning altruism]. . . . Might one distinguish the word '*athara*' from the word '*anāniyya*'? . . . But this love in the human disrupts his sense of ethical and natural obligation, for he does not care if he threatens the interests of others in realizing his own interests, large or small, or simply for entertainment, or envy, to corrupt his nature. This is *athara* [self-love] . . . *anāniyya* [egoism] is innate and natural, meaning the love of a human for himself, whether *athira* [self-loving] and *īthār* [altruistic] . . . as for the man of self-love, he is ill-mannered due to his weak conscience" (162–163). We still should return one day to the subject as Maximos the Confessor analyzed it, and in light of the foregoing we might replace the Pauline translation (Ḥarīṣa) "*'abīdan li-l-athara*" [a servant of self-love]; let us say "*athirīn*" [those who are self-loving].

3. The word here is *anāniyya*, as opposed to *athara*, the latter of which indicates not only the appropriation to oneself exclusively but also an indifference to others. As Jabbour explains in his footnote above, he uses *athara*, rather than *anāniyya*, as the translation of Maximos and Paul's Greek term *philautia* (love of the self).—Trans.

Theologically, we say that God created the spirit and the body together. The body reaches its completion in nine months, whereas the spirit continues to grow, dependent on education and personal struggle. In terms of psychology, the child is very limited; in terms of the body, he is incapable until he grows in stature and age. His mother cares for him, and his attachment to milk and warmth becomes very great. The child suckles with delight, and as soon as he can move, he puts everything in his mouth.

The child is a miser, jealous, and a great egoist. Stories of the jealousy of children are terrifying, wherein one finds attempts to hit, scratch, injure, pluck out eyes, and strangle necks. The mother cannot save children from jealousy, save through enormous effort, and only with relative success.

Everything in the child's life makes the mother into a watchful eye upon her child, but the child is not a doll. The child is a person with an "I" and character. The "I" certainly does not come from nothing.

In our country, sentimental people suffer from fits of infatuation for their children, and so they corrupt them with coddling. The education of a child is impossible without a system of limitations safeguarding the child's life, his health, and development. If the mother leaves the child to roam free, he will put his hand in fire or eat dirt and poisonous substances.

The rearing of even one child is stressful and costs his family a great deal; will the child one day acknowledge the favor?

At a certain stage, the child inclines toward destruction, breaking all that comes into his hands. He plays with dolls one moment, only to smash them a moment later with great delight. His interests are all damage and disturbance. He alternates between amusement and demolition. The family intervenes with gentleness or harshness, a diverse mix of words, with hitting, gestures, methods, or with something else.

On the one hand, there is the father with his own character, the mother with her own character, brothers, sisters, and others all with their own characters; on the other hand, there is the child's "I."

Clashes occur in a thousand ways and only God knows everyone's different reactions. The child thinks, yet his capacity for thinking corresponds to his age. He may often misinterpret and misunderstand things, and all this may leave a significant trace on him.

The child complains about the strictures of his family, about their control over him. The child is aware that he is inferior to them and that he needs them. He is distressed at seeing them as old and himself as young. He is overjoyed if we raise him up in front of a mirror so that he sees himself higher than those present, especially higher than the one lifting him.

From the womb, the life of the child is a knot of complexity. In the womb, the fetus is closed in on itself, undisturbed and in affective happiness and an environment of his own delight. After the womb, he departs to a world of disturbance, in which his place is different from that of the womb, and hence he revolves around himself and his own nourishment.

As a result, the child is an egoist, a glutton, covetous, avaricious, miserly, greedy, preoccupied with himself, closed in on himself, with a limited awareness of his own being, withdrawn into himself, attached to himself (a narcissist in Freud's expression, that is, one who has ardor for himself),[4] attached to his breastfeeding, stubborn, ferocious, jealous, and envious; afflicted by a sense of inferiority that may push him one day into vanities, ferocities, and malice, and this is just a drop in the ocean.

The family works to redress many of these ills, and clashes necessarily occur; avoiding these traumas is impossible. They alternate between coddling and restricting the child, depending on the circumstances or their moods.

This clashing generates negative reactions in the child, and this ends up becoming an ambivalence in him. That is, he loves his family and he hates them (*ambivalence*); even family members are not spared this ambivalence.

The child possesses an extraordinary propensity to identify with the character of his family, their natures, their practices, and their logic, even the ways they judge things, because he has girded himself with their ambivalences.

In our country, we abuse the words "no," "*kʿa*,"[5] "*dū*,"[6] and "shame" for children, to the point that their existence becomes entirely knotted with shame and a sense of guilt. This results in a very strong ambivalence.

4. *ʿĀshiq li-nafsuhu*. See Freud, "On Narcissism" (1914), *SE* 14:67–102.—Trans.

5. According to the Syrian colloquial dictionary of Yāsīn ʿAbd al-Raḥīm, the word *kʿa* means "filth or something dirty, in children's speech. It is a word parents say to children if they want to stop them from eating something." See Yāsīn ʿAbd al-Raḥīm, "Kʿa."—Trans.

6. Another Syrian colloquialism: "a word said to a child to caution him against falling into chasms [*mahwā*, both physical abysses and a metaphor of one's deep

This entails the forceful appearance of aggression and love in the unconscious; the man fights a crippling sense of guilt by duping his soul, deceiving it by preventing it from consciously feeling guilt. This is what explains people's furious explosions whenever we agitate the sense of guilt in them. If they have some etiquette,[7] they will engage in defense to prove that their behavior is innocent, perfect, and pure. This defense is the desperate defense of groundlessness.

1—Ambivalence

The greatest evidence of ambivalence in our upbringing is the evil of the social relation. No one trusts anyone; no one gives credence to the words of anyone; no one has faith in the loyalty of another. The overturning[8] of friendship is common law, and betrayal is widespread. A brother may betray his brother; an only son may cheat his father and his mother, taking their money and then consigning them to a nursing home. Thanklessness is known to be common law.

When an officeholder falls, his beneficiaries are those quickest to discredit and slander him. In the market, every buyer and seller is a double-crosser. Without deception, no one would succeed. Total sincerity is the rarest of goods, while counterfeiting is nearly common law.

As for the wealthy and powerful, they are afflicted by a dangerous disease—a crazed love for praise and flattery. The successful physician in people's view is the one who dazzles, and the illustrious attorney is the one who shows them Paradise in the blink of an eye, while everyone says: the world is halal for the clever.[9] People praise the one who takes many

---

desire]. Perhaps it is an archaeological remnant from Sumerian in which *dū* means 'walk' or 'come.'" (Yāsīn ʿAbd al-Raḥīm, "Dū.")—Trans.

7. *Adab*, the cultivation of character. Jabbour often points out both the necessity of this cultivation and its function in structuring repression.—Trans.

8. *Inqilāb*, this word also denotes a coup d'état and derives from the same root as "heart" (*qalb*), *q-l-b*. The heart is an organ of revolution, overturning, and shifting.—Trans.

9. Translator's Note: *al-dunyā ḥalāl li-al-shāṭir*, meaning everything is permitted; *halal* is counterposed to what is morally prohibited, *haram*. *Al-shāṭir*, moreover, is a double entendre insofar as it is the word for both one who is "clever" and the "prodigal son" of the Gospel parable.

bribes, and they curry favor with the rich man who has accumulated wealth from smuggling and swindling; nor do the majority question the source of so-and-so's riches but they are satisfied[10] in admiring his skill at acquiring illicit money. Jealousy and envy creep in. They curse the sources of wealth while being saddened at their own lack, or they say in fiery bitterness: the world is halal for the clever. The disappearance of sincerity in personal, financial, and commercial relationships is a mass phenomenon.

Double-dealing is common law. A brother cheats his brother at the marketplace and dupes his father. The tongue's speech is amiable and accommodating, yet no one trusts in another. Sons do not trust their fathers, and vice versa. Even our children do not trust their families, accusing them of lying and saying to them in a moment of boldness: "Liar."

Despite all of this, we love sociability and the appearance of sociability because our family coddled us when we were children, and we have spent our lives finding sociability, even a hypocritical one, pleasant. As such, a sincere spiritual life is almost impossible.

These ambivalences of ours are deeply rooted since childhood, and therefore, all of our dealings are corrupt. There is no place for sincerity in our lives or loyalty in our friendships. Is there anyone absolutely true in sincerity and candor in our East? Is there any trustworthy man in whom we put our complete faith, who lives and dies keeping our confidence? In how many people have we placed our trust only for them to be unworthy of it? To how many people have we delivered our neck only for them to cut it?

10. Satisfaction and its attainment is the operation of the pleasure principle. Freud, in his writing "Group Psychology and the Analysis of the Ego" (1921), *SE* 18:65–144, notes the ambivalence of the ego where the "shadow of the object" falls upon it:

> [These melancholies] show us the ego divided, fallen into two pieces, one of which rages against the second . . . We have said that [the 'ego ideal'] is the heir to the original narcissism in which the childish ego found its self-sufficiency; it gradually gathers up from the influences of the environment the demands which that environment makes upon the ego and which the ego cannot always rise to; so that a man, when he cannot be satisfied with his ego itself, may nevertheless be able to find satisfaction in the ego ideal which has been differentiated out of the ego. (68-69)

As Jabbour shows, then, it is out of a process of originary narcissism that the ambivalence toward a wealthy other emerges.—Trans.

I know a person who used to send invoices to his victims who trusted in him.

Doubt is the foundation, trust is the anomaly, and deceit is a means of extracting trust. If there is a benefit or advantage for us, we wage war with the violence of the state against the one at whose table we eat. If he falls, we criticize and publicly denounce him; we may completely turn on him, especially if we gain the favor of his adversary. Even in times of loyalty, our unconscious heart[11] is not pure, and so we criticize an intimate friend in our heart, mocking his conduct and storing up information about him therein. If the times shift, we pour out our cup of rage upon his head. In some places, opportunists curse their former teacher in order to flatter their current one.

In the company of people, we go along with them, flattering them, cajoling them, revering them, and lauding them—that is, if we have not mocked them in secret, or both secretly and openly. When they are absent, we criticize them, shatter their reputation, insult them with calumny, gossip, and slander. If they say something about the other, we hurry to pass on his words and what occurred between him and this other, if we have not slandered him with defamation and falsehoods. The story of slander is the story of every human in our East. It is a common, mass cancer.

If we stop looking for advantage and benefit and provisionally exercise control over deceit, dissemblance, flattery, sycophancy, and complicity, then our unconscious dispositions at least (and often our conscious positions) show themselves to be controversy, opposition, contradiction, quarrel, criticism, complaint, somewhere between a raucous, furious revolt and a silent one, dissatisfaction . . . an inner, or perhaps open, insurrection, a refusal . . .

Discontentment is a crippling phenomenon. We are infatuated with change, and so we immediately applaud any change without having insight or waiting for deeds to be the judge of words. Our heart is constantly overfull,[12] and so we proclaim our filiation to each new sign of change. Yet,

11. *Sarīra*, a Sufi term related to *sirr* (secret); it is also a synonym of *ḍamīr* (conscience). As pointed out by Oddbjørn Leirvik in his research on the latter term, *sarīra* is part of "a typical distinction, found in Islamic Sufism, between *ḍamīr* as 'the inner conscious' and *sirr* as 'the inner unconscious,'" (20–21), a distinction that resonates with Jabbour's usage here. See Leirvik, "Conscience in Arabic and the Semantic History of 'Ḍamīr.'"—Trans.

12. *Qalbunā ṭāfiḥun dawmān*. See ftn. 8 of this chapter.—Trans.

since inversion[13] is foundational, we immediately divide into followers and adversaries.

For some, ambivalence intensifies such that they always take up a contrary and discontented position. The crux is that we do not abide in contentment, and its lack quickly overwhelms us; thus, an internal instability characterizes us. If we were to become aware of our condition and register the conflict of our views and our positions, we would realize that we are ceaseless wheels of change, that logic is absent from our lives, and that cohesion is shorn from how we live. It follows that we neither care about harmony between our past and our present nor are we interested in the integrity of our personal history in terms of its consistent, sequential, and logical course.

Ambivalence makes us indiscriminate in our gentleness or aggression. Our shifting from the utmost bounds of gentleness to those of malice will not, it follows, be denied. Between the two extremes is an ever-incalculable number of distinct positions between pliancy and severity. One may pardon in a moment, or may never pardon. One may rush to the aid of one of his adversaries while a friend rejoices in the affliction of his companion. There is nothing permanent in this. The former may turn quickly to reopen the wound of enmity, while the latter may quickly repent, or marvel at his malicious joy over his friend and attempt to repress the rebukes of conscience, if there is a living conscience within him.

Acquaintance with every state of ambivalence is impossible. Even a single individual knows throughout his life millions of states and alternations.[14] Advancement in age and virtue may alleviate these negatives, whereas he who grows old in iniquity, in rare cases, increases in meanness and vileness.

Poor upbringing in childhood is responsible for intense ambivalence. In every human, there is a propensity for pliancy and a propensity for harsh-

13. *Al-taʿākus,* implying a "mirroring" effect whereby a division is created (in political debate, say).—Trans.

14. If I wanted to write of slanders, machinations, their reports, and their agents, I could produce volumes. This is a common cancer that has been imposed since the dawn of our history thousands of years ago. I leave the matter to the future and to memoirs. In the fifth century, Theodoret of Qūrsh [Cyrrhus] was fed up with the capricious men who would revere him and then turn on him with a vicious aggression. This rapid change of heart is a pernicious illness, lacking stability or temperance.

ness. Solicitude, indulgence, and living in the shadow of the family tear apart pliancy, love, and sympathy, while abuses strengthen malice. These events converge, and then malice grows strong, often clashing with sympathy. Thus, one develops love and hate for a single individual, and this is something deeply rooted in our lives. We love food and we devour it; we love the breast which nursed us, and we bite it.

It was Basil the Great who said that no human escapes transgression, even if his lifetime spans a single day. The divine scripture anticipated Basil, having said in the Old Testament in the book of Genesis 6:5: "And the Lord saw that the evil of the human had multiplied on the earth, and that every imagining of the thoughts of his heart was only evil, every day."[15]

Genesis 8:21: "For the imagining of the human heart is evil from his inception."[16] As for the al-Shidyāqī translation,[17] it reads: "the thought of the human heart . . . since his youth." In the translation of the Seventy [the Septuagint],[18] "the thought of the human." The corrected French translation of Segond:[19] "for the human heart is ready for evil . . ."

1 Kings 8:46: "For there is not one human who does not transgress."

Job 4:17: "Is there a human more righteous than God, or a man purer than his maker?"[20]

Job 9:2: "How can a human be righteous before God?[21]

15. From the Protestant translation. [This likely refers to the "Smith-Van Dyck Bible," a Protestant translation largely accomplished through the work of Buṭrus al-Bustāni. See Abu-Manneh, "The Christians between Ottomanism and Syrian Nationalism"; Hanna, "The Famous Smith-Van Dyck Bible of 1860"; Grafton, *The Contested Origins of the 1865 Arabic Bible*.—Trans.]

16. As such, al-Yāzīgī [This refers to the Arabic translation of the Bible done by Ibrahīm al-Yāzīgī at the request of the Jesuit order in 1881.—Trans.]

17. This is in reference to a translation originally completed in the United Kingdom (Cambridge) in 1857, but which was published in 1983 in Tripoli. The original translation is derived from the Masoretic text (rather than the Septuagint) and the Greek books of the New Testament. See al-Shidyāq, *al-Kutub al-muqaddasa* [The Holy Scriptures].—Trans.

18. That is, the Greek Septuagint, which is used liturgically by the Orthodox Church.—Trans.

19. This refers to the revised French Bible published in 1910 and named after Swiss theologian Louis Segond (1810–1885).—Trans.

20. Al-Yāzīgī.

21. From the Protestant and al-Yāzīgī, revised.

Job 14:4: "Who extracts purity out of impurity? No one."[22]

Job 15:14–16: "Who is the human that he should be pure, or one born of a woman that he should be righteous? Behold, his holy ones He does not trust, and the heavens are impure in his eyes. How much more the abominable and corrupt human who drinks up iniquity like water?[23]

Job 25:4–5: "How might a human be righteous before God or one born of woman be pure? Behold, the moon itself is not luminous in his eyes, nor are the stars pure, so what then of the human, a cadaver, and the son of Adam, a worm?"[24]

Romans 3:10–18: "As it is written, 'There is not one righteous, not one, not one who comprehends, not one who asks after God. They have turned aside, all of them, and become contemptible all together. No one does righteous works, not one . . ."[25]

Psalm 50:5: "Behold, in iniquities was I conceived and in transgressions did my mother bear me."[26]

Psalm 57:3–4: "The dissemblers have turned aside from birth. Speaking lies, they have gone astray from the womb. They have venom as the venom of the snake, as the deaf viper that stops its ears, for it does not hear the sound of the magician, nor the magic of the dazzling sorcerer."[27] Segond translates: "The liars go astray with their departure from the womb (of their mother)."

Proverbs 20:9: "Who says, I have truly cleansed my heart, I have purified my transgressions?"[28]

Ecclesiastes 7:20: "No one is honest on the earth, rendering what is good without transgression."[29]

Isaiah 48:8: "I knew that you betray exceedingly and were called disobedient from the womb."[30]

22. The Protestant.

23. Al-Yāzigī, revised.

24. Al-Yāzigī.

25. Orthodox Archdiocese of Baghdad, Kuwait and Dependencies. [For this Arabic edition, see *al-Kitāb al-muqaddas*.—Trans.]

26. Dayr Mār Jirjis, Dayr al-Ḥarf.

27. Al-Yāzigī.

28. Al-Yāzigī.

29. Al-Yāzigī.

30. Al-Yāzigī.

This is just a drop in the ocean concerning our origin that, from the womb, is wallowing in corruption. The New Testament is more strongly expressive than this in its length and breadth; it would take too long to review all the passages.[31]

The letters of the Apostle Paul to the Romans and Corinthians are replete with examples, and the first letter of John includes some pertinent passages. For our conception is not pure, nor our birth, nor our life. It cannot hurt to cite a passage from John and another from Paul.

The Lord Jesus said: "That born of the body is itself body, and that born of the spirit is itself spirit."[32]

In 1 Corinthians, Paul gave a fruitful interpretation for all the verses that we have mentioned:

> It (the body) is sown in corruption and resurrected in incorruption. It is sown in abasement and resurrected in glory. It is sown in weakness and resurrected in strength. It is sown a body of the soul[33] and raised a body of the spirit.[34]

31. In such a bitter reality, the storms of the passions and interests blow, and justice vanishes. Therefore, complaints about the loss of justice and equality are widespread. Honest, fair, and impartial people are rare because everyone has their passions, interests, and angles. Do you see how the genius of the Arabic language succeeded, in that it named the heart, *qalb*, because it is inconstant [*mutaqallib*], unfixed in a permanent state? Yet it also named it "the core" [*al-lubb*], and thus it appears that it is both the deepest and that which is changeable, inconstant in states and conditions—manifest ambivalence.

32. John 3:6.

33. Thus is the Greek original, and it is supported in the adjoined verse: "living soul" [*nafs*]. It is likewise in the French Jerusalem [translation]. The Jesuit [translation] renders it as "human" [*basharī*] and its equivalents as "animal" [*ḥayawānī*]. Nevertheless, al-Shidyāqī agrees with the French Segond: "natural" [*ṭabīʿī*]. These external differences between translations make the meaning clear.

34. *Jism rūḥānī*. In making a distinction between the vital body (*jism nafsī*) and the spiritual body (*jism rūḥānī*), Jabbour is drawing on a genealogical distinction between *nafs* (psyche/soul) and *rūḥ* (spirit) that has a long history in Arab Christian and Islamic commentaries. Whereas the former is understood as a vital principle of the body (likewise glossed by Jabbour as a Greek notion) the latter is that which is connected to both the divine Spirit and the heart, transcending both passible and intelligible faculties. See Lane, *Arabic-English Lexicon*, "نفس".—Trans.

> If there is a body of the soul, there is also a body of the spirit,[35] as it is written: "Adam the first human became a living soul [*nafs*],"[36] and the other Adam[37] (became) a life-giving spirit.[38] Yet it was not the spiritual that was first, but rather what belongs to the soul. Then, after that (came) the spiritual. The first human is dust from the earth; the second human is of heaven. For that which is in accordance with the earthen likeness will be earthen, and that which is in accordance with the heavenly likeness will be heavenly.
>
> Indeed, flesh and blood are not able to inherit the kingdom of God, nor is corruption (capable) of inheriting the incorrupt.
>
> The dead arise incorrupt . . . for it is necessary for this corrupt (body) to put on incorruption, for this mortal (body) to put on immortality.
>
> And when this corrupt (body) puts on incorruption, and this mortal (body) puts on immortality, at that time the written saying will be fulfilled: "Indeed death has been swallowed up in the victory."[39]

These words are clear concerning our corrupt and earthen origin from mortal Adam. However, Christ is spirit. We die to corrupt and earthen Adam, but in Christ we put on what is heavenly and spiritual; we rise, wearing what is of incorrupt heaven and spirit, which inherits the kingdom of heaven; what is of the body, that is, "flesh and blood," cannot inherit it. There could not be a more eloquent expression.

Each of us falls to pieces, save he on whom his Lord has mercy, just as he had mercy on Paul, about whom the Acts of the Apostles, 8:3, said, "As for Saul, he was sowing ruin in the church, going from house to house dragging out men and women, delivering them to prison."

35. That is, between "*sōma psychikon*," a body of the psyche/soul and "*sōma pneumatikon*," a body of the spirit.—Trans.

36. Genesis 2:7.

37. That is, Jesus.

38. While Jabbour uses "*ḥayya*," meaning living, to describe the soul (*nafs*) of Adam, he uses "*muḥīyyan*"—one of the names of God's Holy Spirit, *al-Muḥī*, the enlivener, and one of the names of God in Islam—to describe the Spirit (*rūḥ*) of Jesus.—Trans.

39. 1 Corinthians 15:42–54, from the Jesuit and the Revised Pauline translation. [The translations refer respectively to the Arabic Jesuit Bible and the Pauline Bible published in Jounieh, Lebanon.—Trans.]

The Acts of the Apostles, 9:1: "As for Saul, he was still spewing threat and murder toward the disciples of the Lord." Paul had alluded to this in his letters and considered himself the first among transgressors.

The Church Fathers touched upon this subject, while Maximos the Confessor expanded on it. In Maximos's view, transgression introduced into Adam corruption, death, and self-love (in Greek, *philautia*), self-love being the mother of the passions.[40] "The passions have their ground in natural passibility."[41] In Greek, the name of this [passibility] is *pathēton*[42] and the name of passion is *pathos*. Passion is[43]

> also a result of a free decision issuing from the spirit. In the beginning, the human chose the law of creaturely birth, which is "the law of the first creation."[44] Hence, transgression was deeply rooted in "the innermost [*bāṭin*] of nature"[45] and, like a dye, suffuses everything.[46] Yet, despite this, this law remains "additive,"[47] additional. It does not follow us into eternal life,[48] although it remains here upon the earth, adhering, as an inherent property, to the purest of natures

40. See Maximos, *PG* 91, 397 D; *PG* 90, 1197 C; *Centuries sur la charité*, *SC* 9, 2.08, 3.08, and 3.56. [For an English translation, see Maximos's *Four Hundred Texts on Love* in the *Philokalia*, vol. 2.—Trans.]

41. [Balthasar, *Liturgie cosmique*, 139. Passibility is translated as *Qābiliyyat al-alam*.—Trans.]

42. Meaning also "suffered, exchanged."

43. The following quote is taken from Balthasar, *Liturgie cosmique*, 139–140. The parentheticals are Jabbour's clarifications of Balthasar's rendering of Maximos's quotes.—Trans.

44. Maximos, *PG* 91, 1276 B.

45. Maximos, *PG* 90, 628 B. [The French reads "dans le sein même de la nature"—Trans.]

46. Maximos, *PG* 90, 249 A. [Maximos uses the same metaphor of dye (*vafēs*) that is used in Islamic Sufi commentaries (especially al-Kashānī) to describe the inundation of the creature by the Uncreated. This is entirely consistent with Orthodox Christian ascetic (and especially hesychast) writings; participation in God's energies is true, uncreated participation in God. Hence the passions, by filling the heart, displace participation in God as He who is not, as what is *excepted* from the mind and the senses.—Trans.]

47. The original term from Maximos's text is *epeisagousa*. —Trans.

48. Maximos, *PG* 90, 541 B.

> in such a way that (these purified natures) are not able to rid themselves of it entirely.[49]

So what salvation is there before death? The itch of transgression remains until death. Every human body became[50]

> a "valley inscribed and eroded by the ceaseless waves (that are the passions)."[51] . . . "By violating (the law of God), transgression entered human nature, and by transgression corruptibility entered reproduction."[52] "The human is frightened by death and attempts to cheat it, under the delusion that survival is easily accomplished through the begetting of children; and so he falls, being a slave to (sexual) enjoyment, in love with life,"[53] "however he begets the dead, for he himself is not everlasting, rather he makes death everlasting."[54] "A mixture of enjoyment and suffering, this is life,"[55] because, "death is existent, in a state of power, becoming tantamount to the judgment of nature."[56]

We amend this quickly [with Balthasar] to say that Maximos said that the sexual act and marriage are not transgressions and they are not evils; otherwise, so too would be the maker of nature, who gave us this way of multiplying. If it were so, we would fall into the blasphemy of the Manichaeans who spoke of the existence of two principles.[57]

Marriage is the union[58] of two parties, and so "the human, by the faculty of union [*hē pros henōsin dynamis*] that he possesses, is the natural

49. Balthasar, *Liturgie cosmique*, 139–140 [Balthasar cites Maximos, *PG* 90, 541 A in this final line.—Trans.]

50. The following quote is taken from Balthasar, *Liturgie cosmique*, 143–144. The parentheticals are Jabbour's clarifications of Balthasar's rendering of Maximos's quotes.—Trans.

51. Maximos, *PG* 90, 425 A.

52. Maximos, *PG* 90, 313 A.

53. Maximos, *PG* 90, 316 B.

54. Maximos, *PG* 91, 437 C–440 A.

55. Maximos, *PG* 90, 256 D.

56. Maximos, *PG* 90, 424 B.

57. Maximos, *PG* 91, 1340 B. [See Balthasar *Liturgie cosmique*, 145.—Trans.]

58. *Ittiḥād*, the same word used when referencing union with the divine in theosis.—Trans.

mediator [*physikōs mesiteuōn*] between creation and God."[59] The love of the two spouses is, according to [John of Scythopolis],[60] a "distant echo of divine love. By this enigmatic image of love and unity, one participates, in an obscure form, in (God's) righteousness itself."[61]

As [John of Scythopolis][62] and Maximos see it, the evil existing in the appetitive [part of the soul] does not reside therein as such but puts that part into conflict with the intellect.[63] Yet it is possible to direct it toward God; harmony between the inclinations of a man and a woman is "impossible if they have not clung to God with unanimity."[64] In my text, *Disclosures in the Constitution of Faith*,[65] I focused both on the existence of the mystery of marriage, carried out according to the blessing of God that makes one out of two, and on their meeting in the church, that is the body of Jesus, within which the two are members.

Moreover, the holy Gregory the Theologian has written, "the laws of nature have been dissolved, the higher world must be perfected."[66] Then Maximos wrote: "What are the laws of nature which are dissolved? It is conception by sowing seed and giving birth in corruption. Those two things that did not leave any sign of their trace on the true embodiment of God and His perfect becoming human."[67] Jesus was neither born through seed nor corruption:

59. Balthasar, *Liturgie cosmique*, 145. [Balthasar cites Maximos, *PG* 91 1305 A B.—Trans.]

60. Jabbour misattributes this quote to Pseudo-Dionysius, which comes from the commentary on *The Divine Names* written by John of Scythopolis (cited in Migne's *PG* as Maximos).—Trans.

61. [John of Scythopolis], *PG* 4, 281 A C. [The parenthetical in this quote is Jabbour's clarification.—Trans.]

62. See ftn 60.—Trans.

63. [John of Scythopolis], *PG* 4, 301 B C.

64. Maximos, *PG* 91, 396 D, cited in Balthasar, *Liturgie cosmique*, 146.

65. See Jabbour, *al-Tajalliyāt fī dustūr al-īmān*.—Trans.

66. Gregory the Theologian, "Oration" 38/2 in *PG* 36, 313 B. [This line is from Gregory the Theologian's oration on the Nativity: the original line reads "*Nomoi physeōs katalyontai, plērōthēnai dei ton anō kosmon.*" See Maximos's commentary on this (Ambiguum 31) in the second volume of Maximos Constas's translation, *On Difficulties in the Church Fathers*, which has emended the many errata of the *PG* edition. For Gregory's sermon, see Oration 38.2 (*SC* 3; 8:106, 11. 9–10).—Trans.]

67. Maximos, *PG* 91, 1276 A B.

It was necessary for the maker of nature, who Himself sets nature right, to dissolve the laws which subjugated nature—the laws by which the resulting transgression of disobedience has been enjoined upon humanity, that they pursue their propagation like a chain, a manner itself characteristic of creatures without speech—in order for the All-Powerful God[68] to bring to good, by His love for humanity, what the human destroyed by carelessness and in weakness.

ιϛʹ

In the beginning, the devil [*Iblīs*] by deception maliciously inspired the human's self-love. He deceived the human by assaulting him with pleasures, separating him from God and others as one having free choice.[69] And since he distorted the uprightness of the human, he divided his nature in this way and fractured it into a multiplicity of perspectives and imaginings.[70] Indeed, people revere the cause of their destruction itself and adhere to the reason for their corruption unknowingly. In this way, the array of human nature is broken into a thousand pieces, and humans, like wild animals, devour the sons of their own nature. The human looks to acquire pleasure and to avoid pain, driven by his self-love, and devises innumerable forms of corrupting passions.[71]

68. *Al-qadīr* (the All-Powerful), one of the ninety-nine names of God contemplated in Islam.—Trans.

69. The "free choice" (*khayār ḥurr*) referenced here is a translation of Maximos's crucial term *gnōmē* (see ftn. 72 of this chapter).—Trans.

70. Self-love [*athara*] for Maximos is: "the passion toward the body" (see Maximos, *Four Hundred Texts on Love* 2.08, 3.08, and 3.57); "the mindless, passional love for the body" (ibid., 3.08). It is "mindless affection for the body" (ibid., 3:57). Therefore, it is a state of lust for the body reminiscent of narcissism for Freud.

71. Maximos, *PG* 91, 396 D. [This passage is taken from Maximos's "Letter to John Koubikoularios on Love." As Grigory Benevich points out, this letter develops a notion of love that figures Abraham as the one who attains the divine perfection of love. The exemplarity of Abraham here recalls his condition as *khalīl,* beloved of God, which resonates in the tradition of Ibn al-ʿArabī familiar to Jabbour (see Translator's Introduction). See Benevich, "Maximus Confessor's Interpretation of Abraham's Hospitality."—Trans.]

We consider this amount sufficient. In sum, Maximos views transgression as a result of a volitional action,[72] from which spiritual death results and which, in turn, causes bodily death; hence, corruption entered us, and our propagation became like that of animals, and so self-love, the mother of all the passions, came to rule over us.

The passions multiplied, tore us apart limb from limb; we devoured one another like vicious animals.[73] Instead of the inclination of our natural will being toward God, the passions entered us, and our will came to be inclined toward evil. For us, conception is an animal conception. We are born into corruption, being susceptible to death and deterioration. Our self-love drives us toward pleasures, and so we dive into them and annihilate ourselves within them amid delusion. Bearing children does not secure the everlasting for us; rather, we increase the number of the dead.

Maximos alludes to the saying of the Apostle Paul in his letter to the people of Galatia (Galatians 3:28)—that within the Christian good news, there is neither male nor female. To this, he adds that there is "neither self-love nor the passions of nature subjected to corruption and reproduction."[74]

How did Jesus save us? Jesus saved us by a conception without seed from a virgin mother who bore Him without corruption, and thus He took on our nature in its entirety, apart from transgression:

> Rather, not choosing the fallen likeness of the bodily human amid corruption, He takes the image of a servant, and accepts being subjugated, in near conformity with us, to the passions of nature itself—yet not to error—as if He was subordinate to it, being He who is without error.[75]

72. Jabbour here is referencing Maximos's concept of the "gnomic will" (*thelēma gnōmikon*); that is, the peculiar state of a will meeting its intention. As opposed to the "natural will," the gnomic will is one developed from a process of deliberation and uncertainty. The human, in short, does not know what he wants. A decisive point for Maximos is that Christ possessed no gnomic will, but only the natural human will and the divine will of God. Those who are divinely perfected on earth likewise no longer have a gnomic will.—Trans.

73. Maximos, *PG* 90, 256 B.

74. Maximos, *PG* 90, 889 C.

75. Maximos, *PG* 91, 1316 D.

"Since Adam voluntarily quit his birth within the theosis[76] of the (Holy) Spirit, he was born bodily into corruption."[77] Jesus was born in a bodily birth,

> defeating by it the power of our condemnation and restoring, in the (*ṣūfī*) manner of inundation, birth in the Spirit.[78] And because He undid the chain of bodily generation in His own being, for our sake, He granted us . . . that we become children of God rather than children of flesh and blood.[79]

Maximos draws here from John 1:13, concerning our birth from God rather than from the body. This is only a drop in the ocean as to what exists on this topic. As regards our salvation in Jesus, we have touched upon this in our writings, *The Mystery of the Divine Economy* and *The Counterfeits*.[80]

We conclude this topic with a text from the holy Gregory Palamas, (a text) faithful to the thinking of Maximos and his counterparts (Gregory of Nyssa and others) on this matter. It pertains to the act of reproduction and birth, which is

> spontaneous, independent of the law of the intellect—and if there are some who control it by force, there are others practicing it with temperance in order to produce children. It bears the signs of the first judgment. For it is corrupt and named thus, that is, corrupt, and no one gives birth save by corruption, it being nothing other than a passional activity issuing from one who did not preserve the dignity that God presented us by nature and who has come to resemble the animals. The conception of the Virgin Mary resulted from the abid-

76. *Ta'alluh*, to participate in God's divinity. This is a translation of the Greek term *theōsis*, a concept found throughout Maximos' writings and the Orthodox monastic tradition upon which Jabbour draws.—Trans.

77. Maximos, *PG* 91, 1348 C

78. *I'āda khalīliyyan (ṣūfiyyan) al-wilāda fī al-rūḥ*, where *khalīlī* and *ṣūfī* are alternative translations of the Greek *mystikos*. The original Greek reads: "*tēn en pneumati mystikōs diōrthōsato gennēsin*." See the Translator's Introduction for more on this peculiar grammatical form.—Trans.

79. Maximos, *PG* 91, 1348 C.

80. Jabbour, *Sirr al-tadbīr al-ilāhī*; *al-Muzayyafūn*.—Trans.

> ing of the Holy Spirit and not from a bodily work . . . not from assenting to a passional whim and the experience of it.[81]

Humans are born like the animals. As for Jesus, He reflected the verse:[82] a virgin woman birthed Him without seed. The Holy Spirit knitted in her womb the human nature[83] of Jesus, and He Himself (that is, the Spirit) births us in Jesus. Our spiritual birth in baptism is the act of the Holy Spirit, like the conception of the Virgin Mary.

Maximos said:

> Christ is ever born in an inundating (*ṣūfī,* mystic)[84] manner from the psyche, taking a body via those who have been saved, and fashioning from the soul that births Him a virgin mother, not bearing the signs of nature subjugated to corruption and reproduction in the relation between male and female.
>
> No one is astonished, then, if he hears that corruption is found before reproduction . . . reproduction begins from corruption and ends in it. Christ does not possess the specific passions of this reproduction, nor of this corruption, "for in Christ is neither male nor female."[85] Paul sees clearly the characteristics and passions of nature subjugated to corruption and reproduction.[86]

Therefore, the psyche/soul is both a virgin and a mother like the Virgin Mary. Mary conceived Jesus by the Holy Spirit, He who became similar

81. Gregory Palamas, Homily 52. [No other attribution appears but this is likely referring to the French translation done by John Meyendorff. See an English translation of this homily for the Entry of the Mother of God, which likens Mary's bearing of Christ to the life of hesychasm, in *Saint Gregory Palamas: The Homilies*.—Trans.]

82. *ʿAkasa al-āya*. The term *āya* is most commonly used to refer to a passage from the Bible or Qurʾān; it also means a marvel or miraculous sign. Here, Jabbour is, presumably, referring to the passage from Isaiah (7:14).—Trans.

83. *Nāsūt*, as opposed to *lāhūt* (divine nature). See Arnaldez, "Lāhūt and Nāsūt."—Trans.

84. *Khalīliyyan*. See the Translator's Introduction for more on this term and its glosses.—Trans.

85. Galatians 3:28.

86. Maximos, *PG* 90, 889 C D. See also Garrigues, *Maxime le Confesseur*, 127–128.

to us in order that we might realize His likeness within us. Transgression dispossessed us of this likeness, yet Jesus restored to our nature its originary eagerness for God; He restored its originary passion for God, and He restored its ultimate aim that is God Himself.

Maximos also said:

> Indeed, the Lord became transgression because of me, according to passibility, mortality, and corruptibility, for He voluntarily put on the condemnation of my nature, though being without that condemnation that belongs to free choice, and did so in order to condemn transgression and the condemnation of my free choice and my nature.[87]

> By His power, He has freed the whole of human nature from the deviation that had mixed with it through the passions, and did so through His body, rising from among us as if some first fruit. He has done so by His subjecting to the natural propensity for passion (that is, the natural leap toward God) the control of evil over nature, (this) control which was at that time governing it, I mean the natural propensity for passion."[88]

Maximos's construction is quite complex, so an explanation follows. Maximos wants to say that the extraneous deviation mixing with our nature through the passions has been subjected to the control of the natural propensity for passion. This propensity is our desire, our originary leap toward God. And therefore, Jesus accepted to be subject to judgment. He took upon his being our entire case[89]—save the inclination to err—even death upon the cross, and by it He passed sentence on the judgment upon us;[90] he freed our natural desire toward God from the control of the distorted passions. He restored to us our natural right to orient toward God in order to realize[91] the [divine] likeness without servitude to the passions; and

87. Maximos, *PG* 90, 408 C D, cited in Riou, *Le monde et L'Église*, 86.

88. Maximos, *PG* 90, 316 C D, cited in Riou, *Le monde et L'Église*, 86. In the latter volume, see also pages 85–87, 103, and 139.

89. *Qaḍiyya*, a word that also means a legal suit or cause.—Trans.

90. Romans 8:3–4 and John 16:11.

91. *Taḥqīq* is a term within Islamic commentaries for the "spiritual realization" of the divine Truth *(al-ḥaqq)* in the encounter with the Real.—Trans.

so we reclaim our right to incorruption, immortality, and indefatigability, and our innocent passion returns to an orientation toward God.[92]

The human is knotted from his beginnings. Cain murdered his brother Abel. On August 9, 1981, a twelve-year-old vendor was slain because he stole a cluster of grapes, and then the family of the deceased slew the killer in the afternoon.[93] News of violence in recent years exceeds every fantasy and police drama, and how many people make these stories their pleasure, though a great number of them fear a cockroach, yet still they delight in the violence of their own thoughts.

Many may wonder at children's ardent love for the sight of violence in watching fallen and obscene television and films. Then videos and the internet arrived, the capstone of misfortunes and disasters, the ruination of children and even adults. The industry's record is a disgrace.

Consequently, our errors in child-rearing remain largely responsible for our alternations between states of pliancy and mercilessness, between sympathy and vehemence. There is neither a clear line nor a definitive border between them for us. There are those among us who are today one way, and tomorrow another; they shift from one pole to its opposite. Today, I enthusiastically say that someone is an angel; tomorrow, I say that he is a devil, without him committing an offense between yesterday and today.

92. For Maximos, John Climacus, and Palamas, the term "passion" [*hawā*] is misplaced, its meaning discarded and distorted by Evagrios and his successors. Authentic passion is one thing, and its distortion toward evil is another. The meaning of this will be clarified presently. I draw our attention to what Maximos said above concerning the rending of our nature into a thousand pieces. This inner rending is responsible for our dispersal and the loss of our way among the turmoil of thousands of reasons that bind us to a thousand opposing, conflicting paths; we squander our energies in what is vain and iniquitous.

93. In February of 1968 (from what I recall), four persons fought over an allegation of bird hunting as they let shots fly against one another. Three died and the fourth went to the hospital; I was told that he died there. On January 1, 1976, two fought, and one or two were killed for the sake of five lira. Violent, international gangs threaten civilization; it requires a radical treatment . . . The civilization of the industrial age has inflicted many negatives upon the Europeans and Americans, and millions are incapable of keeping apace with it. North America's number of homeless varies around 40 or 42 million; that is, around one-sixth of the population.

This is ambivalence. It is the cause of the alternation of our history between construction and destruction. We have a pronounced image of this in the harrowing events of Lebanon. After an amazing and long period of progress, civilizational upbuilding,[94] construction, and cohabitation, the fires broke out. How did people alternate between the positives of building and the negatives of razing? How did this excessively lively, stable, and secure country change to a country of the human's destruction and extermination? How did people change from being affectionate and compassionate in hardships and crises to men of ruthlessness and barbarism?

How did the human become cheaper than a bushel of radishes? The wars exposed the core of the human.

Some will justify this with a billion reasons, yet the true reason is compassion's[95] lack of preponderance over mercilessness in our lives and history; a sufficient preponderance that would be sufficient to restrict viciousness and delimit it enough to protect common life and the country.

A lack of stability is a trait that characterizes all of our personal, national, and religious history in our Mashriq. Indeed, our countries have outdone the world of old in religious fragmentation. There is no deep affiliation, as people adhere to the dead shells of religion and not to the theological-*ṣūfī*-ascetic depth of religion. We are affiliated with religions, but we do not embrace them to the degree of their becoming a personal dye, coloring every mote of our being. Our religiosity is superficial because we are unable to throw ourselves into the turmoil of spiritual struggle.

The aforementioned non-preponderance of compassion and attachment causes many to shift from allegiance to allegiance; it is easier than drink-

94. *ʿUmrān*, the central term in Ibn Khaldun's *Muqaddima* and its study of the dialectic of civilizational upbuilding and destruction, which Jabbour is likely referencing here. As in this text, Ibn Khaldun contemplates the vicissitude of history as a divine limit: "Civilization [*ʿumrān*] decreased with the decrease of mankind. Cities and buildings were laid waste, roads and way signs were obliterated, settlements and mansions became empty, and dynasties and tribes grew weak. The entire inhabited world changed. The East, it seems, was similarly visited, though in accordance with and in proportion to (the East's more affluent) civilization. It was as if the voice of existence in the world had called out for oblivion and restriction, and the world had responded to its call. God inherits the earth and whomever is upon it" (vol. 1, 64–65).—Trans.

95. *ʿAtf* most precisely means to be inclined and thus has the additional meanings of affection, regard, mercy, and compassion.—Trans.

ing a cup of water. It makes them like quicksilver. And how often do we complain about those like quicksilver? I have seen with my own eyes someone conclude an agreement with their right hand and break it in less than half an hour, and allies renege on their oaths the next day.[96] This is common law: this is the character of wolves.[97]

This dearth of compassion leads to lying, dissemblance, perfidy, mistrust and suspicion, to appropriation, egoism, self-love, utilitarianism, avarice, and greed; it makes deceit halal.

When we think we have an interest, we justify a white lie. But there is no lie, save a pitch-black one. In the name of interest, we allow ourselves every overstepping, inversion, betrayal, perfidy, and breaking of contracts and accords. It is no wonder that the Frenchman La Rochefoucauld[98] explained all forms of human behavior through egoism.

No matter how much shame exercises control, utilitarianism breaches its walls. We are shamed at times, then we rid ourselves of shame because we cannot bear the rebuke of conscience, and so we appear as if we have not committed an offense. Our hatred for the censure of conscience is obscene.

With this, things keep their course, sometimes toward construction, sometimes toward destruction, alternating day and night, yet without long-term future development. Our condition mutely sings out: "My inclination is whatever passion desires." Passion blinds both sight and insight.[99]

96. The practice of swearing an oath with the right hand has a particular history in Lebanon and Syria, one related to swearing one's allegiance. See Dylan Baun's chapter "Fighting the Punks" in *Winning Lebanon* for an example of this practice among sectarian militiamen.—Trans.

97. A clear reference to the Latin proverb *homo homini lupus* [man is a wolf to man] that first appeared in Plautus' play *Asinaria* (*The Comedy of Asses*) but was repeated in Thomas Hobbes' *De Cive* as well as by Freud in *Civilization and Its Discontents*.—Trans.

98. François de La Rochefoucauld (1613–1680) was a French writer and moralist known for his *Maximes* and is frequently referenced by Jacques Lacan in his seminars. See Rosso, *Procès à La Rochefoucauld*.—Trans.

99. *Al-baṣar wa al-baṣīra* (see ftn. 1 in chapter 1). The latter refers to spiritual insight or discernment and thus constitutes part of *maʿrifa* (gnosis). The use of this dyad of outer sight and inner sight—a corollary of the *ẓāhir* (manifest) and *bāṭin* (hidden) and Jabbour's own reference to the "counterfeit"—is found all throughout Islamic tradition, including influential authors such as Abū Ḥāmid al-Ghazālī and Ibn al-ʿArabī.—Trans.

It is the blight of vision. How painful it is to see people whose soul is the object of desire. They disavow that a given person, for example, has any virtue even while he has merits and even if he has some ills. There is neither impartiality nor justice in judgment! And the worst of them are those who were the greatest beneficiaries of this person; they become ingrates possessing incomparable impudence.

This is only a drop in the ocean; what is worse is what is known of those who hurt family and friends on behalf of the devil or for fleeting gain. This harm reaches, at times, the point of threatening the life of a relative or a friend with murder.

How were they deprived of a life of compassion during childhood? It is the human alternating between the holiness of the Virgin Mary and the depravity of using grenades, pistols, and daggers. Whoever betrays one person over a dollar becomes ready to betray another. The prisons are teeming with repeat offenders. Each man's fate is fixed by his own custom,[100] and whoever is accustomed to betrayal is fated to be treacherous. One does not trust the man at his side, however gentle and amiable, because his very gentleness exposes his veiled intentions to betray and its instrument. Al-Mutanabbī[101] said: "Injustice is one of the innate traits of souls; if you find one of integrity, it is by some deficiency that he does not do injustice."

We say, "The key to the stomach is a morsel," and the key to evil is a step. When one has slipped into evil once, one is made ready to repeat it. If the most spotless worker in the world takes a bribe once, then the thought of bribery will seek to entice him.

Let's return to betrayal, since its appearance is a danger. It does the utmost ill to the relationships of family and friends; it disturbs social relations since slanders multiply and people are then suspicious of one another even in

100. *Li-kulla imrā'in min dahirih mā ta'awwada*. The opening line of a poem from al-Mutanabbī (see the following footnote) rehearsed for the poet's patron, Sayf al-Dawlah, on Eid al-Adha in AH 342. This wonderful English translation is that of Suzanne Stetkevych, and it can be found in the sixth chapter of her book, *The Poetics of Islamic Legitimacy*, 187.—Trans.

101. Abū al-Ṭayyib Aḥmad bin al-Ḥusayn, later known as al-Mutanabbī, was born in AH 303 and became a famous panegyrist in the Aleppine court of Sayf al-Dawlah. His compositions in the contemporary Levant and wider Arabic-speaking world are often used as proverbs. See an Arabic collection of his writings, *Dīwān Abī al-Ṭayyib al-Mutanabbī*; Hamori, "Al-Mutanabbī."—Trans.

the familial environment.[102] Slander is a hidden harm and a disease that decimates like a secret, malignant cancer. It is an iniquitous aggression.

We do not know when the trusted friend or the relative will betray us. Worse still is that the betrayal often comes from one in whom you have the utmost trust, as was the case with Indira Gandhi, the daughter of the famous Nehru and daughter-in-law of the famed Gandhi. She resorted to the violence that her father had fought against, as had her father-in-law. She remained confident in her guards from the Sikh sect, a sect doomed to be subject to violence.[103] She was not wary of them. It was a blind and futile trust, and she paid an exorbitant price; it put an end to her life. She did not read well the book *Kalīla and Dimna* of Ibn al-Muqaffaʿ, even though its origin is Indian.[104] And even if she had read it, she would not have benefited from its lessons. In one interesting story, one animal rebuffed the seeming assurances of another, and then told him what he meant by this: whenever I recall your son's murder of my son, and you recall my fracturing of your son's skull, the thought of revenge will come again to each one of us.[105]

102. For a study of political life and the marked increase of suspicion within Syrian society under Hafez al-Assad's government, see Wedeen, *Ambiguities of Domination*.—Trans.

103. Jabbour is referring to then Indian Prime Minister Indira Gandhi's general militarism and most specifically to her government's 1984 Operation Blue Star, a brutal military assault on the Sikh Golden Temple in Amritsar and another 125 Sikh shrines in Punjab that saw hundreds of Sikhs killed, arrested, and disappeared. Gandhi was killed several months later by her Sikh bodyguards in retaliation.—Trans.

104. The *Panchatantra* or "Five Treatises" is an ancient set of Sanskrit fables, which were later translated into Persian and Aramaic; in AD 750, it was translated from Persian into Arabic by Ibn al-Muqaffaʿ under the title *Kalīla wa Dimna* (the names of two jackals who feature prominently in the structure of the fables). Ibn al-Muqaffaʿ was a Persian scholar who served in both the Abbasid and Umayyad caliphates. The volume—exemplary in its literary style, its status as wisdom literature, and its continued life in the modern Arabic-speaking world, not only in the form of textual schooling, but also as oral proverbs—is an apt citation given Jabbour's concern over education.—Trans.

105. This is a paraphrastic account of the story known in its Arabic version as "Bāb ibn al-malik wa-l-ṭāʾira fanza" (The king's son and the bird Fanza), in which the bird Fanza takes revenge on the king's son for murdering her child; the king's attempt to entice the bird to come back to him—with assurances that

Of course, I do not call for resentment and grudge; rather, I know what is in the hidden depths of the human: stores of betrayal, vileness, and baseness. Pedagogy saves the human to some extent, for the home is the foundation, and the mother's hands weave nobility within her children. The father, the mother, siblings, and grandparents bequeath laudable traits to a great extent. For whoever is of an honorable origin preserves the dignity of his origin.

An essay in Issue 9, 1985 of the Russian journal *Philosophical questions*[106] mentioned that, in the mind of the child, the mother's image remains the closest one to him. Accordingly, the exemplary image of the mother in the child's mind forges his conscience to a great degree, molds his ethical disposition, and constructs his personality. Still, for every rule there is an exception.

Ambivalence [*taḍādd*] is not confined to the psyche but may extend into language. In the Semitic languages, there are a number of words called "contronyms" [*aḍdād*], that is, a word which has two contrary meanings. I have written two chapters in a document published in Paris in 1960 concerning contronyms in the Arabic language. Professor Jacques Berque expanded the ambit and gathered twenty-five contributors, publishing [with Jean-Paul Charnay] a volume in 1967 entitled *L'ambivalence dans le culture arabe.*

The first part of my contribution was a study of contronyms, in which I classified and sorted them. In the second part, an analysis appeared in the light of psychoanalysis and its theory of ambivalence;[107] it was entitled, "Ambivalence."

I did not investigate this subject further for lack of time and its intractability. Indeed, I later found the ambit of ambivalence in the Arabic language to be dozens of times greater than I imagined. Every writing on contronyms fails to exhaust the material. Mr. Tawfīq Zā'id informed me that he translated his doctoral dissertation on "contronyms" into Spanish; the late professor of Arabic language at the University of Damascus, Ribḥī

---

she had already taken her revenge by attacking his son and so their relationship is still in balance—is met with a skeptical response similar to the one recollected here by Jabbour.—Trans.

106. No further bibliographic information is provided, but this is likely a reference to the preeminent Soviet materialist journal *Voprosy Philosofii*.—Trans.

107. See Jabbour, "L'homonymile des Addad."

Kamāl, who contributed a chapter to the book along with us, prefaced it.[108] Mr. Zā'id mentioned to me that my research was very reminiscent of his dissertation, but I was not pleased with the caliber of my own research. If my interest were to hold, and the matter to draw me in, I would examine the dictionaries and unearth from them what I could by publishing a book in several parts. In an article published in the journal *al-Maʿrifa*,[109] I mentioned the incapacity of the Arabic dictionaries and the abundance of terms within which contronyms are buried under a single title; for example, the word *jawn.*[110]

Ambivalence is a problem in the hollow[111] of every human, but it is so pervasive for us as to exceed the limits of intelligibility; our language bears witness for us. Since completing this book on November 14, 1983, my knowledge of it has increased, as has my surprise at the extent of the extraordinary ambivalence in the Arabic language. I have not sufficiently accounted for it in writing.

2—The Ambivalence of the spirit and the body

We said previously that the human's bodily development is natural from the time of the womb; as for the development of the psyche, it will be quite limited if society does not assume responsibility for it. The body temporally

108. See Kamāl, *al-Taḍādd fī ḍawʾ al-lughat al-sāmīyya* (Ambivalence in light of semitic languages).—Trans.

109. Jabbour, "Munāqashāt ʿan fiqh al-lugha wa al-taḍādd fī al-lugha" [Discussions on philology and ambivalence in language] in *al-Maʿrifa* (November 1981).

110. This word denotes both black and white color, and therefore can also indicate an admixture (of, say, red into black). Interestingly, the word is also used to denote this shift in color with the sun's setting. This is found in some of the oldest Arabic dictionaries, such as al-Jawharī's *al-Ṣiḥāḥ*.—Trans.

111. *Jawf*, a term that has a specific history in Qurʾānic commentary as it is used to contrast creatures to God, the latter being described as *al-ṣamad* (one who is steadfast, solid) in Surah al-Ikhlāṣ (Q. 112). Ibn Kathīr's magisterial 8th century (AH) exegesis of the Qurʾān notes that "*al-ṣamad* is that which has no hollow [*jawf*]," and, he adds, "this is very strange." "Our lord . . . is He who is steadfast [*yaṣmad*] toward him in need, He who has perfected his sovereignty, and He is steadfast [*al-ṣamad*] which has no hollow [*jawf*], He neither eats nor drinks, He is who endures after His creation." Ibn Kathīr, *Tafsīr al-qurʾān al-ʿaẓīm*. Surah 112, *al-Ikhlāṣ*.—Trans.

precedes both psychological and ethical, and, therefore, religious and spiritual development.

In the view of Maximos the Confessor and his counterparts, it was Adam's transgression that brought us down to our current level. Multiplying through procreation at present—after our expulsion from paradise—gives priority to the body rather than to the spirit. Hence, the body's activity precedes the activity of the spirit; from the womb, the former exercises its functions in a mechanical manner. It is endowed with the powers of the psyche, which are confined to the body at the start. Only after a time does the body shift from understanding by means of images to understanding by means of words and ideas.

Concern for the necessities of the body initially precedes any other care. The child fears the punishment of hunger just as the adult fears death. This reality causes the child to become established, with his feelings, concerns, desires, cravings, requests, and delights connected to his body. The process of his ethical, religious, and spiritual advancement emerges, and then it clashes with the whole array of habits and practices that had suffused him for the sake of the body's functions. The body in its foundation is weak because it bears in its being the corruption from the moment of Adamic error—susceptibility to death and annihilation.

Wresting the child away from concentrating his "I" around his body and from pivoting around it toward a centered ethical life is no easy matter. And what if we want to raise him spiritually? The severe family errs just as the lax one does. A wise blend of leniency and firmness is necessary in order to establish a strong and compassionate character. Character education is important. However, are not "Adamic" mothers, and even virtuous ones, guilty of being concerned for their children's bodies, such that they are exceedingly neglectful in remembering the spirit? In this case, excessive compassion is harmful and destructive.

After the fall of Adam, implanting the spiritual life within children is like introducing one foreign body into another. In the image of the ladder inscribed on the Arabic translation of the book *The Ladder to God*,[112] trans-

112. This is in reference to the Orthodox icon named after John Climacus's work, the earliest extent example of which is a twelfth-century image at Saint Catharine's Monastery in Sinai. The icon depicts monastics ascending thirty rungs (the thirty steps of the spiritual life) to heaven while demons attempt to drag them therefrom.—Trans.

lated by the Monastery of Dayr al-Harf, we see that some have fallen from the beginning of the path, some have fallen in its midst, and the last have fallen even from a certain height. The spiritual life is not possible without the pressure on one's existence that the spiritual fathers demand, as noted in the book, *The Way of the Ascetics*.[113]

The war between the spirit and the body, about which the Apostle Paul spoke, becomes fated for the human who strives toward God.

From our beginnings, we are joined to the body; if the spiritual masters have bemoaned the rarity of ones who are spiritual, then the reason is that we live first for our bodies, while religion and ethics are introduced to us as a foreign body that the family plants within us with relatively poor skill, but God knows.

The family seldom succeeds in orienting all its children successfully toward the spiritual life, and we often see one of them diverge and deviate, accompanied by eccentric reactions to his family.

As such, the spiritual edifice is always a powder keg, because it sits atop a mass of desires, needs, and passions that were once the weft and warp of the human's existence,[114] before he embarked on the spiritual path. The self-confidence of someone who claims spirituality is an incurable illness.

The fetus grows in the womb from day one until its birth, without any contribution from the family. The mother does nothing for it to develop from a delicate cell into a complete human.

The human attains complete bodily development before any spiritual receptivity, and the principal reason for this lies in the slowness of the processes of transference from the body to the spirit. This is, moreover, the view of scientists who assert that the activity of the psyche is entirely connected to the genesis and maturation of the nerves; this also means that precedence is given to bodily, rather than spiritual, growth.

113. A work by Tito Colliander originally written in Swedish and titled, *Asketernas väg*. It is unclear what language and translation Jabbour is citing here, but he himself did an Arabic translation in 1981 using the French translation of the original. See also the English translation by Katharine Ferré and published by St. Vladimir's Seminary Press that same year.—Trans.

114. The original diacritics have "sudā kiyān al-insān wa luḥmatahu [warp and weft of the human's existence]," but we have assumed in this translation that "sudā" is an erroneous, or perhaps colloquial, transcription for *sadā* (a warp).—Trans.

Owing to the ferocity of our bloody and long-term war with the things of the body, it is no wonder that we see people who are oriented around the body, and that we ourselves also remain spiritually underdeveloped.

3—The sense of guilt

The child's sense of his incapacity and of his need for others is a sense that his family is greater in both stature and capability than him, of his family's supervision over him, his inner and outward rebellion against them, his aggressive intention against his family, his jealousy of them, the interminable surveillance of the family, and of the family's rebukes and restrictions. All this forms a yoke around the child's neck, regardless of the positive aspects of these things.

Everything encourages the development of the child's sense of guilt and the growth of checks within the conscience. The child identifies, to a greater or lesser extent, with his family members' consciences and even their feelings of guilt. The child has a strong propensity to identify with his family; yet, there remains for the human his own originality and singularity. However much he resembles his family, he remains distinct from them. His temperament may come as a reaction to that of his family, and then we are surprised, uttering the proverb: "The thorn leaves behind a rose, and a rose leaves behind a thorn."

Excessive indulgence is equivalent to excessive restriction, and this explains the ingratitude of an undutiful only child. Indulging someone who is deprived is more beneficial than indulging someone who is spoiled, at times, exceedingly so. Someone who is deprived is invigorated through indulgence and comes to value his family, whereas someone who is spoiled is content only with abundance upon abundance. The deprived may be content with a single lira while the spoiled are discontent with a thousand; the rule is relative. The human is an inconstant creature.[115]

How does the child face this sense of guilt? Education and the conditions of upbringing generate this feeling within him, but we cannot determine the matter theoretically. When we study the human, we must consider each person as a specific case; hence, general principles are few. However, the knowledge of those experienced orients the work. These issues pertain

115. *Mutaqallib*, in reference to the propensity of the heart to overturn (see ftn. 31 in this chapter).—Trans.

to the child and his family, to their particular singularity, their general and specific situations, and each of their specific levels of thinking and understanding.

The existence of the sense of guilt is a vital necessity, first for the growth of our ethical character, and second for our spiritual growth. As for the Sophists, who claimed that the education of a child is possible without the sense of guilt, they were ignorant of spiritual matters, which we will analyze presently.

A well-trained scholar may excel in instructing a child without the sense of guilt, but a well-raised person still has a certain manufactured quality, and nothing guarantees that he will then be successful in educating his own children or grandchildren. Nature has its limits; it retaliates, even after generations. Someone may succeed in papering over the instincts, but he will not succeed in doing this for his sons or grandchildren. The conflict between the conscience and the instincts is a specific and delicate matter. One cannot bury the conflict forever, and there is no evidence that this conflict might result in a higher degree of character.

Psychoanalysts observe issues from a lived perspective. They remove impediments from the life of the patient so that he can proceed in life as a normal person; as for the extent of his capacity for spiritual luminosity, that is unknown and private.

The human remains wrapped up in earthly conceptions. The removal of impediments is important, but it is not everything. It is possible for the family to deepen the sense of guilt or to lessen it such that it can become superficial. Liberal classes make the sense of guilt superficial, ethically speaking, while the opposite may occur for both categories [that is, liberals and traditionalists]. An excess of sympathy or severity may corrupt the son of traditionalists. Liberals may, for a number of reasons, impart exemplary limitations on their child. One may grow up hostile to his family's behavior. The family may deliberately raise their children contrary to how they were raised. The variations exceed every number or count.

The child's reactions to his inferiority or superiority are innumerable, and his shifts are uncountable. Every aspect of the human is shiftable and transferable from one state to another. Neither science nor scientists, but only our Lord, is Omniscient and All-Aware in this arena.[116] A reasonable

116. Both *al-ʿalīm* and *al-khabīr* are among the ninety-nine names of God in Islamic tradition; Jabbour, moreover, is playing on the use of the same roots in

education may encourage the child to develop a moderate sense of guilt accompanied by a moderate reprimand. If the family wants to impart on him their own nature in every case and brand him with their consciences perfectly, they will burden him. He must be treated as a child with limited energy. Therefore, the proximity of the mother's age to the age of her child will be beneficial for education.[117] A reasonable distance in years makes the mother flexible and fresh, such that she deals with the child flexibly and kindly, and not with the hardness of a forty-year-old. Here, too, exceptions appear.

In a well-tempered state, the sense of guilt remains active in both consciousness and the unconscious without irresolvable crises of conscience and without extensive indecision that kills the freedom of initiative, proficiency in settling matters, and the ability to make sound ethical decisions in a timely manner. Those who live their lives in ethical indecision are incapacitated by a sense of guilt deeply rooted in both consciousness and the unconscious.

Poor education and the child's reaction(s) may cause the sense of guilt to be embedded deep within the unconscious, accompanied by an inner psychological anguish, to a degree that fluctuates throughout the individual's life between a consciousness of his guilt and self-punishment for it. This issue may result in neurosis[118] and the paralysis of the patient's life; it may also result in crime, as one commits infractions to obtain punishments, even if they are minor ones, and hence, there is the danger of sadism in poor education. It may eventuate in madness. It may lead one to take temporary refuge from it in order to freely live a life of guile, deception, profiteering, and pleasure. It may also result in hypersensitivity. The conflict between love and enmity, compassion and hard-heartedness, may lead to what is a false success in love, meekness, pliancy, and kindness; yet, the

---

denoting the practice of scientific knowledge (*ʿilm*) and scientific expertise (*khibra*). God, Jabbour implies, is *the* scientist.—Trans.

117. An age gap between spouses is a catastrophe for them and their children; a successful marriage tends to be between a man and woman in which the man is older than his spouse by a reasonable number of years, in such a way that harmony between the pair is easy, from which the children likewise benefit.

118. *Al-ʿuṣāb al-nafsī*, the technical term in Arabic for neurosis, but one that, as in English, immediately ties the condition of the soul/psyche (*nafs*) to the nerves (*ʿaṣab*).—Trans.

tension remains in the unconscious, and the sense of guilt remains surreptitiously in the unconscious, inciting one's guilt.[119]

People of this kind build their ethics according to the outward appearances of virtue, without extinguishing the sense of guilt in their unconscious.

In fact, they realize a good ethical balance. Some of them appear meek, blessed, and compassionate, while others appear honest, blameless, and just.

Yet can any one of them bear to be exposed to criticism? Can they bear to encounter a discerning spiritual father casting light on their counterfeit positions? Do they not esteem their virtues largely in keeping with repression, one which intensifies their hidden sense of guilt within the unconscious?

Is it not from their mouths and their kind that we hear: "My son is the finest son, my school is the finest school, my clothing is the finest, my house is the finest home, my organization is the finest, my house's furniture is the finest furniture . . ." The list goes on. So, is our brother the most perfect of God's creatures, free of all faults and defects? These virtuous ones join their virtue to pride and egoism, with both assuming the appearance of a virtue; nevertheless, arrogance is still arrogance and egoism is still egoism.

When interacting with these people, the most arduous thing is to rouse their sense of guilt or their feelings of inadequacy. When they realize that their cardboard castles are in danger of collapse, they turn into the most adroit lawyers, apoplectically defending themselves.[120] They lack cool nerves and the capacity to face the situation as it is; they cannot bear a simple shock to their cardboard castles.

Some who claim ethics arrive at the conviction that they are free of faults, that they have successfully buried the sense of guilt. They say: "We do not kill, nor are we sexually immoral, nor do we steal, nor do we bear false witness, so what remains of our transgressions?"

119. See also Freud, "Some Character-Types Met with in Psychoanalytic Work" (1916), SE 14: 309–33.—Trans.

120. For some, deep feeling reaches the point of a powder keg, exploding into tears, sorrow, and regret, or it flares up in anger and incites resentment. Internal pressure makes the nerves of the skin very sensitive, unable to bear a scratch. True capaciousness of heart, not its counterfeit, is victorious over wrath and teaches one to bear others patiently, such that their love grows in the breast.

In social life, these people are useful because the number of wrongdoers decreases considerably; however, Christian ethics are much higher than this.

4—The sense of guilt and the spiritual life

We saw that the human is knotted from his childhood by a number of issues and that the struggle for life is a principal motive. His connection to his digestive system is a vital one, lest he die, and the focus of his digestive system is to acquire various pleasures. His self-love is centered on his body and transforms his gluttony for food into a hunger to possess everything. His love for his own being drives him to tighten his grip on all that falls into his ambit. Throughout his life, he remains focused on his own being. Sometimes these abuses reach the point of using his family and others as means for himself.

Education is what makes someone receptive to others. One's respect for the individuals in his family, and others, as persons who deserve all our respect and love, is a spiritual level out of reach, except for the one whose life the Gospel and the Holy Spirit have transformed.

Envy and jealousy are two decisive factors in development. One spends his life comparing himself with others, endeavoring to be superior to them. Life is a battle, made of rivalries and conflicts.

Sexual life is a foundational problem, founded on bodily and vital needs. Unleashing it is devastating for others, and even for the wanton himself. There must be limits, precepts, and control over the psyche.

The spiritual life is carried out on the foundation of putting to death the works of the body and enlivening the works of the spirit (see Paul). Paul also discussed the conflict between the spirit and the body.[121]

This conflict is a true reality from which there is no escape. Within it are instincts, drives, desires, cravings, and passions. Each of them clashes with the Gospel. However much I try to overlay my soul with virtues, in the depths of my psyche there are aggressive drives and cruelty. I may use cruelty even against my own soul and cause it illness, oppression, mortal dangers, and serious risks. I may be excessive in food and drink in order to destroy and ruin my body; I may discipline it to the extremes of abstinence such that I pay the price of excessive illness and nervous disorder; and I

121. Galatians 5:16–26.

may exacerbate my egoism, self-love, and self-interest, and hence be hostile to the rights of others and their boundaries, exposing myself to their reprisal.

I am vulnerable to all manner of abuse; I abuse my psyche, others, and the material world to the point that it is impossible to be just and to use anything chastely.

I need to plumb my depths so that I come to know not only my malicious actions and corrupt speech, but also the precise movements of the passions—that is, the roots of evil pervasive within me.

The sense of guilt is a wise guide for those who live life in the spirit, but it has a specific nature; it is not entirely buried in the unconscious. This sense emerged during childhood, yet it was not buried completely; a part of it remains in the field of consciousness, guiding those who live life in the spirit to righteous work. It does not act with oppressive force as in the case of children who end up as psychiatric patients; it works with relative gentleness.

The spiritual man uses the sense of guilt to warily and artfully gather all his energies against his passions and his evil. The spiritual man stokes this consciousness into a fever in order to extinguish pride. Pride is the devil's transgression. When the devil tempted Adam and Eve, he tempted them with theosis, and this is even more atrocious than pride.

Obedience and service may well surmount stiff-necked insolence; still, the sense of guilt remains a blade that smites the height of arrogance, false theosis, and empty self-importance.

The spiritual human knows that the cravings of the body remain alive as long as the blood flows in the veins, and that obeying their needs depletes the energies of ordinary people, because they live for their bodies. Therefore, he knows that victory over the body does not exist save in death.

Greed shifts from one object to another, so too does gluttony. One may be greedy for knowledge and its like, or for possessing things of a religious nature, or for wealth. Pride does not sleep, and vainglory is a worm that neither sleeps nor rests.

On the path of the spiritual human, the objects of the drives and passions are transformed, and hence the objects themselves come to be of an ethical and spiritual kind. This is a very important principle: the transference and transformation of a person's conduct is a crucial feature.

The truth is that the human is still a windblown feather. However much we subdue our passions, the grinding war intensifies, and the chief passions appear intractable and are not easily conquered; what always follows is an acute and growing sense that we are the greatest of transgressors who have not yet made any notable progress.

The sense of guilt drives us to struggle evermore, since we have not reached a sufficient point. When we fall into this trap, we spiritually perish and delude ourselves into thinking that we have come to safe shores, when in fact, we are in the midst of a merciless war.

The sense of guilt is the greatest incentive to refuse contentment, the cessation of struggle, and a satisfaction with the existing situation or our current condition. Indeed, it assures us that we are a trash heap, that we have not yet made a beginning, and that our whole struggle is paltry in relation to what it must be. Indeed, it is the engine (the motor) of the spiritual life, which is stymied when the former stops running. Hence, the ones who live life in the spirit deepen it greatly, as we will see in the next chapter.

CHAPTER

6

THE CONFESSION OF TRANSGRESSIONS

The human is neither an angel nor a demon. The Apostle James said of the tongue: "Anyone who does not stumble in speech is a perfect man, likewise capable of ordering his whole body with a bridle . . . The tongue is a small organ that boasts in lofty matters. The tongue is an inferno too, truly a world of iniquity! It pollutes the whole body, setting one's life ablaze, while the inferno stirs it up. No human has the strength to suppress it; it is an unrestrained evil, overflowing with deadly poison—by it we bless our Lord and Father, and by it we damn those people who were made in the likeness of God . . ."[1] This is our reality. We are in a constant conflict between the passions of the body and the ascents of the spirit. This battle only ends at the moment of our last breath.

The Apostle James raises the issue of controlling the tongue. We may control our actions and so abstain from murder, sexual immorality, or theft. However, we remain largely incapable of restraining our tongues. Our evil shifts into our speech, and after a long struggle, we may be victorious; so then the evil moves into our thoughts, where it is a catastrophe. Victory over thoughts is arduous. After an immense struggle, the holy ones arrive at a disinclination toward the musings and thoughts that the devil tries to hurl upon their spirits, compelling their minds to ruminate on the remembrance of the name of God that thus becomes the object with which their minds are preoccupied.[2]

1. James 3:2–12.
2. Cf. the writings of Diadochos of Photiki.

I know a person who fought against the custom of taking an oath with his right hand for forty-four years; despite this, he would see himself in his dreams swearing with his right hand. The spiritual struggle against transgressions is a vocation that one practices over the course of a lifetime, day and night.

A great ascetic may be inattentive and become enticed by thoughts of disputes in his youth with his childhood peers. The conflict between the thoughts of the body and those of the spirit may lead the perfect ones to stray into a battle of the thoughts that has no relation to the authentic war of the spirit and the body.

Monastics may deviate in their ardor for spiritual cleanliness. They overdo their care for the cleanliness of the body and the monastery and exceed a reasonable ascetic limit. I may fast from food while frequently partaking of seeds, nuts, coffee, and tea. I may fast so harshly that I return, after a time, to my gluttony, making up for what I missed. Someone may not be an adulterer, but he might not deal with his spouse in a suitably Christian way. Married life is not without restrictions, for it obliges a spousal respect for one another's character, each other's ways of being, and perspectives.

The dead body does not commit adultery, but is it pure for this reason alone? Purity is purity of the spirit. I may deal with others in a myriad of ways without gathering the elements necessary to be free of egoism, abusiveness, rudeness, and excess. This is owing to a lack of necessary respect, one free of any contempt, internal and external, or any complaint. It is nearly impossible to safeguard my relationship with others from something negative, even if I have, by and large, succeeded in viewing them as if they were Jesus Christ. Faults exist within us, even if we attain near perfection.

Evagrios named thoughts spirits, that is, evil spirits. These spirits descend upon us suddenly and steal the serenity of our minds, disturbing and polluting the mind if they can.

Safeguards might break down, and then I injure others unintentionally, even with a passing joke that did not account for the other's current psychological state, with a contemptuous tone, or by some other gesture.

I may suppose that my familiarity with so-and-so allows me to return his greeting while I sit at my table, without great care or deference. Nevertheless, family and friends are those who censure more than others. My respect for people must be ever enkindled, and I cannot become accustomed to a lack of reverence for any person, even a child.

Familiarity does not justify indifference to the dearest of relatives and friends. They, too, are human, whom the devil may try with misunderstanding.

I may spend a lifetime without harming anyone. However, are my thoughts clean? If anyone wounds me or disdains me, does my psyche remain staunch? Do thoughts and revolts of anger not stir up therein? Are not the delicate and sensitive those most susceptible to injury from criticism? One is at a loss as to how to deal with them.

I may not infringe on any person's right, and yet, do I keep calm nerves if a person snatches five lira from my hand? Do I rejoice if someone takes something belonging to me, even with my knowledge? Do I remain mute and dumb if people curse me?

Do I rejoice if I see my companions succeeding over me? Do I rejoice in people's joys? And do I grieve over their grief?

The list is long, and I would not wish to imitate the holy Peter of Damascus (eleventh–twelfth century) in enumerating a long list of errors. Better yet, in my view, is to let the Holy Spirit inlay my intellect and heart with the verses of the New Testament so that the Lord Jesus Himself may teach me what He wills and what I must do, and in order to make known to me my terrible and utterly fallen state. There is an additional way, and that is to recite the prayers before communion, the Jesus canon,[3] the prayers of Ephrem,[4] and

3. A reference to the canon (a set of thematic texts) to Jesus Christ said after the prayers for the departed. Jabbour composed an Arabic translation, *Qānūn yasūʿ*.—Trans.

4. This refers either to the penitential prayers or, more likely, to the *Spiritual Psalter* of Ephrem the Syrian (d. AD 373). The former are integrated into every weekday prayer during the Great Fast. In contemporary Orthodox Christianity, they are interspersed with prostrations and read as follows:

O Lord and Master of my life, do not give me the spirit of falsehood, inquisitiveness, love of leadership, and vain speech
Bless me, your erring servant, with the spirit of chastity, humility of thought, patience, and love
Yes, O my King and my God, grant me to know my faults and failings, and not to pass judgment on my brothers, for you are blessed unto the ages of ages. Amen.

the canon of Andrew[5] until one internalizes them. Then begin prostrations and prayer, for praying with the holy ones puts us in their company.

The Apostle Paul said that nothing good dwells in his body[6] and that he was the greatest of transgressors.[7] So, where do I, the iniquitous wretch, stand?

Whenever we plunge into an examination of our psyche, we realize our emaciation and the calamity that comes from our wallowing in iniquity. Those fleeing from themselves and from God do not wish to know themselves in their true state. They hurry off, like expert lawyers, to defend themselves, justifying their condition with vapid excuses.

The ones who live life in the spirit are violently opposed to the disgrace of self-justification; the only reasonable thing for them is to accuse the self of being a singular web of iniquities. They see nothing in the self but transgressions' pollution; this is what Abraham, Job, Isaiah, and Paul felt in the presence of God.

Those unlike them are eager to justify their own being, and it is, therefore, difficult for them to open up and be guided. Those who live life in the spirit take hold of the sense of guilt as a fire iron in order to be spurred to the remembrance of their transgressions and to find cause to rebuke themselves.[8]

The *Spiritual Psalter* was translated into Arabic by ʿAdnān Ṭarābulsī, with an introduction written by Jabbour. An English version (translated from Russian) appeared in 1997. See Ephraim, *Spiritual Psalter.*—Trans.

5. This penitential canon, composed by Andrew of Crete (known in Arabic as Andrew of Damascus), is chanted with prostrations during the first and penultimate weeks of the Great Fast. See Jabbour's Arabic translation of Andrew's composition, *Qānūn al-tawba*.—Trans.

6. Romans 7:17–18.

7. 1 Timothy 1:15.

8. In the typika after the *makārizmī* [in Greek, *makarismoi*; that is, The Beatitudes from Christ's Sermon on the Mount], a prayer says: "Pardon, forswear, and forgive us O God, our voluntary and involuntary stumblings, by word and deed, with knowledge or without knowledge, and grant pardon to us all." In it, we ask for pardon for all transgressions that we have committed without knowledge. Of course, the reckoning of God distinguishes between the one who has come to know much and the one who has come to know little (Luke 12:47–48), even though an iniquitous deed remains an iniquity. And therefore, those who suppose that they are free of error as long as they are not active in iniquity err. Laziness,

By this, they exterminate the enemy of the spiritual life that is self-admiration. Of course, the ones who truly live life in the spirit are sadists who subdue their masochistic psyche,[9] and this is what vexes analysts and atheists.

Sadism and masochism become a danger if they become illnesses. If I do good to one who is poor, it inspires me to think that I am a do-gooder. If I visit the sick or the imprisoned, it inspires me to think that I am gracious. If I make prostration or partake of the Oblation, it inspires me to think that I am pious. If I am kind to people, it inspires me to think that I am a great human being. If I overcome a temptation, it inspires me with the intoxication of victory. If I am silent, it inspires me to think that I am an ascetic. If I put on rags, it compels me to appear as though I am a re-

---

negligence, disregard, indifference, and slowness are signs of spiritual weakness; a lack of struggle is a great spiritual weakness. If we are not spiritually feverish, we are lukewarm, and spiritual tepidity is a dangerous disease. Disregard is a transgression as much as perpetration is a transgression. Whoever disregards doing good errs. Disregard may be the most grave of someone's transgressions, for it paralyzes all his movement: neither vinegar nor wine (in colloquial Arabic: neither a fork nor a knife). [Both adages imply the problem of tepidity and ambivalence—neither sour nor sweet, neither sharp nor blunt.—Trans.]

9. In a somewhat playful manner, Jabbour is referencing Freud (and possibly Lacan) on sadism and masochism. The former took up the concept from Marquis de Sade and Richard von Krafft-Ebing. These processes are the passive and active forms of a drive to be satisfied in a sexual object. Freud takes sadism as a "masculine" aggression that is inverted in the "feminine" passivity of masochism. Lacan's assessment, distinct from Freud's, sees sadism as a "disavowal" of masochism and, as such, the latter cannot be derived from the former. "The economy of masochist pain," Lacan says, "ends up looking like the economy of goods" (*Ethics of Psychoanalysis*, 239). This resonates with Jabbour, whose subsequent lines here make clear that one derives a primary satisfaction at the site of the existential self (*dhāt*) via the good of the other; the psyche is primarily "masochistic" in the sense that it derives its essential self-possession (*dhāt*) through an imaginal and passional circuit with that which is not the self. Lacan sums this up in recounting the story of Saint Martin sharing his cloak with a beggar, noting that "our own and our neighbor's [good] are of the same material," but also raises a question: "What can be behind" or beyond "having needs that have been satisfied"? (186). See Sigmund Freud, "Three Essays on the Theory of Sexuality" (1905), *SE* 7:123–246; Jacques Lacan, *The Ethics of Psychoanalysis*, 186 and 228; Lacan, *The Four Fundamental Concepts of Psychoanalysis*, 185–186; Lacan, "Kant with Sade."—Trans.

nunciant. It is impossible for me to undertake any work, speech, or thought without it lurking at my heel, so that I stumble into self-admiration. If I am a stingy miser, donating a piaster is more costly than saving a city from hunger. How many people break our heads boasting in trivialities, mentioning alms when they are not something to be mentioned in the world of righteous deeds?[10] How many do good deeds not out of kindness or spiritual drive, but for the sake of appearances and boasting? And to have their names etched onto the walls of churches or in the pages of journals and magazines! This is a common offense of the rich; all their good works are for the sake of ostentation, appearance, pride, and boast. Exceptions are few. How many of the rich will not donate even a piaster, except when they might reap from it self-admiration and vain, worldly glory, even from the closest of family and friends! This is an incurable disease for the rich and for politicians. If I wanted to speak about the sources of capital, I would have many experiences to relay.

In sum, a spiritual ethic is not the basis of people's dealings. For the cause of reaping capital, people greatly tolerate their consciences until wealth becomes a god to them, and they leave the worship of the true God. We know, spiritually, that the adherence to material things on the whole, and even to immaterial things, is idol worship. Jesus alone is righteous because He draws together everything to which the human cleaves, and when the human is interested in something other than Jesus, he is lost. Nothing can take the place of cleaving to Him.[11]

Yet, is this common? No. Therefore, all of us are a pit of iniquities, and no one can rightly attribute any virtue to his soul. The decisive proof is our shared unwillingness to die as a martyr. We are counterfeit Christians all; whoever does not say to Jesus, through the voice of his condition, day after day—let my blood be shed for your sake—will not advance one step

10. *Iḥsān,* the concept of righteous action. It appears in the Qur'ān multiple times and is articulated broadly in Islamic and Arab Christian traditions. Mustafa Shah notes that this term is also important in Islamic Sufi discourse, being used to indicate spiritual perfection. See Shah, "Iḥsān."—Trans.

11. Some are afflicted with a burning passion for the Holy Scripture, prayer, hymnody, care for the poor, but without a mad passion for Jesus. The human is capable of this. In psychoanalysis, we call the dissociation between the sexual component and the affective component isolation, as was the case with Don Juan. The crucial thing is the person of Jesus.

in the spiritual life. Counterfeiting, the greatest of ills, is what I describe in my book, *The Counterfeits*.[12]

The correct introduction to the confession of transgressions is the demolition of self-admiration and pride; the successful means is deepening the excavation of the sense of guilt. This is the lightbulb that is brought into our insides to illumine them and image them, just as physicians do.

Christianity says that the human reached a bottom even lower than wallowing in transgressions, to the point that there was no means of rescuing him, but God pitied him and brought about the only possible means of doing so—the incarnation of Jesus, Son of God, and His death upon the cross.

Who am I that I merit the death of the Son of God? I am a worm, not a human.[13] I am an animal.

Who am I that He should die for my sake? I am the lowest of refuse in creation. He is God, the one who is Omnipotent in everything, and I, on the other hand, am what kind of "I"? I am a void,[14] or rather, I approach a void because a void is the loss of existence, and the loss of existence is not evil. I am a creature wallowing in iniquities, plagued by transgressions, as near as possible to a void. A void is not the enemy of God, whereas I, the erring one, am at enmity with God through my transgressions. Cattle lack an intellect and freedom, and so they are not culpable, whereas I possess a free intellect and am culpable for my crimes. Whenever I am armed with this sense, spiritual progress is possible and my virtues will be the fruit of a correct, not counterfeit, struggle, by the aid of the Holy Spirit, who safeguards me from the black bile[15] so that my humility may be holy and not suicidal.

How do we confess?

We recall that the monastics in the fourth century would disclose all of their thoughts to a spiritual elder; does this resemble psychoanalysis?

12. Jabbour, *al-Muzayyafūn*.—Trans.

13. Psalm 21:6.—Trans.

14. *ʿAdam*, a term encompassing "lack," "nihility," and "nullity." Jabbour's usage of *ʿadam* parallels Lacan's use of *faille*, which he uses to denote the "rift" or "fault" that constitutes the subject. See especially Lacan, "Presentation on Psychical Causality."—Trans.

15. That is, melancholia.—Trans.

Psychiatric patients are knotted by a repressed inner conflict that needs to be aired, making way for the repressed to enter into the field of awareness and be incorporated into the conscious "I." As for the monastics, their personalities are unafflicted, and their sense of guilt does not pass them by unaware. They contend with errors and the passions face-to-face according to their capacities for discernment and wisdom, training in the battle between the spirit and the body. In this battle, the weapons are numerous, as are the ruses of the devil. In it, the monastic comes to recognize the passions and their modes of concealment. The light of the Holy Spirit and the Gospel slowly imbue the monastic with a knowledge of the various types of transgressions and evil thoughts.

The monastic is a human who has withdrawn from the world, and so it is then incumbent upon him to make war on every manner of attachment to money, possessions, food, drink, and clothing. He did not abandon wealth only to cleave to a collection of books, for example, or icons, or something else. The hand of the monastic does not grasp at anything; it is open to the point that he gives away his clothing should someone ask it of him. The monastic does not crave to possess anything (I am not, by this, encouraging would-be thieves to rob monks.)

Wisdom intervenes for the good of the divine economy.[16] The monastic is a human who withdraws from the world, disdaining station and rank in order to live in humble service to the brethren. Obedience and service come to be more precious to him than every rank. The monastic vows integrity, and so it becomes necessary for him to contend with every single form of the body's ardor; his eyes do not love seeing. His ears do not delight in hearing save in hearing the words of God and the praise of His glory. His lips do not love food, nor does his tongue love prattle. His touch does not delight in feeling anything. His heart does not incline toward bodies, nor does it pause before their beauty. Indeed, God has bewitched the monastic and enchanted his innermost core. God is the limitless beauty, while what assails the monastic is ephemeral.

The monastic has renounced himself,[17] and therefore he is not prideful or self-conceited, nor does he boast in himself. The monastic put his psyche to death. Thus, he is not spiteful, he does not become angry, nor

16. See chapter 1, ftn. 8.—Trans.

17. *Kafara bi-nafsihi*. Jabbour is inverting the typical use of *kafara*—which is both to be thankless regarding the benefits of God and to renege on one's ac-

does he hate. He does not harm, think evil, or deal in an evil manner, and he does not return anyone's evil with evil.

For the monastic, the law of "an eye for an eye and a tooth for a tooth" has killed itself. He responds to evil with good, triumphing over evil by good. If his enemy hungers, he feeds him, and if he thirsts, he gives him drink. He rejoices with those rejoicing and grieves with the grieving.[18]

The monastic loves and prays for all people. He does not return insults with insults but with righteous deeds and prayers.

The true monastic is the living, not written, Gospel. The Holy Spirit causes the written Gospel to be incarnate in his life, so that we see in this monk the image of Jesus Christ.

All of this is theoretical and needs to be realized. Virtuous lay people [*ʿalamānī*] may be in the image of Jesus more than monastics. It is an individual matter as to whether the monastic is more competent in the life of holiness than the people of the world.[19] Virginity allows for the sanctification of all time to God, whereas the labors of the world's people are many. Virginity is a great gift, yet where are those who are deserving of it? It is a diamond neck collar[20] searching for someone good and beautiful to encircle. But where is this excellent one? The truth is that the human has stalled on the path of virtue, be it a monk or a common person, a virgin or one married.

If the virgin at the monastery suffers from a war of evil thoughts, the married one suffers from wars of deeds, sayings, and thoughts, while the clergy in the world suffer very greatly. The monastic is not stripped of everything by merely entering the monastery; he remains a human. His entrance into the monastery represents one step in a million-mile march. The

---

knowledgement of God (*kufr*)—in marking by it the ascetic disposition toward the lower world (*dunyā*) and the psyche/soul (*nafs*).—Trans.

18. Romans 12.

19. *ʿĀlam*, by which Jabbour distinguishes between two terms for "the world." The term *al-ʿālam* is used to refer to the created world (used as a translation, say, of the Greek *kosmos*). As here, it can be used to refer to those who are "in the world," that is, not a monastic. The word *al-dunyā*, in contrast, refers to the lower world and is correlated with terrestrial things as opposed to spiritual things. This is consistent with an Arabic usage that is very present in the Qurʾān and Islamic traditions. See Abrahamov, "World."—Trans.

20. *Ṭawq*, a word that connotes something (in the form of a contronym) that is both burdening and capacitating.—Trans.

war of thoughts is an unceasing battle, day and night, and one encounters in it the devil, with all the weapons of evil, taking advantage of the monastic's passions and inclination, all in order to befoul him.

God himself allows for the war to intensify so that the monastic becomes trained in it, uprooting one transgression after another.

Repression in childhood precipitates the curtailment of the sexual instincts and the aggression instinct. Repression is a choke throttling the drives and instincts,[21] but this yields only minor virtue in proportion to its minor caliber.

The monastic, then, exists between two fires: first, the site of his conscience and intuitive sense [*shuʿūr*], which is greatly expanded by the activity of the Holy Spirit and the Gospel; second, the site of his evil thoughts and passions, that is likewise broadened by the activity of his sense of guilt and the breadth of his knowledge about it. His conscience is living, not sleeping, while his passions are very ferocious, unyielding for as long as he lives.

Each of these two horsemen attempts to occupy the psyche of the monastic and to drive the other from it. In the end, the millstone of the grinding war turns; victory for the former this time and for the latter another time, until God grants victory to the monastic at the moment of death in a final, heavenly triumph.

In this battle the monastic stumbles many times; but what is the cure? The Apostle James left us a very wonderful sentence. He said:[22] "Mourn your miseries, lament, and weep, so that your laughter turns into lamentation and your delights into melancholy. Be humble before the Lord, and He exalts you."[23]

Paul said: "I am a wretch." Lamenting errors and the fate of one's being is an essential monastic object. Among the most famous mourners were Ephrem the Syrian, Isaac the Ninevite, Andrew of Damascus, and the monastics mentioned in the fifth rung of *The Ladder to God*,[24] by John Cli-

21. *Muyūl* and *gharāʾiz* respectively.—Trans.

22. The current translation is precise in rendering the Greek meaning. We have taken from the Arabic translations the best of what matches the Greek original. The first phrase is derived from a phrase that Paul used (Romans 7:24), "I am a wretch [*shaqī*]," the second meaning is "lamentation," and its third meaning is "weeping."

23. James 4:9–10.

24. *Al-Sullam ilā allāh*; in English translation, *The Ladder of Divine Ascent*.—Trans.

macus. All of them were sons of our Middle East, and there are many others. Lamentation is a foundational object in all ascetic writing, and its sibling is weeping. Symeon the New Theologian was a fount of weeping and lamentation and writes of them. It is said that tears etched furrows into the cheeks of Ephrem the Syrian. The Apostle James advised that laughter should invert into lamentation and delight into "melancholy" (the translations also give us "grief" and "sorrow," but the term has a depressive tone, so I prefer "melancholy").[25]

The monastic laments and weeps over his errors, bewails his wretchedness, and is melancholic. His laughter sinks into lamentation, and his delights into melancholy.

There is much of this in the Psalms, and the subject is reiterated in the New Testament.

Hence, on the one hand, the monastic sets his sense of guilt ablaze, and, on the other, he mourns his wretchedness, laments, weeps, and is melancholic, humbling himself before the Lord. When he attains humility, our Lord God raises him up. "Blessed are the sorrowful" is, in the Greek, "blessed are the lamenters," originally, those mourning the dead.

This is the path of genuine repentance. This is the soil of repentance, cleansed of invasive weeds for the sowing of perfect virtues. The kingdom of God is not one of eating, drinking, and wantonness, but of asceticism, rigor, pure prayer, and righteous works. The way is miserable and riddled with dangers. Therefore, there is a pressing need for a spiritual elder to lead the monastic and the non-monastic alike, that lamentation may be an opening to spiritual perfection and heavenly joy.

How does the spiritual elder guide the monastic?

The elder is a human who is practiced in the forms of the monastic life. He is a person possessing a history of human relationships since his mother's womb. His life in the monastery and his training have altered a great number of his states and conditions, and so he has become an expert in the

25. *Kaʾāba* is related to depression and so to the "black bile" that Jabbour referenced earlier. Appropriately, it is also related to the term the Egyptian poet Mohammad Abu-Zaid used in his inaugural Arabic translation of Freud's 1915 text "Trauer und Melancholie" ("Mourning and Melancholia," *SE 14*:243–258) in 2009, titled *al-Ḥuzn wa al-iktiʾāb*.—Trans.

human passions and demonic warfare. The elder is deeply rooted in humility and thus has attained the gift of discernment,[26] which has made him into a spiritual expert in spiritual warfare.

The winds of God came upon him, and so he became a monk; but he needs leadership. The Muslim Sufis have said: "As for whoever does not have an elder, the devil is his elder."

Spiritual guidance is an important spiritual institution. John Climacus opposed a solitary ascetic life and favored a life of communion until an individual matures, only then becoming a hermit if he willed it. In the communal life of the monastery, the monk is trained in purification and humility, and submits to guidance. His dealings with the brothers keep him in human contact; this is necessary for controlling a sharp temperament, wrath, exasperation, anger, and all aggressive movements directed externally. Anthony the Great and his company are those monastic founders whom the compassion of God united and thus they shone. We, then, are oriented both toward an elder and the monastics who follow his guidance.

The elder is a human, as are the monks. One of them is an expert and the others are inexperienced; they may often, or even always, be younger in age than the elder. The elder is a leader, and the monk is one of his men[27] who is under his authority and his obedience; the obedience required is a complete one.

How do the two sides face each other? The simple fact of the elder being a leader and the monk being one of his men raises the issue of the relationship of the head to the subordinate, and vice versa.

The monastic cleaves to his elder, and so what kind of trust is between them? It is a trust that will emanate from the sum of the monastic's history. He may relate to his elder with an explosion of trust, like one who falls into ardor, vexed in bewilderment and ecstasy. It may be tepid, or it may be at some point between the two poles of ardent mad love and tepidity. The degrees between the two conditions are innumerable. The pair, one standing before the other, poses all the problems of the human's relation to the other, as contradiction (*ambivalence*) is an inseparable part of the

26. *Tamyīz*, in Greek *diakrisis*. This term is also important in the writings of al-Ghazālī.—Trans.

27. *Nafar*, a word that implies both a military man under the authority of a commander (a "soldier" or a "private") and more broadly one of the leader's kinsmen (see Lane, *Arabic-English Lexicon*, "نفر").—Trans.

human's formation. On the one hand, the monastic will alternate between the manifold negatives of doubt, misgiving, loss of trust, rebellion, jealousy, envy, contempt, disdain, soft or harsh criticism, movements of wrath, anger, agitation, and sometimes even aggression, hatred, disgust, scorn, ennui, discontentment, and weariness. On the other hand, amidst the manifold positives of love, we might mention: respect, sobriety, proper adherence, proper obedience, complete obedience, upright love, radical love, gentleness, kindness, affection, and meekness. The end is love without corruption, just as the Apostle Paul said.[28]

There is a love tarnished by passion. The ardent desire of Qays and Layla[29] is love, yet it is a love connected to gender. Stripping love of gendered passion[30] is an extremely arduous spiritual process. The monastic spends his life striving to succeed in this, to arrive at the pure love that is a blessing from the Holy Spirit and one of His fruits.

Love is an important human affect. It is the strongest of the affects, as we see in the life of lovers. Christianity is established upon love. God himself is love, as John the Evangelist taught us,[31] but the Holy Spirit clarifies our love of the passions until it becomes pure, one of His ripened fruits that the Apostle Paul numbered.[32]

28. Ephesians 6:24.

29. An ancient Arab story about the poet Qays ibn al-Mulawwah and his mad love for Laylā bin Mahdī, hence the more commonly known title of the story *Majnūn laylā* (Laylā's madman), *majnūn* or "madman" being the epithet Qays earns for his ardor. Despite being enamored with one another from childhood, the love that the pair shares remains unrequited; the zeal and madness of Qays for Laylā becomes the very trait that keeps them apart. Laylā is eventually married to another, and Majnūn (Qays) retreats to the wilderness, where he later dies. The story has produced an impressive array of literary works spanning centuries and multiple languages, most prominently the Persian poet Niẓāmī Ganjavī, and a play by the great Arab poet Ahmed Shawqi. Moreover, the story has been interpreted in Islamic Sufi writings as a contemplation on the mad passion of the spiritual seeker for God. See Seyed-Gohrab, *Laylī and Majnūn*.—Trans.

30. Freud used a term that guides our meaning here. Its French translation is *désexualisation*, even though the concept of sublimation [*al-tasāmī*] for Freud is not a spiritual or ethical concept. [See Freud, "The Ego and the Id" (1923), *SE* 19:1–66.—Trans.]

31. 1 John 4:8.

32. Galatians 5:22.

Love may be confused with sex, as in the life of lovers and married persons who are distorted sexually, and it may be mixed with a high degree of violence. A mother who is excessively affectionate corrupts her children, ruins their upbringing, and harasses her spouse. The mother who loves her spouse and children to the point of controlling them with excessive affection exercises a harmful sovereignty over them. It unconsciously deprives them of freedom of movement and comportment. A mother takes charge of all matters on the pretext of serving her spouse and children with righteous and perfect service, but she rather impedes their freedom. It is better for them to have a role in the home and not be idle.

The mother who intervenes in every affair of her spouse and children, on the pretext of eagerness and solicitude, harms the growth of their characters and her own receptivity. Dealing with another human requires a great deal of respect for his person, his freedom of disposition, without an excessive exertion of sovereignty or censorship, or even without an overflow of gentleness and affection.

Love builds up human character, filling a person with affects formed out of respect, admiration, and an appreciation for the freedom of the beloved. A cognizant love is accompanied by self-control. Every excessive inclination gives birth to complaint, even if it was unconscious and did not produce an over-correction. Pure love is devoid of the impediments that an immature and impure love may sow. The admixture of violence with love may reach the borders of criminality; there are incidents of jealous partners who torture their spouse, even sometimes to the point of murder, and there are criminals who pursue sexual murder, known in French by the name "vampires."

Undoubtedly, violence plays an important part in life, though of course I do not mean harmful violence. The human is strongly disposed to stand out.[33] Movement in all its variety requires struggle, and struggle requires expending energy, and the expenditure of energy, usually, requires that the psyche be coerced into struggle or else it will be slothful. When a person has become accustomed to struggle and labor, it becomes a spontaneous and urgent need, except for the indolent and their ilk. Labor is a great means

33. *Istaʿadād li-l-burūzan.* Recall that Freud describes the ego as the *projection* of a surface that is the limn of the body. The "I," as Lacan insisted, is thus split between the *conatus* of its 'speaking-out' and its insertion into the symbolic apparatus.—Trans.

of filling a void, of combating restlessness, discontentment, and weariness. Labor molds the body and leaves a great impact upon the soul.

One's work makes up the principal phase of life, and whoever fails in his profession fails in his life. One's work is a great force in the stability of the psyche; it is like a marriage between a number of psychological aspects. Someone without work lives in agitation, worry, strain, dejection, confusion, and crisis; when he returns to laboring, he settles into harmony, ease, and gratification. Idleness is the mother of vices, whereas labor over many hours is the daily anchor of the human's psychosomatic activity.

Sometimes, a person becomes irritated with the duration of labor and craves idleness. Yet, no sooner do the days of leave or yearly vacation come than he is discontented and craves to return to work, because the emptiness has constricted and besieged him. Some people labor excessively, to the point that work becomes their passion and obsession. Some people are incapable of sitting, so they always remain on the move and working. They relish labor as others relish the pleasures of food. However, all this vitality and energy is capable of transforming into violence, cruelty, harshness, aggression, and evil. This one, too, is capable of being struck by repression such that his vitality weakens and his character collapses. A violent shock can shake one's being, even if one's character is relatively solid.

In other words, our strength is capable of being used up in positive things and squandered on negative ones. Even work is one means of turning our thoughts from the passions; we forego evil thoughts by our occupation and dedication to labor. Spiritually, labor is a necessary precondition of being united to prayer. It gives us rest amid our face-to-face confrontation with the passions at certain times of the day. However, it cannot redirect our longings toward Jesus, which only prayer can do.

Love may be mixed with egoism and utilitarianism,[34] and this is often so. A mother may love herself in her child, or she may set her hopes on his future and his sympathies for her in her old age and later years.

34. The famous French monastic [*rāhib*, literally, "God-fearer"] and writer La Rochefoucauld [1613–1680] made egoism the motive of human conduct. The truth hurts. However, and indeed unfortunately, humans are egoistic and utilitarian to various degrees. All the problems between the mother-in-law and the daughter-in-law originate, on the one hand, from jealousy and an excessive attachment on the part of the mother to her son, and, on the other, the wife's egoism

Deception and double-dealing may also be mixed in, opening the door to base goals. A French woman once recalled to another: "Nineteen times I saved so-and-so's wife from falling into the snares of the sycophants. I was telling her: 'You poor thing, they are deceiving you for their base goals, they do not love you.'"

How easy is this path, as Ahmed Shawqi[35] said: *By their talk of beauty, they deceived her / The belles, praise misleads them.*

How ignorant are the likes of these victims of false praise, the families of whom did nothing to alert them to this danger, and how many are they? Wicked men know that this is a weak spot for women.

Among the episodes of tribulation recounted by the holy Dorotheos of Gaza is one concerning himself. He found that his views coincided with his elder's, and so he fell into tribulation—namely, that he had no need of the elder's consultation as long as their thoughts coincided. His psyche resisted, and he made a decision to this effect: even if our thoughts coincide, my thinking is not correct unless the elder agrees with it. Hence, what is correct is only what the elder says. In this way, he escaped the trial and returned to an unreserved reliance on his elder.

Love and hate are not the only axis of these relationships. The elder instructs the monastic in the principles of prayer, fasting, and asceticism, as well as in the attainment of the virtues.

Prayer takes precedence because it is the yeast of the monastic's life. It leavens fasting, asceticism, and the virtues. Gregory of Nyssa named it the "leader of the choir of virtues." Ephrem the Syrian, Mark the Ascetic, and John Climacus called it "the mother of the virtues."

The masters of monastic leadership in our contemporary world are found in the monasteries of Mount Athos. One is fully trained in prayer first, then released to the heights with the study of religious texts. Their favored prayer is the Jesus prayer: "My Lord, Jesus Christ, Son of God, have mercy on me." The Russian ascetics added to it, ". . . have mercy on me, a transgressor."

We know from a newly discovered writing from a monastery in Egypt, the writings of Diadochos of Photiki, the book *The Ladder to God*, and

---

in monopolizing her husband and separating him from his family; this is distorted love.

35. One of the most famous modern Arab poets and playwrights.—Trans.

the *Two Centuries* of Hesychios of Sinai, that this prayer is very ancient,[36] contrary to what Father Irénée Hausherr claimed.[37]

The spiritual writers—and especially those at the monasteries of Mount Athos—connect this prayer to breathing.[38] That is, the monastic repeats the prayer at a pace with the frequency of his breath. It is truly the zephyr of the spiritual life. For the name of Jesus is the mightiest strike force, razing the strongholds of the devil and his tribulations. John Climacus advised us to smite and scorch the devil with it.

All spiritual life is of relative and limited benefit if we have not opened our chests wide to Jesus. This is accomplished by wringing the psyche in fervent, enkindled prayer, nourished by a fiery faith in Jesus and the scorching flame of desire.

Fasting, asceticism, and the virtues revolve around this orbit. Even studying the Gospel is only of relative benefit if it has not been leavened by prayer and the blessing of the Holy Spirit. This training requires specific raw materials and a requisite pliancy within the individual so that the monastic is able to absorb the training. If the monastic is long in the tooth, of a harsh temperament, or a hard nature, his capacity will be limited. It is something related to the capacity for affective communion, which is connected to each individual's upbringing. There are persons within whom there is a propensity to mix with the other, and there are persons who can only mix relatively or superficially. There is one who opens his heart, and there is another who is incapable of opening it totally or even relatively.

36. Jabbour is referring to Hesychios of Sinai's Greek maxims, which were incorrectly ascribed by Jacques-Paul Migne to Hesychius of Jerusalem (*PG* 93, 1479–1544). These maxims, which mention the Jesus prayer, were included in the first volume of the *Philokalia*, as are those of Diadochos of Photiki. An English translation of the former appeared as Hesychios the Priest, *On Watchfulness and Holiness*, in Palmer et al.'s translation. Jabbour is arguing against Irénée Hausherr's dismissal of the claim that the Jesus prayer is an ancient practice. See Hausherr, *Noms du Christ et voies d'oraison*.—Trans.

37. My book *Yasūʿ am yhwh?* [Jesus or Yahweh?] highlighted the importance of the name of Jesus. Chapter nine of that book is much more complete than [the research of] Irénée Hausherr and Lev Gillet as a source for the name Jesus in the Bible and as a name for supplication and other things. There are also prayers of the Orthodox Church, of an overwhelming multiplicity, that are based on the name of Jesus.

38. *Tanaffus*, the same root (*n-f-s*) as in the term *nafs*.—Trans.

People are raw material. Viscid materials adhere, while others do not, meaning that the existence of a human's propensity to be viscid, to cohere with the other, aids him in adhering or not. You meet a person, and in minutes he makes you a brother and you him, whereas you spend a lifetime with others without cleaving together. Viscidity does not mean what we say in colloquial language about some people: "He is clinging, oppressive." Viscidity here is a comprehensive and affective coming together.

At times, the monastic may see in his elder his father, in terms of authority; at other times his mother, in terms of affection; at other times, his brothers, in terms of rivalries and a friendship tinted with jealously and envy; at another time, his schoolteacher; and at other times, his companion, and so on. His disposition in facing these images reflects his affects toward these aforementioned people. But things progress for the better until the relationship becomes one of mature persons who are in perfect or near-perfect openness, one to another. Each of them has covenanted with God to live for God, and thus divine blessing has consecrated them both.

In this way, the mercilessness of the soul shatters to become sweetness and pleasantness. O how terrible is this mercilessness! In this way, the torpor of feeling and of the senses shatters, and then the monastic becomes a fruitful site of gentleness, of great soul, and of extraordinary manliness.[39] Mercilessness and torpor are diseases impeding the growth of love. In this way, the other becomes our center, and from him we move with ease toward God. All of this demands perfect obedience from the monastic. But is attaining the highest degree of obedience an easy matter for a monk? The monastic's success in obedience might well be the foundation of his success in the whole of spiritual life. Why?

Arrogance, anger, aggression, and sexual revolt flare up in the monastic with force, rising from the bottom to the top, then the nerves and psyche tense in an aggressive, ascending movement. The movement of obedience is a descending movement; through it, the obedient one ends up in control of his nerves and comes to reduce the ascending movements. This one

39. *Rujūla*, a term that is likely a direct translation of the Greek *andreia*, which is used throughout Greek ascetic teachings, connoting boldness and courage.—Trans.

buries arrogance, egoism, self-love, and he obtains humility, pliability, tractability, and meekness. Through obedience, one can bridle all manner of passions with ease.

The monastic acquires magnanimity[40] in times of agitation, becoming meek and long-suffering since he who obeys his elder in total obedience possesses the protection of his command. Control over one's own being is an extremely arduous matter. All the world's warriors may be incapable of controlling themselves. So, if a monk controls himself, it is he, not they, who is brave in the world.

Christian virtues are the fruit of a ferocious war with the passions, not the fruit of wrestling with the psyche. There may be someone who is broadly capable in the external world, yet he is incapable of dispossessing himself by cutting back on his smoking.

The obedient monastic who bridles the movements of his passions will be one of rare strength. It is the strength that moves mountains, of which the Lord Jesus spoke—that is, "the mountains of transgressions," as Maximos said. This movement is more difficult than moving physical mountains. The spiritual elder may not be the ultimate goal, but, even so, obedience to him does its work, as we see in *The Ladder to God.*

None of this comes to pass without struggles that span a lifetime. Within these struggles is the devil, lying in wait for us, looking to wage war on us through dissatisfaction, restlessness, ennui, and weariness, especially from noon to the afternoon. The battle is like any other battle; it exhausts a person's energies. The heat of the day affects temperament. As soon as noon approaches, weariness will have gnawed at us to some extent.[41]

Of what kind is this war?

It is a war between the conscience and our yearning for God on the one hand, and the body on the other. The body attempts to utilize the sources of

40. *Raḥāba al-ṣadr,* literally "capaciousness of the chest."—Trans.

41. See *The Ladder to God* [*of Divine Ascent*], section 18:24–25, concerning the progression of meekness for attaining humility. The meek is victorious over agitation, tantrums, and excitement, such that arrogance can no longer prompt him to agitation, tumult, and vigor. In arrogance there is a violence. Meekness transforms that violence into a gentle integrity.

our strength, to exhaust them in its pleasures, while the conscience and the desire for God stand before it as an invincible rampart. Whenever a monastic advances spiritually, he is indifferent toward his body; he has monopolized the sources of his strength in order to exhaust them in spiritual things.

Whenever the monastic makes progress, the body's discontent increases, like a snake whose tail is seized by a hedgehog. Whenever the latter squeezes it, the serpent's clamor and buffeting of the hedgehog increases. The monastic may fall into excess and extremism. So the task of the elder would be to orient him, to keep him within defined and reasonable limits, as the more the monastic constrains and represses his body, the more its fury rises in revolt.

Of course, to be successful, one must have a defiant and courageous posture. A reasonable degree of extremism is necessary. The warm winds of faith and renunciation are what call the monastic to be separated from family, the world, and possessions, in order to live for his Lord alone. The monastic does not cling, neither to people nor to the earth; he lives in contempt of the world and its wealth. Bravery is the stamp of the monastic in particular and the Christian in general.

Those who imagine that the monastic is a coward or one afflicted by psychological trauma are in error. Medically speaking, this idea has been refuted. Psychological trauma in particular and psychological illness in general cause the sources of the patient's energy to be wasted in unconscious psychological conflict, while the monastic requires both conscious and unconscious energies.[42] Patients are afflicted by a conflict that strikes at the lower powers with ruinous force, by which the higher powers come to a be a poor guide.

These people are in need of medical treatment to restore harmony between these conflicting powers. Once harmony has returned, the patient will always require that the conflict not be repeated. As for asceticism, it is a procedure in which the higher powers wrest away as much of the poten-

42. The highest Christian model is the martyr [*shahīd*], because he dies out of love for Christ and the church, and the monastic is a living martyr. The traumatized psychological patient's powers are squandered; so, how could he possess the bravery of the martyrs? The monastics are courageous champions, daring, not idlers or freeloaders. They bring God down to earth. Who was capable of this in the first place, save the Virgin Mary?

tialities of the lower powers as possible. The ill are incapable of this, for they, even after healing, will be like a "cracked" crystal, ill-suited for the life of the monastery and what it holds concerning the bravery of asceticism.

Symeon the Stylite,[43] Anthony, and their followers are the true champions of history after the apostles, in the same manner as the martyrs. Did the holy Fathers not say that the monastics are martyrs?

In the early church, the apostle and the martyr occupied the first two ranks. The desire for witness was their shared stamp. A letter from Ignatius of Antioch[44] to a Roman family is an attestation to a desire and fiery yearning for a martyr's death.[45]

Origen said:

> In the early church, the first sacrifice, following the apostles, (is) the sacrifice of the martyrs. The second is the sacrifice of the virgins. The third is the sacrifice of the unblemished . . . However, one must not look to the bodies of the unblemished and virgins as a holy oblation, pleasing to God, for the mere chastity of the body alone.[46]

Origen coined this term: "martyrdom of conscience."[47]

In the persecution of the year 177, the faithful of Lyons (France) said of the martyr Attalus: "He was always among us a martyr of the truth."[48]

43. I composed his Eastern life with great scientific precision and admiration in 1990. It was published in 1992.

44. See the translation [from Greek] by Patriarch Ilyās IV, *al-Ābā' al-rusūliyyūn* [The Apostolic Fathers].

45. See a summary of the studies from which we have only drawn a small portion in Kirchmeyer, "Grecque (Église)," in *Dictionnaire de spiritualité.*

46. Commentary on the Letter to the Romans 9:1 in *PG* 14, 1205 A. Moreover, in his book *An Exhortation to Martyrdom*, Origen groups the unblemished with the martyrs (paragraph 15 in *PG* 11, 581 D). I have used the term *muḥṣinīn* [unblemished] instead of *'afīfīn* [abstinent] to reserve the term "abstinence" [*'iffa*] for the ascetics specifically. The term unblemished [*muḥṣina*] is applicable to a married woman and others, and I have used it in the masculine without restricting it to the feminine alone.

47. *An Exhortation to Martyrdom*, paragraph 21 in *PG* 11, 589 D. He expounds on the book of Numbers 10:2 in *PG* 12, 639 A.

48. Eusebius, *Ecclesiastical History* 1.43 in *PG* 20, 425 A.

Basil the Great spoke on martyrdom through intention:[49] "I regard, sincerely, whoever dies as a martyr to be a happy man, that you may become a martyr in intention."[50]

In his sermons, Pseudo-Makarios likewise proceeded in a wondrous way:

> If we willed to bear all hardships and tribulations with ease, then death for the sake of Christ would be the object of our desires and would be ever before our eyes. For He has enjoined us that we might follow Him, bearing His cross, that is, that we be prepared and ready for death . . . Does it grieve the one who desires death for the sake of Christ to bear sorrow and adversity?[51]

It is truly a marvelous text. The true Christian is ever ready for death for the sake of Christ. We will see that Anthony the Great was burning with this desire.

We arrive now at the crux of our subject concerning the martyrdom of the monastics.

The martyr faces death in an instant and passes on to his Lord, whereas the monastic faces martyrdom every day and every moment in the course of life, crucifying his psyche with Jesus in asceticism and struggle, putting his own being and its passions to death daily.

Athanasios the Great recalls Anthony the Great's continuous desire for a martyr's death:

> He was indeed spurred by a great desire for martyrdom, however, inasmuch as he could not surrender himself, he served the confessors of the faith. And when the judge saw his courage, his companions' courage, and their desire for martyrdom . . . he would have had martyrdom; however, the Lord preserved him for our benefit and that of others, that he would be a teacher in asceticism . . . When the persecution ceased, he returned to the monastery in order to live the hour

49. *Niyya*, a concept important in Islamic commentaries as well. Al-Ghazālī for example, references the need for *niyya* before any act toward God. See Wensinck, "Niyya."—Trans.

50. Homily 19, "On the Forty Martyrs" in *PG* 31, 508 B.

51. *PG* 34, 949 B; see also Theodoret, bishop of Cyrrhus, *Treatment for the illnesses of idolatry*, chapter 8 in *PG* 83, 1021 A; and Gregory Dialogos, Pope of Rome, "Dialogues" 4.95 in *Patrologia Latina* 77, 428 A.

> of martyrdom in his conscience, imposing on himself a greater and more intense asceticism.[52]

Further on, we will look at the holy Gregory the Theologian's text, in which he considers the baptism of tears more arduous than the baptism of martyrdom by blood.

Diadochos of Photiki (mid-fifth century) said that no human can attain perfection while in the body except the holy ones who come to martyrdom and perfect confession.[53]

The Desert Fathers themselves are of this view. Anba [Father] Bitimios related once, concerning Anba Makarios the Egyptian,[54] how two strangers settled in Scetis, became ascetics and, after an ascetic struggle, fell asleep in the Lord. When the fathers came to Anba Makarios, he guided them to the cell of the two ascetics, saying: "Come, behold the martyrdom of these two young foreigners."[55]

52. Athanasios, *The Life of the Holy and Great Anthony*, paragraphs 43, 46, and 47 in *PG* 26, 912 A B. This text reveals the wisdom of Anthony, who did not deliver himself to martyrdom frivolously. Instead, God preserved him for another martyrdom: a martyrdom within the conscience, through asceticism. In this way, the ascetic arrives at the station of the martyrs, a dual band of brothers. Origen advised against rushing headlong into martyrdom. The matter requires equanimity and poise. If the battle falls to us, then it is on us to face it with the confession of faith, and to die as martyrs for the sake of the truth. For there, we are facing an exigency. We must not facilitate others' perpetration of the crime of our murder; otherwise, we would be self-loving and motivated by self-love (according to [Origen's commentary on] John 1:28 and 23). In other words, if a martyr's death comes, then there will be a thousand upon thousand welcomes, but with the composure and the understanding of discernment. The matter is exacting and left to a living conscience, illumined by the Holy Spirit in offering up the self as a sacrifice, albeit willingly, as long as God is well-pleased in its offering as an actual oblation, so that our blood would be shed like that of the martyrs.

53. See *On Spiritual Knowledge and Discrimination*, paragraph 90, *Philokalia*, vol. 1.

54. The term "Anbā" is of Aramaic origin and appears in the Greek New Testament [in the form "Abba"] three times (Mark 14:36, Romans 8:15, and Galatians 4:6). It means "Father" [in Arabic, *ab*]. We use it in the vernacular for young children when teaching them the words: "*Abbā, Abbā, Abbā.*"

55. Makarios, Saying 33 in the Greek [*Apophthegmata tōn Paterōn*], while it is Saying 19 in the translation of the Frenchman Guy [*Paroles des anciens: Apophtegmes*

Longinos said: "Give blood and receive spirit."[56] We come now to two remarkable texts by Ephrem and John Chrysostom, two sons of our immortal country. Chrysostom said in praise of the martyr Thecla:

> She guarded this virginity, which is, if well-considered, a great martyrdom before martyrdom itself. For the pleasures are merciless tormenters of the body, crueler even than tormenters, torturing with fetters not made by human hands. They injure the psyche by means of the eyes and by means of the ears; they bring the firebrands of licentiousness to the garments of the soul.[57] They flog the mind with a cruel whip; they torture us in wars that are constantly novel. (If we triumph over the eye, they make war on us through the ear; and if we triumph there, they make war on us through ugly thoughts). When our vigilance causes us to overcome every one of its snares (that is, pleasure), then pleasure will also come during sleep, fighting against us through shadows. Therefore, (we face) an endless cycle of wars, neither beginning at sunrise nor desisting at night . . . All this made virginity a long martyrdom for this blessed virgin, Thecla. She contended against pleasures just like the martyr (contends) by facing savage animals. She battled thoughts just like they battled abuses. She struggled with passional imaginings as if she were struggling with

---

des Pères du désert], and found in *PG* 65, 277 B. [For an English translation, see Saying 33 of Makarios in *The Sayings of the Desert Fathers*, translated by Benedicta Ward.—Trans.]

56. Longinos, Saying 5 in *PG* 65, 257 B. [Benedicta Ward translates the entire saying as follows:

> Abba Longinus said to Abba Acacius: "A woman knows she has conceived when she no longer loses any blood. So it is with the soul, she knows she has conceived the Holy Spirit when the passions stop coming out of her. But as long as one is held back in the passions, how can one dare to believe one is sinless? Give blood and receive the Spirit." (*The Sayings of the Desert Fathers*, 123)

This follows the thinking of the soul as both feminine and a virgin mother, as Jabbour tracked earlier in Maximos.—Trans.]

57. Jabbour has rendered the Greek term *gnōmē* (see ftn. 69 and 72 in chapter 5 of this text), the will to know or perceive, as *thiyāb al-nafs*, the garment of the soul/psyche.—Trans.

> the tortures of the executioners. Yet she too won the victory to that measure, in this heated and sundry war, because the holy fire of her soul was of a greater heat than the fire of nature.[58]

What caught my eye in this text is that pleasure abates before the campaigns of watchfulness,[59] and so it seeks refuge in dreams in order to agitate our frame of mind during sleep, and to drain our watchful, spiritual resolve. Today, the dream is no longer a mystery and an enigma. During therapy for psychiatric patients, the dream is broken up into its elements by special craft and skill, following the scientific rules of psychoanalysis.

Indeed, many of the Fathers discussed dreams. John Climacus treats the issue in his writing, *The Ladder to God*.[60] Their treatments are valuable in a number of ways, even if their times did not allow for the greatest depth. Thanks are due to Freud for the invention of a scientific method in the analysis of dreams, because, with it, astonishment and bewilderment have ceased. Still, their full analysis is completed in therapy, even if analysts know by experience the meaning of many dreams merely by hearing them narrated.

During treatment, the dream is broken up into each of its elements, such that its hidden meaning will be clarified, sometimes with difficulty and at

58. *PG* 50, 745.

59. *Yaqaẓa*, a translation of the Greek ascetic term *nēpsis*.—Trans.

60. *Al-Sullam ilā allāh*. See the third "rung" of *The Ladder of Divine Ascent*, "*Peri xeniteias*," what translator Lazarus Moore perceptively renders as "On Exile or Pilgrimage," since the estrangement implied here also implies "a notion of movement" (see his ftn. 1, page 63). This is reflected in the eighteenth-century Arabic translation of a manuscript housed at the Monastery of Mār Jirjis at Dayr al-Ḥarf, wherein the same chapter title is translated as "On blessed estrangement" (*fī-l-ghurba al-ḥasana*). In the subsection of this chapter, "Concerning dreams that beginners have," John writes, "A dream is a movement of the mind while the body is at rest. A phantasy is an illusion of the eyes when the intellect is asleep. A phantasy is an ecstasy of the mind when the body is awake. A phantasy is a vision of something which does not exist in reality" (3.26). Dreams, the text argues, become a site in which divine estrangement risks being compromised by vainglory. For the manuscript of the Arabic translation housed at Mār Jirjis (1766 CE), see *The Ladder of Divine Ascent*, fol. 2r–133v, the Hill Museum & Manuscript Library, https://w3id.org/vhmml/readingRoom/view/125961. —Trans.

other times with intense distress. In the course of the dream-work,[61] there is sometimes a lucidity that we do not enjoy in watchfulness.

The Fathers discovered some important points spiritually, discerning from them both the spiritual condition of the monastic and the distincton between his sexual feelings and sheer sexual activity. The degree of uncovering that we mentioned earlier was very high, and with it, the activity of the body [*jism*] no longer exercises dominance over the sensations, because the senses have been entirely directed to God.

In the life of those inundated by God[62] (that is, the Sufis, the mystics), withdrawing from that which is material is fitting. The Apostle Paul mentions being snatched up into the third heaven, saying: "I know a man in Christ from fourteen years who was snatched into the third heaven. Was it in the body? I do not know. Or was it outside the body? God knows. Rather, I know that this man was snatched into paradise. Whether it was in the body or outside the body, I do not know. God knows. There he heard the mystical words that the human is not permitted to utter."[63]

As for Ephrem the Syrian, since it was his habit to innovate and excel, he said:

> In your person, in your freedom, be a martyr and judge, be a warden of your psyche, crucify your body every night in prayer, and when you get up, interrogate it as to whether sleep defeated it. So, be an inspector of its nighttime vigils. Establish a covenant with your members in all earnestness. If you have not sunk down into sleep from the time of evening, then consider and count yourself with the martyrs. Do not allow sleep to overcome you at night; do not spoil your victory. Make your soul a martyr of nighttime vigils, and let this martyrdom be

61. The Arabic phrase *ʿamal al-aḥlām* is a translation of *Traumarbeit* (dream-work), which Freud details in the sixth chapter of *The Interpretation of Dreams*, wherein he analyzes the central procedures by which the dream-work is effected, namely condensation and displacement: "The whole mass of these dream-thoughts is brought under the pressure of the dream-work, and its elements are turned about, broken into fragments and jammed together—almost like pack-ice." Freud, *The Interpretation of Dreams* (1900), *SE* 4:312. See also *Introductory Lectures on Psycho-Analysis* (1916), *SE* 15:1–240.—Trans.

62. *Khalīliyyīn ilah.* See the Translator's Introduction for more on the use of these terms.—Trans.

63. 2 Corinthians 12:2–4.

> established between you and God . . . The martyrs gave witness in the day, while the ascetics (gave witness) during night vigils. Witnesses tell of the martyrs' victories before kings, but the Son of the King (that is, Jesus) described the promises made to the righteous, like (those made) to the martyrs. The martyrs are crowned with fire, those vigilantly keeping vigil. The sword made the martyrs renowned, and this too is the aim of the ascetic. The martyrs suffered from hunger, and the ascetics, from affliction. The martyrs were tortured with thirst; the penitents by mortification. The martyrs tasted pains, and the ascetics repented.[64] The martyrs won the kingdom by their steadfastness,[65] and the virgins by their chastity. The bodies of the martyrs were beaten with rods before the judges because of their sure hope, while vigils mortified the bodily members of the ascetics, keeping vigil because of their vows. The former witnesses were victorious over their oppressors, and the athletes of the wilderness were victorious over tribulations. The martyrs beheld the mystery.[66]

With these two important texts, those of Chrysostom and Ephrem, we have concluded this subject. They offer a clear image of the life of ascetics and monks, as well as what takes place within its mystery. Chrysostom lived in Antioch and Ephrem in north-east Syria. The two of them represent the

64. The comparison of repentance with the martyr's pains is quite significant, and it agrees with what we have said in this book. It is not an invention, playacting, or a jest, but a wringing out of the psyche by agonizing pain. Therefore, how negligent are they who partake of the Oblation [that is, the Eucharist] without wringing themselves through the winepress of repentance in order to cut off the ugliness of their transgressions from every taste and flavor, else one is conquered by the devil and one's desires. This will take us to the Palamas's view shortly.

65. *Ṣumūd*, a modern term that is used to refer to Palestinian determination in the face of political domination and expropriation. Jabbour links this determination to martyrdom.

66. See Lamy, *Sancti Ephraem Syri hymni et sermones*, vol. 4, 214. In 1973, KU Leuven in Belgium published a new, fully revised edition of Ephrem's writings to mark sixteen centuries since his death in AD 373; it is worth our attention since Syriac is the sister of Arabic, and so, where are the people of brotherhood? [The latter is possibly a reference to Beck's German translation (some of which was translated into French) of Ephrem's Syriac corpus, some of which was published in 1973, in the *Louvain Corpus of Oriental Christian Writers* (*CSCO*)—Trans.]

first generations of ascetics. They left many marks on monastic and ascetic life in the See of Antioch; what's more, Chrysostom trained people in the monastic virtues.

Those who extract from oblivion every human energy,[67] igniting them in prayer, asceticism, and the virtues, are not like us. Indeed, they are humans who have ascended to a rank above humankind. They are those who made the decision that the life of the world is a deception and a delusion; they are not like the rest of humanity.

A Protestant Frenchwoman asked another, "Why do the great women artists end up in the monastery?" This was the answer: They experienced the deception of the world, its delusions and pleasures, and found that the happiness of the world is temporary, transitory, and empty. It is an illusion within a false illusion. They knew people and knew the falsehood of their affects, the dissemblance of their relationships, and the carnality of their feeble love. They knew that only a few would accept to be honorable spouses to women artists; anyone honorable would refuse to even deal with them, let alone marry them. They reached the bottom of experience in matters of the body and the world; they found everything void and a grasp of wind, and so they rejected the world and its ilk.

This inner revolution[68] is based on the failing of a tremendous hope in the world and its vanities, and on the realization that flight from the world is correct; and so they collected their scattered powers. This is easy for them when the strength of will is in abundance. The matter requires only a shift from one military camp to another. They were fedayeen troops[69] in service

67. *Insān*, the term for the human, derives from the root ā-n-s, implying an intimate link between oblivion (*nisyān*) and the human. In Orthodox monastic tradition, and as Islamic commentaries also note, *nisyān* is countered by *dhikr*, the remembrance of both God and death. See the *Tafsīr al-qur'ān al-'aẓīm* by Ibn Kathīr (d. AH 774 / AD 1344) and his commentary on Qur'ān 20:115, in which he notes: "إنما سمي الإنسان لأنه عهد إليه فنسي." (But he was called *insān* because he was enjoined yet forgot).—Trans.

68. *Inqilāb* (see ftn. 8 in chapter 5).—Trans.

69. The term *fidā'iyyūn*, meaning those who sacrifice themselves, emerged through the anti-colonial struggles in the Mashriq. It first referred to irregular civilian resistance to the British occupation of the Suez during the mid-twentieth century; the more well-known usage, from which Jabbour is likely drawing, refers to those fighting to free occupied Palestine.—Trans.

of the body, then they moved to the freedom of the spirit and its supremacy.

It is no wonder that Chrysostom said that he did not know a great saint who had not previously been a great transgressor, meaning that the strength wasted in grave offenses is redirected toward serving God. These are the penitents, not the traumatized. Their powers are marshaled, not sunk within the unconscious. The people of the earth are more sagacious and astute in this generation than the children of the Kingdom. Their capacity for transformation is preserved, whereas the hardening of the now-desiccated faithful strips them of freshness and pliancy.

CHAPTER

7

THE ESSENCE OF MONASTIC CONFESSION

The monastic confesses to his elder every thought that wanders in his mind throughout the day and night, and he must not conceal anything. The holy Cassian mentions a monk who remained troubled for ten years until he disclosed what it was to his elder.

In terms of total divulgence, the repentance of monastics resembles the psychoanalysts' treatment of patients. The analyst[1] treats conflicts that occur in the unconscious, while the elder is predominantly concerned with the conflict that occurs in the field of consciousness.

The monastic experiences a certain amount of repression, one which necessarily passes from childhood to adolescence, adulthood, and old age, but his resulting conflicts remain conscious.

The monastic's elder needs—in order to better direct him—the complete divulgence of what is happening within the monastic, so that the light may be universal, without darkness, hiddenness, or falsehood. Novices stumble if they are deprived of guidance. The guide eases the path for them, saving them from wasting their energies in vain. The guide handles matters with wisdom, understanding, sagacity, and cognizance, saving novices from the hardship of treacherous and perilous ground as well as from ruinous deviations. The elder is the "master of skilled craftsmanship." As for the

1. I always mean Freud's school of analysis. Its technique for analysis is schematized in several writings, the broadest of which is a book by the Englishman Edward Glover, *Technique de la psychanalyse.*

monastic, he is naive, with neither firsthand knowledge nor the experience of age. He is a green recruit.

The elder[2] slowly draws the monastic away from every species of attachment, and how many there are! Each one is a kind of ardor. Ardor is not specific to those men and women who become infatuated. The gambler is a passionate lover; the zeal for reading is ardor.

The human is extremely attached to his needs. For someone who passionately loves his stomach, the existence of someone like Symeon the Stylite, who abstained from food during the Great Fast, and the existence of a great number of ascetics who ate once a day, or every two days, or every fourth or seventh day, is a miracle. And what did they eat? Stale bread, salt, beans, and water.

In the wilds of Egypt, with its arid climate, the ascetics' hours of sleep were few. In the regions of the Syrian Stylites (specifically, the provinces of Aleppo and Idlib), the arid climate does not allow the Stylite to sleep much. The holy Arsenios did not sleep at night in Egypt's wilderness, but spent the night praying in vigil from sunset to sunrise.

These ascetics—with little food, little sleep, and in constant watchfulness—are nothing but the summits of a bravery of the soul. They needed supernatural energies to master themselves and to restrict their bodies to the most minute quantities of food, drink, sleep, and rest, remaining chaste toward all passions and pleasures of the body. This psychological control would be impossible if it were not for its effect on the nervous system and its ancillaries.

Psychiatric patients suffer from acute nervous disorders, from disorders in the glandular functions, the digestive and urinary systems, and even cardiac dysfunction. As for the monastic obedient to his elder, the wisdom and discernment of the elder keep the former within reasonable boundaries and thus he exerts control over his nerves and the functions of his other members, unless there are other causes at work; not all bodies are equal. The body of Symeon the Stylite was a solid rock. But God may see in our illness a means of debasing us and teaching us humility.

2. I reiterate: the elder is not necessarily a priest. Symeon the New Theologian spoke of the capacity of monastics, one of which, in his day, was to receive the confessions of the people. The one confessing needs to be a seasoned and skilled expert, not a priest without expertise in these matters.

The monk's candor prevents secrecy. Secrecy hurls the monastic into unconscious conflicts that utilize shame and the unconscious sense of guilt, and by this, he slides toward a life in the crypts. Airing things in the light is the enemy of the hidden things that belong to unconscious repressions. The Lord Jesus taught us that what transpires in darkness is itself darkness, and that the son of the light welcomes the light, so that his works may be accomplished in God.[3]

The chief reason for keeping vigil is to avoid entering into a lengthy sleep by which watchfulness is weakened, since in sleep the reposed animal is revived. The human who diminishes his watchfulness and lessens his vigilance weakens his watch over his own being; he loses the logical cohesion between his thoughts and imaginings and then retreads the remote past.

The discovery of the mysteries of dreams by psychoanalysis revealed their links to childhood and the unconscious. A thousand states lie between the dream and watchfulness. Dreams are tied to the unconscious, and so people fancy them prophecies, vainly insisting on this . . . [4]

The ascetics keeping vigil shift the role of the unconscious to the lowest level possible, extracting the sources of energy invested in the exigencies of the body, its desires and cravings, in order to marshal them in service of the spirit. As a result, they undertake acts of transference:[5] expanding the field of conscious awareness at the expense of the unconscious so that the monastic's life may become enfolded in spiritual watchfulness and spiritual attention to the furthest extent possible, bringing the [divine] light into his life.

Symeon the New Theologian discussed this divine light, which enlightens the entire spirit and body to such a degree that, for the illumined, the signs of darkness vanish, and so one appears completely as light. He said:

3. A reference to one of the priestly prayers said during the Divine Liturgy of John Chrysostom, itself taken from Matthew's Gospel (chapter 5).—Trans.

4. For more on dreams' relation to prophecy, see Ibn Kātib Qayṣar's *Commentary on The Apocalypse of John* and Stephen J. Davis's commentary on it; John Climacus, *The Ladder of Divine Ascent*; Ibn Khaldun, *Muqaddimah*; and Freud, *The Interpretation of Dreams*.—Trans.

5. *Taḥwīl*, a translation of Freud's concept of *Übertragung*. While it is most associated with the forms of displacement between analyst and analysand (transference and countertransference), the word "transference" is also used to speak of "shifts" in the libidinal cathexis of the psyche.—Trans.

"Its rays dawn a little, then it allows itself to be seen, like a firebrand in the midst of my heart and my reins, circulating ceaselessly, enkindling the whole inside of my bowels and making them to be light."[6] So, then, the light pervades, spiritually and bodily, his entire being.

Within Symeon's theology of the divine light, one also belonging to Palamas and the whole of our tradition, we say: God is light. He illumines us by His light so we may become light. By His light, which illumined us with light, we see Him as light. He is all in all. By His light dwelling in us, we see Him as light. By God who is in us, we behold God.[7]

Palamas said:

> Whoever participates in the divine energy himself becomes light. He is united by the light, and with the light, he sees with complete lucidity all that remains concealed from those who do not have this blessing. For in this way he surpasses not only the bodily senses but also all that he is capable of knowing (by his intellect) . . . For pure hearts see God, . . . who, since He is light, dwells within them and discloses Himself to those who love Him, to His beloved ones.[8]

Maximos the Confessor, anticipating them both by centuries, said: "With the passage of time, participation in divine illumination causes him (that is, the human) to be a luminous soul in his entirety."[9]

The Holy Fathers knew the issue of transference and discussed it. Maximos the Confessor spoke about it at length, and the monastics of Mount Athos wonderfully epitomized it.

Gregory of Nyssa said:

6. Koder (ed.), *Syméon le Nouveau Théologien*, 84–85, in *SC* 174.

7. The texts of Symeon are numerous. The collection of Basile Krivochéine [Archbishop Vasiliĭ] is best. As for Palamas, there are a number of texts and citations by previous Fathers: Vasiliĭ, *Dans la lumière du Christ*, 229–255; Gregory Palamas, *Defense des saints hesychastes*, 144, 190, and, 458, 460, 504, 524, 668, 670, 710, 712, and 718; John Meyendorff, *Introduction a l'etude de Gregoire Palamas*, 243–245.

8. Homily 53 "On the Entrance of the Lady," 176–177 (Oikonomos edition). [See Palamas, *Tou en hagiois patros hemōn Grēgoriou*.—Trans.]

9. Maximos, *Four Hundred Texts on Love* 2.48; Pseudo-Makarios the Syrian is the father of this luminous theology. There are excellent citations in the translation [of Elder Sophrony's *We Shall See Him as He Is*] by the monastic Sister Maryam (Hudā Zakkā), entitled *Muʿāyana allāh kamā huwa*.

> Indeed, the virginal life seems to me to be a means and a strength, a life of greater divinity. It equips those who live in the body to be ones likened to the natures of the bodiless . . . in order that our free and emancipated psyche be raised, to the greatest extent possible, to divine joy and blessing. It will not direct its gaze toward anything of the earth, and it will not take its allotment from the pleasures awarded to ordinary life, but it will transfer[10] its capacity for love away from bodily things so as to behold noetic and immaterial beauty. We have devised the virginity of the body to equip the psyche in such a manner that, through it (that is, virginity), the psyche is made to completely forget the bodily movements (issuing) from nature, leaving no need to indulge them through the gratification of the inferior inclinations of the body.[11]

Pseudo-Makarios, stressing the necessity of completely restricting our love to God, said:

> Those who do not follow the teaching of the Lord, those who do not renounce themselves so as to love none but the Lord . . . are swallowed up and perish. Only those who have loved God alone with all their will, and have been separated from all love of the world, will be able to lead the fight to the end. Yet we find very few who have fashioned for themselves a love like this, who have turned their backs on all the pleasures of the world and its objects of desire, bearing with patience the assaults of the evil one and his trials. . . . This is absolutely necessary if one is to be plentiful in faith, patience, courage, steadfastness, long-suffering, hunger and thirst for righteousness, zeal, implacability, good judgment, and understanding. For the majority of people wish to win the kingdom without labors, wars, and sweat of the brow: this is impossible.[12]

10. *Tuḥawwil*, where the original Greek word used in the text is *metathēsei*.—Trans.

11. "On Virginity," *PG* 46, 348 B. [The parentheticals in this quote are Jabbour's insertions.—Trans.]

12. Homily 3, paragraphs 5 and 6 in *PG* 34, 472 B, as well as Homily 4, paragraph 15, *PG* 34, 484 B C. See also *PG* 34, 500 B and 509 B.

As for the monks of Mount Athos, they said in the *Tomos* (that is, the letter) of 1339,[13] which they drafted largely in defense of Palamas:

> If the body is to participate with the soul in the good things of the indescribable coming age, then it is affirmed that the body will participate with the soul according to its ability from the present time . . . for the body itself has an experience of divine things when the passible energies specific to the psyche are found not moribund, but transformed[14] and sanctified.[15]

Palamas himself took on the task of clarifying this text (relying on Gregory the Theologian and Maximos the Confessor) in the most beautiful manner: "Owing to a fear of God, the passible part of the psyche, rather than dying and remaining passive, is transferred into an energy pleasing to God, generating a salvific humility and a lamentation that garners forgiveness."[16] This magnificent text anticipated Freud by more than 550 years. The energy that is transposed into an inflection[17] is what forges the spiritual human. As for what is not transformed, it sinks into the crypts. Freud refuted religious models because he learned from them the ills of a staid religious education in leading to the development of psychological illnesses.[18]

13. For a recent translation of this letter into English, see Russell, *Gregory Palamas*.—Trans.

14. *Muḥawwala*, a translation of the Greek word, *metaskeusthentos*. The translation of this passage by Jabbour—which heavily emphasizes the transformation of the *passible energies* of the psyche, rather than of the body—evinces his insistence that the concept of transference exists in these pre-Freudian texts.—Trans.

15. *PG* 150, 1233 B.

16. Palamas, *Defense des Hesychastes*, 356. Palamas fell asleep in 1359, Gregory the Theologian in 389/390, Gregory of Nyssa in 395, Pseudo-Makarios in 430(?), and Maximos in 662. They anticipated Freud, and so they are his ancestors.

17. *Tataḥawwal fi al-taṣarruf*, translated more colloquially, "changes into action." However, what appears to be decisive for Jabbour (and likewise for Maximos) is the *deflection* of this energy of the psyche. Hence, we have rendered *taṣarruf* through the more technical but equally valid mathematical and grammatical translation, "inflection."—Trans.

18. Jabbour is, most likely, remarking on Freud's *The Future of an Illusion* (1927), *SE* 21:1–56. As the following paragraphs show, it is part of Jabbour broader argument against a repressive model of ethics (that he associates with Freud's European experience of Christianity, as well as the writings of Evagrios and Kant).—Trans.

There is a religious pedagogy that forges the types of people who erect an ethics upon repression. Likewise, there are types of human character that take their appearance from religion and their façade from ethics.

In Freud's theory, reaction formations (*formations réactionnelles*)[19] are moral reactions that repress the instincts. Meekness represses anger, for example. Therefore, in Orthodoxy, true ethics are of a *ṣūfī* nature. Within them, meekness is a new *ṣūfī* acquisition based on the transference of anger into love, gentleness, and sympathy toward the existence of the other as a Christ disclosed before me.[20]

Palamas continues his clarification:

> Indeed, the teaching passed down to us tells us that dispassion does not consist in putting to death the passible part [of the psyche], but it is transferred from evil toward the good by orienting it, in its formation, toward divine things following its complete deflection from evil and its inversion toward the good. For us, the man who attains a state of dispassion is one who no longer attains any ugly habit but comes to be rich in righteous habits. He is characterized by his virtues, just as the passional ones (that is, people having the passions) are characterized by ugly pleasures. He is one who has subdued the appetitive and incensive desires,[21] the two which

19. In German, *Reaktionsbildung*. See Freud, "Three Essays on the Theory of Sexuality" (1905), *SE* 7:123–246.—Trans.

20. *Ka-masīḥin yatajallī lī*; Jabbour is drawing on the imagery of the feast of *al-tajallī* (known in English as the Feast of the Transfiguration, see ftn. 1 in chapter 3 of this text), which in Orthodox practice commemorates the disclosure of Christ's divine light to three of his disciples on Mount Tabor. The theology of this event—which was a crucial touchstone for Gregory Palamas's defense of the hesychast claim to attain a vision of the divine light—is rooted in the notion of transformation and transference that Jabbour conceptualizes. That is, *tajallī* names the disclosure of Christ as the image of what cannot be seen, neither by the mind nor the body.—Trans.

21. Palamas is referencing the two lower aspects of the soul/psyche, the appetitive (*al-shahwāniyya*, Gr., *to thymikon*) and incensive (*al-ghaḍabiyya*, Gr. *to epithymitikon*), to which the higher noetic part (*al-dhihniyya* or *al-ʿaqliyya*) is also added. These passible aspects of the soul/psyche are thus not truly distinct; as the Greek terms suggest, the primary drive (*thymos*, drive or wrath) obtains a vector in the form of an object (*epi-thymos*, something upon which this vehemence or

compose the passible part of the psyche, (having subjugated) these energies of the soul through inner knowledge, discernment, and judgement, just as the people of the passions subject their intellects to their passions. For the ill use of the energies of the psyche is that which gives birth to the odious passions, just as it gives birth to the abuse of the inner knowledge of beings, "Did not God confound the wisdom of this world?"[22] However, if we use these energies as is fitting, we will reap the inner knowledge of God through the inner knowledge of beings, because we will have comprehended the spiritual meaning of beings and practiced the attendant virtues with the aid of the passible part of the psyche, which works in conformity with the aim that God intended for it when He created it. Through the appetitive desire, we adopt love, and through the incensive desire, we take on patience. So, it follows, this describes not one who has killed the passible part of his soul (as then he would not manifest the movement, nor the work to acquire a divine state, a relationship with God, and the inclinations of the spirit of divine things), but one who has subjugated it, in order to move, as is fitting, toward God, with endless thanks to Him.[23] Thanks to this remembrance, he will come to possess a divine inclination and be impelled toward a better acquisition as well—that is, the love of God. By this love, he is perfected in accordance with the Holy Scripture, the precious given commandments,[24] from which he

---

drive falls). The direction of this drive (toward or away from God) is what is at stake in the process of transference. But insofar as they denote a vector, none of these faculties is responsible for the disclosure of God, a fact that marks a distinction from the rational (the noetic qua reasoned) contemplation of God emphasized in Latin Christian traditions. For more on this genealogy of the soul, and the distinction between the intellect and reason, see Bradshaw, *Aristotle East and West*; Vlachos, *Orthodox Psychotherapy*; Isṭfān, *Aʿmidat al-īmān al-urthūdhuksī* [Pillars of the Orthodox faith].—Trans.

22. 1 Corinthians 1:20.

23. The remembrance [*tadhakkur*] of God or the remembrance of Jesus is an ancient object of Eastern Christian spirituality. See Diadochos of Photiki, Chapter 98 of his *On Spiritual Knowledge and Discrimination*, *SC* 5, 156 [Places (ed.), *Diadoque de Photicé*; see also the *Philokalia*, vol.1]; John Climacus, *The Ladder of Divine Ascent*, Rung 28 in *PG* 87, 1112 C.

24. 1 John 4:19 and 5:1–2.

> learns pure and perfect love for the neighbor. He puts them into practice and acquires them; moreover, it is then impossible not to acquire dispassion.[25]

Palamas follows up this discussion with a focus on the benefit of acquiring this second state of the psyche in spiritual struggle. This same state "gives birth to a great, sundering hatred for the ugly conditions of the psyche and ugly dispositions. This hatred for evil gives birth to dispassion which, in turn, gives birth to love of the singular good (that is, God)."[26]

He insists on the obligation of offering

> the passible part of the psyche to God, living and active, so that it may be a living sacrifice. For the Apostle (Paul) himself said concerning our bodies, "I ask you all, then, O brethren, through the mercies of God, to offer your bodies as a living and holy sacrifice pleasing to God. This is your intelligible [*nāṭiqa*] worship."[27]

The al-Shidyāq translation used the term "intelligible" [*nāṭiqa*] rather than "rational" [*ʿaqliyya*], and both are correct. However, the ancient Arabs translated this Greek term[28] with Aristotle; thus we say an "intelligible animal [*ḥaywān nāṭiq*]."[29] The Jesuit translation used the term "spiritual" from the original French in the *Bible de Jerusalem*. The French footnote mentions that the intended meaning is a worship different from the Jewish and pagan worship established on animal sacrifices. Concerning this, God has de-

25. Palamas, *Défense*, 360–362. [The parentheticals in this quote are Jabbour's insertions.—Trans.]

26. Palamas, *Défense*, 362.

27. Palamas, *Défense*, 362–364. [The parenthetical in this quote is Jabbour's insertion—Trans.]. The verse cited from Paul's Epistle is Romans 12:1, Revised Translation.

28. The original Greek used by Paul is "*tēn logikēn latreian*." *Nāṭiq*, as Jabbour notes, is the proper translation of the Aristotelian notion of *logos*, insofar as *nāṭiq* also refers principally to the enunciation of speech. Moreover, Jabbour is referring to the concept that the human is a "*zōon logon echon*" (a creature having *logos*) attributed to Aristotle. For a discussion of this concept, see Heidegger, *Plato's Sophist*.—Trans.

29. See Mark Swanson's discussion of the term "nāṭiq" in Muslim-Christian debates in "Ibn Sabbāʿ," 920.—Trans.

clared through the lips of Hosea: "I desired mercy, not a sacrifice. The knowledge of God is more than burnt offerings."[30] In Romans too, Paul had said: "God is the one whom I worship in my spirit."[31] It follows that the intended worship is the offering of the human himself as a sacrifice of the intellect, differing from the sacrifice of animals without reason. The Apostle Peter taught that we are all priests in offering these rational sacrifices, that is, ourselves, to God; he said: "And you all also, like living stones, build up yourselves as a spiritual house for the holy priesthood so that you may bring acceptable spiritual sacrifices to God by Jesus Christ."[32]

Palamas interprets the text as the orientation of "the members of the body and its senses to the heights—that is, that we may raise our senses, members, and our whole body to God."[33] He adds:

> The body is not joined to the spirit save by means of this passible part of the psyche . . . The Apostle Paul said: "So put to death your earthly members: sexual immorality, impurity, profligacy, malicious appetite, and avarice, which is the worship of idols."[34] This means all earthly activities, not the activities of the Holy Spirit that are perfected by means of the body, nor the divine and blessed passions, nor the energies of the soul destined by nature to give birth to these passions.[35]

Palamas quotes John Climacus: "Direct all of your desire toward God: let your anger strike the serpent alone."[36] He adds:

> Hatred of evil as well as love of God and the neighbor are two activities specific to the passible part of the psyche; by this energy specific to the soul, we love and uproot evils. What, then, do we put to death? We must put to death this energy's attachments to ugly things, directing it in its entirety toward the love of God, in accordance with

30. Hosea 6:6.
31. Romans 1:9, Jesuit translation.
32. 1 Peter 2:5, Revised translation.
33. Palamas, *Défense*, 364
34. Colossians 3:5.
35. Palamas, *Défense*, 366.
36. Rung 26 in *PG* 88, 1068 C. In March 1993, I completed a booklet on the sacrifices and vows of the church; the Holy Scripture abolishes the sacrifices of the Jews and satisfies it by the sacrifice of the cross.

> the great commandment that has been given: "Love the Lord your God with all your ability"—that is, with all your energy. What is this energy? It is without a doubt the energy of passion, because this is the loving part of the psyche. It is, then, predisposed in this way to love God, for this loving part raises—above earthly things—the other energies of the soul and turns them in the direction of God. So, it is predisposed to love God, granting purity to prayer.[37]

He continues: "We drive away from us every base desire and work, in order to become men of the desires of the Holy Spirit, like Daniel the Prophet, in that we live and move in these desires with perfect thoughts, marching ever forward with courage."[38] He cites Gregory the Theologian, clarifying:

> The divine desire, then, purifies all the faculties of the psyche, the body, and their two energies, and so secures for the mind a continuing purification, making the human capable of receiving the divinizing blessing . . . (Gregory the Theologian says that) by this purification (God) creates humans that have the appearance of God,[39] He speaks to them when they reach this stage as if to close companions . . . Because He is God, He unites with the divinized ones and causes them to know Him nearly as perfectly as He Himself knows those whom He knows[40] . . . In God they know God.[41]

He returns, at the end of the text, to the subject of the transference of energies, saying:

> The hatred of evil and love toward God as well as the neighbor are two specific activities of the passional part of the soul. By this specific faculty of the psyche we love, uproot (evils), and become united, or we remain strangers. Those who love the greatest good, then, ef-

37. Palamas, *Défense*, 368–370.

38. Palamas, *Défense*, 370.

39. *Maẓhar allāh,* a translation of the Greek term *theoeidēs* used by Gregory the Theologian.—Trans.

40. Gregory the Theologian, Homily 45, paragraph 3 in *PG* 36, 628 A.

41. Palamas, *Défense*, 716–718. [The parentheticals in the preceding quote are Jabbour's clarifications.—Trans.]

> fect a transposition of this faculty and do not put it to death . . . they cause it to work in love toward God and the neighbor.[42]

We have cited Palamas at length because he epitomizes and clarifies the Orthodox inheritance, and specifically that of Maximos the Confessor. Some of the weightiness in the translation can be attributed to the length of his expressions, and so they must be studied thoroughly. Here, this point also obliges us to cite the following passages from Maximos the Confessor, now that Palamas has made it easier for us to understand him. Maximos says:

> Baptism gave birth to us through faith in Christ; it gives us the blessing of adoption, but in a state of potentiality and not actuality. The active state is based on the deep knowledge of God and encompasses all the faculties of a human who is aware that it is God who has given birth to him. It adds to faith the deep knowledge of God and, in itself, realizes the divine likeness, the object of its knowledge. The first birth (that is, baptism) is distinguished by the fact that the human will has not been divested entirely of all bodily adaptation, so as to fuse with the (Holy) Spirit. He does not forcefully carve out free choice; rather (the one who is baptized) molds it according to his desire for theosis.
>
> So, any human who has received the (Holy) Spirit of adoption—the seed that capacitates the human's likeness to God for whoever is born of it—but has not entrusted his whole existence to God,[43] allows his psyche to be inclined toward other things and, in his will, still cleaves [to them] in full awareness, and even with the action of the water and Spirit, the inundating[44] (mystic, *ṣūfī*) water. In this condition, one can purify his conscience through ascetic practice, at

42. Palamas, *Défense*, 2:722–724. [The parenthetical in the preceding quote is Jabbour's clarification.—Trans.]

43. That is, despite baptism (see John 3:5). This original Greek passage (for which, see *PG* 90, 281) is heavily paraphrased by Jabbour. Of note is his translation of the Greek term *gnōmē* (the will to perceive and know) with *nafs* (the soul or psyche). For a full English rendering see Maximos Constas's translation in *On Difficulties in Sacred Scripture*, 109.—Trans.

44. *Khalīliyyan,* a translation of *mystikon.* See the Translator's Introduction for more on this term.—Trans.

which time the purifying (Holy) Spirit realizes in him the perfection of his attachment to the good, thanks to the knowledge that accompanies this practice.[45]

The passions were not created, in the beginning, with nature . . . for they were interposed like a graft that has been grafted to the irrational part of the psyche, because of the fall from perfection. . . . At the moment of disobedience, the likeness of dumb cattle appeared in the human, for once the dignity of the intellect is darkened, it is fitting that human nature should take on, as a just punishment, the signs of irrationality that it has so unhesitatingly brought down upon itself.[46]

The intellect acts according to its nature when the passions remain subordinate, contemplating the causes of beings and advancing toward God through them (that is, beings).[47]

The devil oppressed the human race by this law (of transgression) by causing the human to transfer the desire of his soul from the lawful to the unlawful, and to deviate toward disobeying the divine commandment. The effect of (this) disobedience was the loss of incorruption, (which is) the gift of divine blessing.[48]

The virtues adhere to the psyche by the activity of creation itself; therefore, as soon as one is completely separated from delusion, the psyche radiates in that very moment by nature's specific virtue. Whoever is not deprived of good sense is lucid; whoever is neither cowardly nor reckless is brave. . . . According to nature, the intellect is

45. Maximos, *PG* 90, 281 B. [The parentheticals in this quote and those that follow are Jabbour's clarifications.—Trans.] Cf. Diadochos of Photiki's "Cent chapitres sur la perfection spirituelle" in *SC* 5; Garrigues, *Maxime le Confesseur*, 125–127.

46. Maximos, *PG* 90, 269 A.

47. Maximos, *Four Hundred Texts on Love* 4.45.

48. Maximos, *PG* 90, 905 C.

> perspicacious. . . . Wrath is courage; appetite is prudence. So, by eliminating what is aside from nature, that which is according to nature cannot fail to appear perfectly singular, just as by removal of rust the shine and splendor of the iron (appears).[49]

So, once we put aside that which is a stranger to nature, we make nature shine.

We heard Maximos state that self-love is the mother of the passions. "Whoever eliminates it easily rejects other offenses, with the aid of God."[50] Anti-egoism is love. No ruse of the demons is ever able to succeed in "provoking passion, neither in a state of waking nor in the midst of sleep, as long as love and control over the self are both undertaken in the soul."[51] "But whoever has self-love indisputably has all of the passions."[52] What is to be done?

The Fathers distinguished between the object, the imagination, and the passion. They took evil to subsist in passion. If you saw something or imagined it without passion, you were sound; therefore, the monastic resists the passions connected with images. His entire struggle "against the demons aims at separating the passions from imaginings, otherwise it would be impossible to guard his inner freedom when he looked on things." When we have distinguished between the two sides, between passion and the imagination, nothing remains save "the simple concept."[53]

Maximos goes on to say that it is possible to extricate the two powers, the appetitive and the incensive, from their irrational state so that they may become intelligible. At that time, they become two forces like no other, fit

49. Maximos, *PG* 91, 309 C.

50. Maximos, *Four Hundred Texts on Love* 2.08. Maximos takes transgression to be an inner stranger, one that radically corrupts, just as rust corrupts iron; in the language of law, it would be falsifying the truth by interposing insubstantial phrases into an authoritative attribution [*isnād*], in order to corrupt its true meaning; it is the deformation of the truth [*al-ḥaqq*]. Therefore, the lie is very dangerous because it is a deformation of the truth, a psychological torsion against the truth, and Jesus is the perfect truth. The lie distorts truth; this distortion is a gaping wound for Jesus, the truth.

51. Maximos, *Four Hundred Texts on Love* 2.85.

52. Maximos, *Four Hundred Texts on Love* 2.08.

53. Maximos, *Four Hundred Texts on Love* 3.40–3.43. [Jabbour is referring to Maximos's description of *logismos psilos*.—Trans.]

for the good and for felicity. They then enter their authentic natural orbit—to direct the human toward what is created for him according to the thought of God, according to the causes (*logoi*)[54] existing in God since the beginning. The principles (*logoi*) are joined to the Cause (*Logos*; i.e., the Word)—that is, Jesus. This transference leads to an orientation of the intellect toward God with all the capacity of the incensive power and the flame of the appetitive power now transfigured into love:

> Let our intellect move, then, and so let it search for God, for thus it contends with the appetitive power to desire Him, and with the incensive power to keep hold of Him. Or better—if we desire more precision—let our intellect extend in its entirety toward God with the incensive power, like a rope, energetically supporting it, and let it be enflamed by the appetitive power's zeal to the utmost (here, the adjective "utmost" describes the zeal, not the appetitive power).[55]

Before these words, he enjoined us to stifle anger infatuated with corrupt pleasures. Anger may set its energies to the service of pleasures. And we, by nature, are connected with pleasures through a terrible power—that is, by way of the senses. Through this, an irrational power takes root in human nature.[56]

But there is a "reprehensible passion of love. It is that which grants a material thing to be an object for the intellect, and (there is) a circumscribed passion of love; (it is this passion) that connects (love) with God."

The human is infatuated with what he cares for. It turns "his desires and his love" either toward God or toward "the facts of the bodily passions."[57]

Hence, there is "a blessed passion (specific) to holy love that binds the intellect to objects of spiritual contemplation, one that causes it to prefer the immaterial thing over the material, and the divine and spiritual over the sensible."[58]

54. Logoi, causes, principles, is the plural of logos, Jesus is the Logos—that is, the Word of God (John 1:1). In the theology of Maximos and his counterparts, the logoi, principles, exist in God as the origin for beings. Vladimir Lossky considers them to be the divine energies. [See also Lossky, *The Vision of God*.—Trans.]

55. Maximos, *PG* 90, 896 A and 897 A; *PG* 91, 1665 D.

56. Maximos, *PG* 91, 373 D.

57. Maximos, *Four Hundred Texts on Love* 3.71.

58. Maximos, *Four Hundred Texts on Love* 3.67.

> When the human's intellect entirely turns toward God, even his desire enables a burning love of God, and even the incensive energies are reoriented, driving toward divine love. For, with time, participation in divine illumination has made his soul completely luminous, since he has collected every capacity of his lower powers within his being: he has turned them (that is, the capacity of his powers) toward a burning, unwaning, and limitless love of God, completely transferring them from the earthly to the divine.[59]

Joseph Pegon, in his introduction to Maximos's "Centuries sur la charité"[60] notes that Evagrios used the term *ekkoptein*, meaning "to be severed, to be repressed," whereas Maximos used terms for emancipation, liberation, transference—*epistrephein*—and the quiescence of the utmost dispassion—*apatheia*. There is no victory for the will after pulverizing the instincts. It is a blessing that God thought us worthy of them, and through them "our powers of passion and affection are directed in their entirety toward Him (that is, God)."[61]

We note that Maximos used the term transference, a term that we reiterated through the word "intelligible."[62] The Greek verb [that is, *legein*] is derived from the term *Logos*. Jesus is the *Logos*, that is, "the Word of God, the Father." This word has many meanings, and in Maximos's lexicon, it has specific semantics. The *logoi* are the innermost causes of things (the principle, the foundation, the efficient cause) that exist in God, and Jesus himself is the *Logos* of the Father.

By this, Maximos shifts the appetitive and incensive from the unintelligible world to the intelligible world through, he says, transference. The result of transference, through the blessing of God, is an inner unity, the incensive discharging into the channel[63] of the appetitive in order for both to be united by the intellect in its fiery turning toward God.[64] That is, the

59. Maximos, *Four Hundred Texts on Love* 2.48.

60. See *SC* 9.—Trans.

61. Maximos, *Four Hundred Texts on Love* 2.59–2.60.

62. *Maʿqūl.* The Greek word that Jabbour presumably intends is *logikos*.—Trans.

63. This language is very reminiscent of that used by Freud in *Beyond the Pleasure Principle*, specifically his speculation on the psychical systems in the fourth chapter.—Trans.

64. See our introduction to *Qānūn yasūʿ* [The Jesus canon], where Maximos cites the fissure of the three energies, the noetic, the appetitive, and the incensive,

incensive power comes into the service of love, supplying it with a brave and powerful activity.[65]

This language immediately reminds us of psychoanalysis and its theory of sublimation [*taṣʿīd*] (or, as some translations have it, *al-tusāmī*) and of other things in analysis. Transference, *déplacement*,[66] is the foundation of sublimation. Yet, the difference is considerable. Freud did not give sublimation ethical implications, as it pertains to very early sexual impulses within his broader theory of the meaning of the word "sexual." The topic is difficult and vast; I leave it for another occasion.

Freud did not speak of sublimation in adulthood. His specific concern is for the sexual thing, not for a "genital thing" specific to adults.[67]

---

because of error and the fall; hence, divine blessing in spiritual struggle restores its unity and cohesion. The inner separation disappears. For error has torn them apart, riven them into not only a thousand, but thousands of pieces.

65. The ordering laid out by Jabbour, following Maximos and with its origins in Greek philosophy (see Plato, *Republic*, Book iv, 434 D–441 C), is helpfully clarified in the Greek terminology. *Thymos*, the incensive power, is an originary heat (see Plato, *Cratylus* 419E) that sets upon things as a desirous force (*epithymitikon*). In that sense, the originary "heat" of the incensive falls upon objects and becomes the appetitive. In this, there is also a reprisal of the question of the drive and its object between Freud's original theorization and Lacan's amendment in *The Ethics of Psychoanalysis*—namely, the question of whether, in sublimation, it is the *aim* of the drive or its *object* that is shifted.—Trans.

66. Displacement, *Verschiebung*, is a concept Freud developed, along with condensation (*Verdichtung*), particularly in *The Interpretation of Dreams*:

> In the dream-work a psychical force is operating which on the one hand strips the elements which have a high psychical value of their intensity, and on the other hand, *by means of over-determination*, creates from elements of low psychical value new values, which afterwards find their way into the dream-content. If that is so, a *transference and displacement of psychical intensities* occurs in the process of dream-formation, and it is as a result of these that the difference between the text of the dream-content and that of the dream-thoughts comes about. (324)

Here the reader may also note that "overdetermination" is another way of describing the fundamental ambivalence of the psyche, as well as the operation of the cure, treated in this book.—Trans.

67. The distinction here, between the "genital" (*tanāsulī*) and the "sexual" or "gendered" (*jinsī*; the word *jins* also denotes a category or species) is reminiscent of

In contrast, transference does appear for Freud; the drive shifts to new objects (vehicles) and new aims. Sublimation itself is transference. During therapy, the patient's affects—in their negativities and positivities, past and current—are transferred onto the doctor. This transference, *transfert*, has a substantial role in the healing of the patient.[68]

The matter needs its own specific monograph to make use of the material, one that would satisfy the specialists. All of this makes it clear that Maximos is a great authority in global thought. Maximos excelled in speaking about the work of differentiating between the passion and the object of the passion until nothing remains of it except the concept. In psychoanalysis, too, there is something of this. Repression befalls the instinctual drives such that ideas, including obsessive ones, remain in an obsessive neurosis.

A division may occur within the unconscious between two components of the instinct, the sexual and the affective, and it leaves traces according to the type of illness. Don Juanism[69] enters the scene. Don Juan fancies himself a philanderer while in actuality he is deluded. The analyst corners one of this kind in a session, then the latter's tongue slips, revealing him to be afflicted by sexual impotence, covered up by a false Don Juanism (*pseudodonjuanisme*).

Maximos extolled the illumination that enlightens the whole of the human, such that all darkness is removed from him (as stated by Symeon the New Theologian and Palamas after him). For not everything in the human is luminous.[70]

Lacan's theorization of "sexuation," that is, the inscription of the subject qua sex within language. See Lacan's twentieth seminar, *On Feminine Sexuality*.—Trans.

68. Jabbour is at pains to show that the site of the cure is found in this exchange, not in repression, and to do this, he is reprising Freud's theory of psychological development through Maximos's ontology of passibility. In other words, the insistence here is that sublimation is not a form of repressing the passions but of energizing them toward God. This displacement is transference, and it means, counterintuitively, that dispassion is found in the "liberation" of passional life, not in the successful attainment of its object (which is ultimately death), but in its correct vector (inclination) and thus manner of being (in Maximos, *tropos*).—Trans.

69. A psychological condition that enters psychoanalytic diagnoses with Otto Rank's 1922 essay, "Die Don Juan-Gestalt."—Trans.

70. Maximos, *Four Hundred Texts on Love* 2.48.

Freud considered the region of the conscious to be minuscule compared to the region of the unconscious.

Maximos's words on the intelligible and unintelligible, the lower human energies, and their transference from the earthly to the divine are reminiscent, in part, of Freud's on the conscious and unconscious. The culture of Maximos is Greek, and Greek thought centers logic. Therefore, one of Freud's decisive roles in the history of the science of the psyche was to shift attention, in a serious way, from the intelligible to the unintelligible and from the conscious to the unconscious.

Maximos was a great spiritual monastic. He treated matters spiritually and ascetically without plunging into the depths of the unconscious. Even so, he was aware of what darkness and elements of barbarism there are in us,[71] which exist alongside lucidity, judiciousness, and logic, deviating toward the beastly and the asocial. In his turns of phrase, the reader is reminded of the six traits that were once described by Ernest Jones, the great British psychoanalyst: "sexual, brutal, beastly, irrational. . . ."[72] The concept of transference for Maximos is not far from another concept of Freud's. Transference is connected to the freeing of energy and libidinal investment (*investissement libidinal*).[73] The objects with which the human becomes infatuated monopolize his affective attentions: if he ardently loves his body and it has a great influence, his energies turn toward the pleasures of his body, resisting everything that troubles his pleasure.

Maximos—and after him Diadochos of Photiki—showed great interest in the pleasure principle. Freud himself was interested in this subject and published his research in 1920 with the title *Beyond the Pleasure*

71. In the gospel account of the rich man and Lazarus (Luke 16:19–31), we see the dogs pity Lazarus, whereas the heart of the rich man is hardened against him; he falls because of the hardness of his heart, being devoid of pity, less even than that of the dogs, for the pains of the other; he ends up in a hell of eternal torment. Hardness of heart is filled with aggressions. Greed for possessions and other things, as well as gluttony, are the two types of indomitable ferocity.

72. Ernest Jones, cited in Roland Dalbiez, *La méthode psychoanalytique*, 1:473. [The traits named by Jones, as cited by Jabbour in his French essay "L'interprétation psychanalytique des *ad'dad*," are "règnent le refoulé, l'actif, le bestial, l'infantile, l'alogique, le sexuel,"—repressed, dynamic, animalistic, infantile, illogical, and sexual. See Jabbour, "L'interprétation psychanalytique des *ad'dad*," 298.—Trans.]

73. For Freud, "libidinal" [*lībīdawī*] is the adjective corresponding to the noun, libido.

Principle,[74] in which he treated the issue of the pleasure principle and the reality principle. Reality gradually brings us out of the pleasure principle to make us realistic.[75] Maximos addressed the subject theologically, ascetically, ethically, and with great skill, taking asceticism and its pains to be our path toward exercising control over the possessing pleasures, as the power of this pleasure within us is transferred to a blessed life with God.[76] The pleasure principle and pain are both crucial for Maximos:[77]

> (Christ) the Lord, when He became a human without accepting that unrighteous pleasure—which has brought the just condemnation of death upon nature—would prevail in His birth according to the flesh, and since He obediently accepted death in accordance with nature in the passible part of nature—that is, He suffered—He reversed the work of death so that, in Him, death would no longer be a condemnation of nature but, in a clear manner, (a condemnation) of error. For death could not be a condemnation of nature in one (that is Jesus) who was not born of unrighteous pleasure; but it (the death of Christ) was necessary for the annihilation of the transgression of the

74. Translation by Isḥāq Ramzī; the titles in French and English are (although we prefer the English translation): *Au dela du principe de plaisir* and *Beyond the Pleasure Principle* [see *SE* 18:1–64].

75. *Wāqiʿīn*, implying more than "realists," as in English. For Jabbour, it connotes one who lives in an ethical relationship to the reality principle.—Trans.

76. Maximos, *PG* 90, 625 D–641 B.

77. Maximos writes in his Response to Thalassios:

> And because it is the nature of every evil to be destroyed together with the activities that brought it into being, [the human] discovered by experience that every pleasure is inevitably succeeded by pain, and subsequently directed his whole effort toward pleasure, while doing all he could to avoid pain, fighting for the former with all his might and contending against the latter with all his zeal. He did this believing in something that was impossible, namely, that by such a strategy he could separate the one from the other, possessing self-love solely in conjunction with pleasure, without in any way experiencing pain.

In *On Difficulties in Sacred Scripture* 1.2.14.—Trans.

> first father (that is, Adam), by whom the terror of death seized the entire human race.[78]

Narcissism[79] for Freud is reminiscent of Maximos's self-love. The narcissist ardently loves himself [lit. his soul/psyche], while the self-lover has ardor for his body. Freud treated matters from the perspective of pure psychology; Maximos was concerned primarily with the ethical side of the issue.

For Maximos, many points revolve around self-love veiling itself beneath numerous goals that have the appearance of righteousness but are devoid of its inner core.[80] This reminds us of what some call unconscious drives—*motivations inconscientes*. Not all motives for our behavior are conscious, ethical, or righteous. Unconscious drives infiltrate all human behavior. We recall that within the human is a conflict. Unconscious drives infiltrating our ethical life corrupt our paths.

Origen dealt with the issue of coming to martyrdom, and he advised against rushing into it with fervor and without composure, so that we would not provoke the other to commit the crime of our murder. If it were unnecessary and we did not shout a warning to them to save them from this crime, then it would be a self-love incentivizing us toward martyrdom.[81]

If egoism hides even in our desire for martyrdom, pushing us actively to martyrdom, what other space could be safe from its dangers?

Jesus gave us an image of the self-loving human in the parable of the rich man and Lazarus:[82] wealth, a life of luxury, and fine clothes. The rich man did not pity the wounds of Lazarus, who craved the crumbs that fell from the rich man's table. The dogs licked Lazarus's sores, calming his burning sores with their saliva as though it were a kind of balsam, but, in contrast, the rich man was hard of heart and, with stinginess, did not even favor Lazarus with crumbs. Even the popular saying for miserliness, "a dog

78. Maximos, *PG* 90, 633 C D.

79. In French, *narcissime*. I prefer Maximos's self-love to Freudian narcissism, two very important subjects pertaining to the personal growth of the child's "I." Adults are annoyed by the child's egoism, his investigation of everything, to which he rushes while crying out "me, me, me." This is a delicate phase in the child's life for the healthy development of the "I," as he is surrounded by risks.

80. *Kunh*.—Trans.

81. Origen on John 1:23, 28 [*PG* 14].

82. Luke 16:19–31.

doesn't go for a bone," is incorrect, as here the dogs licked the wounds of Lazarus.

The saying of the Lord Jesus teaches us that the miserly, luxuriating, and self-loving human is inferior to the dogs. In the Gospel and the Epistles, the worship of wealth, miserliness, avarice, and ambition is an infidel to God and an idol-worshiper.

Therefore, Maximos said of the human:

> He came to resemble cattle.[83] With this heightening of ignorance, which was wrought by the transference of the natural intellect into a state contrary to nature . . . he was joined to the enjoyment of material things that he discovered, yet as much as he stuffed himself in this enjoyment he enkindled within himself the flame of self-love. To the degree that there was this flame of self-love, he invented many means of pleasure, which are both self-love's fruit and its end.[84]

Falsehood, dissimulation, and deception are often nothing but a trace of the effects of self-love. If it were not for religion, family, and society pruning many of its branches, self-love would be the sole, absolute ruler, ruthlessly enslaving us. It is most obvious with children, for they are the sum of egoism; for them, even the growth of the "I" (*moi*) is bursting with it.

The rich man's hardness of heart, which we witness in the aforementioned parable, is the mark of a self-loving human who neither concerns himself with the life of others nor is conscious of it.

How wounded are we by the behavior of those who do not consider others in their dealings? They behave as though the other person does not exist, or they are indifferent to him, to his needs, opinions, interests, feelings, sentiments, and circumstances . . .

If it is incumbent on the true Christian to die for others just as Christ died for him, then how greatly does self-love govern people when no one will sacrifice a lira for the sake of the other? The egoist is an adult child. The one who raised him did not sufficiently separate his "I" from his self-love.

No sooner does the strength of the child come to the fore in performing actions—like extending his forearms, falling to the ground, and taking steps, alongside his mother's doggedness in fulfilling his needs—than his "I" (*son moi*) begins to emerge. Its conspicuousness reaches quite a

83. Psalm 48.—Trans.
84. *PG* 90, 253 B C.

troubling level when he interpolates his "I" into everything; he looks to obtain everything and do everything. This is a natural phenomenon.

The growth of the "I" is a predetermined necessity for us to become proper humans, whereas it is the obligation of the educator to rear the child so as to eliminate self-love, egoism, a love of hoarding, jealousy, and envy, and to orient the child toward others with respect, gentleness, sympathy, generosity, and sociability. For neither is an expanding "I" nor an advancing self-love good. The person possessing a complete character gives without apology or regret. This is the person who emulates Jesus; he dies even on behalf of enemies, not only on behalf of kin and companion.

How do people regard one another in this bitter reality? In people's eyes, is the other only something they can profit from?

Is the unconscious drives' control over us ever less than ninety percent? God knows. However, we know that the human is wrapped up in himself like cabbage leaves. In marriage, the wife is suppressed if her husband is an egoist; he sees in her a means to an end.[85] The wife of an egoist spiritually suffocates.

Education only increases this regression. Pampering and coddling increase children's self-love. Families complain about their children being obtrusive in their demands, and some of them have lost a great deal of sensitivity; they have no pity on their family but insist that their desires be fulfilled, even if it is a yoke upon the family's neck.

Many families complain about their offspring's lack of sharing in their pains and troubles. Truly, the real shame is in their ill upbringing, since we have not raised them to be free of self-love; rather, we bring them up as persons delicate in feeling and abundant in tenderness. We nourish their self-love and their own incomprehensibility to themselves. Mothers often raise the body of the human, not his spirit; is he a puppy?

A mother once told me: "I raised my son without coddling, but on a foundation of not depriving him of anything." So, I said to her: "Pray and

85. In Christianity, the man is a hypostasis [*uqnūm*, the word for a hypostasis of the Trinity] and the woman is a hypostasis. In Christ, equality between the two is assured. In various societies, the woman is stripped of her dignity, made to look like a servant to the aims of the man, as if she is an animal or like one. Some regressive people forbid women from performing their religious obligations; this barbarous vision of women is evidence of the primitiveness of its proponents. And such barbarism is not confined to the Third World.

fast. In Psalm 50, one finds: 'For in iniquities was I conceived, and amid transgressions my mother bore me.' You have responded to the needs of the part bound by iniquities, not to the needs of the spirit."

I advised the mother: "Deprivation is more beneficial than excessive giving; deprivation strengthens will and character." After a successful trial with her child, she came to support my opinion.

There are marvelous texts in *The Garden of the Monks*:[86] "Truly, no beast, if you honor them, will do you harm, save the body; truly, if you are good to the body, it will do you harm. . . . Whoever honors the body has, along with it, honored the demons, which have deluded it since ancient times . . ."[87]

This is enough without going into detail. Otherwise, it will expand into a whole volume of topics with a very particular grammar that is difficult for readers to understand.

The difficulty in this is what pertains to the heart. People surmise that the heart is the center of life. If their hearts are gripped by something, they die of fear. The heart itself is greatly affected by the states of the psyche. We have learned that the pressure rises and falls immediately with sorrow and gaiety; and some psychiatric patients are struck by paralysis, seizures, blindness, or muteness.

If I have, in many places here, been prejudiced against tenderness, it is because of the risk of an early (that is, childhood) repression of anger and ferocity, or what psychoanalysts call the aggression instinct. However, Palamas and the Fathers said that this power is latent in the soul. The concept of instinct is obscure, and its use by psychoanalysts has the air of philosophy. There is no scientific definition for instinct.[88]

There is a class of addicts in society: hashish, opium, morphine, marijuana, spirits, tobacco, qat,[89] nuts, reading, excess of food, gambling, . . . and all this is connected to the problems of early childhood. There are

86. *Bustān al-ruhbān*, sometimes known in English as *The Paradise of the Desert Fathers*, is a collection of ascetic writings from the Desert Fathers of Egypt, transmitted and collected in the Coptic Orthodox tradition.—Trans.

87. *Bustān al-ruhbān*, 192.

88. Jabbour's reservation here echoes that of Lacan, who insisted on the distinction between the concept of drive (*Trieb*) and instinct (*Instinkt*).—Trans.

89. *Catha edulis*, a flowering plant and stimulant grown mostly in Ethiopia.—Trans.

people who are enamored with reading to the point of exhaustion. Some of them lose the strength of character; others are struck by exhaustion, such that they take medication or enter clinics and hospitals. There is no state of the soul[90] that does not leave a trace on the body, and vice versa, for the body leaves traces on the soul.

The ascetic restrains the exigencies of his body gradually, drawing out of it all the energies exploited for its needs.

There is a world of difference between a human who ardently loves his stomach, devouring food with a boundless lust that comes upon him as a tiger upon its prey,[91] and the human who habituates his soul to eat with great moderation and at restricted times. The sleeping animal within the first person awakens, while the second person gradually shackles it with fetters. An excessive attachment to food turns the human away from the capacity to gather his psyche into the hands of God. An overstuffed belly is the enemy of prayer and of chastity. As for the human who trains his stomach, he will have collected his strength to make use of it in chastity and prayer so as to turn his senses, thoughts, and cares to God. He forgets the things of the body.

Those who become uneasy in speaking of fasting flee from the truth, because they have not tasted the sweetness of pure prayer and ardently love their stomachs. If there were not a sweetness to pure prayer more delectable than honey, the ascetic would not live out decades weakened in body, done so as not to be preoccupied with his stomach over God. For either the body will be the center of our concerns, or God will be our center.

I remind us once more, finally, that repression is established in childhood, and the best types of education are blends between gentleness and firmness, so as to strongly establish one's character. Still, love, affection, sympathy, and success are dependent on a thousand factors; the error of Adam and Eve bequeathed us some troubles that nothing can lift from our shoulders, except the compassion of God, by the blood of Jesus Christ, Who purifies us of our failings.

90. *Ḥāla nafsiyya*, so also a psychological state.—Trans.

91. A trustworthy witness reported to me that a certain man was gulping down half of "a stuffed sheep," in other words, that he was barbaric. He commanded his guys to completely strip a Bedouin woman to force her to have intercourse with his donkey. It was about to happen, but someone with dignity intervened. The stomach is the source of this idea.

The Hesychasts

This research obliges us to touch on the subject of the "hesychast"[92] monks of Mount Athos, but it has many ramifications. The matter requires another occasion, as it consists of a set of precise physiological, psychological, and spiritual issues.

The hesychasts pray sitting on a small chair, inclining their heads. They reiterate the Jesus Prayer with every breath. The Jesus Prayer for them (before their successors in Russia added the phrase "me, the transgressing one") is: "My Lord Jesus Christ, Son of God, have mercy on me" ("me, the transgressing one" in the Russian addition), while they slow their breathing. Consequently, they recapitulate what Diadochos of Photiki and John Climacus called the cleaving of prayer to our breath.

The two Fathers Hausherr and Jugie violently challenged this method, even if the latest entry in the Catholic Dictionary about Gregory Palamas was good on the whole, as Meyendorff saw it, and which Sergei Verhovskoy summed up in his Russian book *God and Man* in 1956,[93] a book that is being translated, I hope, into English by his students at St. Vladimir's Seminary in America.

The truth is that this challenge is profitable, just as is Father John Meyendorff's defense against it in his book *Introduction à l'étude de Grégoire Palamas.*

The proposition changes in light of contemporary research into psychosomatic medicine and psychophysiology. The unity of the human as a person encompasses spirit and body united together without division, meaning there is an exchange of influence between the spirit and the body.

Hence, control over the embodied activities of our nerves leaves traces on the psyche. Excessive spiritual or mental tension is accompanied by a tension in the nerves. Spiritual pedagogy and guidance can utilize the science of these states of tension, in order to train the monastic in the various modes of governing his being, guiding his prayer along with relative

92. *Al-hudūʾiyyūn*, meaning those who are quiet or still and so a literal translation of the Greek term *hēsychastēs* (those practicing stillness).—Trans.

93. Originally published in 1956 in Russian, *Bog i chelovek: uchenie o boge i bogopoznanii v svete pravoslaviia* (God and man: The doctrine of divine knowledge in the Orthodox world). An English translation has not yet appeared. Of particular note is Verhovskoy's commentary on the distinction between the created and uncreated Divine names.—Trans.

perfection, freed from errors. This governance can also imply a new repression and unnecessary exhaustion.

The question is multifaceted; those who are unfamiliar with this subject cannot make much use of it.

Monastic obedience plays a positive role in training the monk to order his psyche. It requires comprehensive training at the hands of an experienced specialist. Indeed, I can affirm that the monastics of Mount Athos are correct, and their method has guided the monks on Athos toward the ordering of the soul, the accurate execution of continuous prayer, an inner stillness, and the sharpening of the discriminating sense. I have personally felt their wonderful influence. Spiritual guidance brings them to an inner peace amid the energies of the psyche.

CHAPTER

8

The Question of Psychosomatic Medicine, Philosophically Considered

Palamas said: "The body is not connected to the spirit by means of this passible part of the psyche." He also said:

> Hatred of evil as well as love toward God and the neighbor are the two specific activities of the passible part of the psyche. . . . Those who love (the greatest) good, then, come to relay this faculty and have not caused it to perish. They cause it to work in a love toward God and the neighbor.[1]

Earlier, he averred the necessity of offering "the passible part of the psyche, living and active, to God so that it is a living sacrifice," and, initially, he spoke in favor of the transference, rather than the death, of the appetitive part, which remains affective.

This is only a drop in the ocean of what is in Palamas and of his predecessors who influenced his thinking. They are monists, not dualists. In *The Mystery of the Divine Economy*[2] and elsewhere, we presented their monistic thinking, which does not differentiate between the psyche and the body, the unity of which is not sundered save in death. The activity of the body is not independent from the activity of the psyche; neither is the activity of the psyche independent from the body. They are interdependent.

1. Palamas, *Défense*, 368–370. The full quote was cited in the previous chapter.—Trans.

2. Jabbour, *Sirr al-tadbīr al-ilāhī*.—Trans.

Hence, Palamas and his counterparts have opposed some contemporary philosophers, even before the advent of the latter, who separate the spirit and the body, or make the activity of the psyche appear successive to the activity of the body.

With this, the Fathers have touched upon a branch of medicine more recently known as "psychosomatic medicine," which is connected to psychoanalysis and psychiatry and which is gradually playing a part in extricating numerous patients from the care of a general medicine that is impotent in the face of many of its clients' issues.

Psychosomatic medicine discovered the effect of affective life, in its appetitive and incensive parts, on the body, and this is what we saw previously in Palamas. Love and hate are two activities specific to the passible part of the soul, connected by means of the body to the spirit. It also discovered that traumas to the psyche primarily affect sexual function. Psychoanalysis uncovered the role of ongoing sexual repression in childhood in the development of illnesses in the soul, just as the repression of the incensive power fractures the energies of the psyche, weakening one's character.

I have drawn attention to the aforementioned words of Palamas, which oblige us to offer to God "the passible part of the psyche, living and active, in order for it to be a sacrifice of love. . . ." Some pious people suppose that excessive softness, ignorance, and meekness are the stamp of piety, and hence they repress their incensive power.

Meekness is the fruit of a bitter struggle, not the daughter of folly and blindness; it is the courageous fruit of transforming the incensive power into a general openness toward the other, with munificence and generosity. Novices go astray because they stifle anger and aggression instead of transforming it. Intense internal psychological pressure intensifies their dermal and internal sensitization, weakening their firmness and their resolve. This statement is important.

The passible part must remain active and vital, so that we offer it to God as a living sacrifice, not a dead cadaver. Those who have been raised since childhood to be repressors ossify, and they lose the vitality of love. The Gospel asks us to refrain from fornication and bodily perversions and from every ugly bodily craving; it does not ask us to abrogate love. Sex is connected to love for married persons, such that if the two are split through repression, one becomes psychologically ill. Even if they are only separated to a degree, the equilibrium of the person will be affectively disturbed. Therefore, neither excessively maintaining the chastity of the body nor extremism in sobriety and primness are sound states, unless abundant care for the chastity of the spirit accompanies it. The body without the spirit is a cadaver. The Sufis are ardent lovers in an amorous rapture, but their lover is God, not the body.

Orienting our hatred toward evil, about which Palamas spoke, is to orient our anger and capacity to contend with evil. When we are victorious over our evil affects and inclinations, we arrive at a state of dispassion, which transposes us to a pure love of God.

This union between the incensive and appetitive powers is crucial, and we have presented it in *On Repentance*, quoting Maximos the Confessor and Symeon the New Theologian.[3] The cessation of dissonance between our intelligible powers and the appetitive and incensive denotes our return to a paradisal state. Our powers harmonize,[4] having one aim, union with God, together with all the powers of the psyche. The intellect prays, the heart loves, with each of its human energies, with patience, beauty, steadfastness, and a wondrous control of the body, for the body itself—according to Maximos, Palamas, and their contemporaries—participates in the divine glory and in the transfiguration, like Christ on Mount Tabor.

In psychosomatic medicine, one finds stunning things concerning the influence of affective states on the body. The vegetative (or autonomic) nervous system—*neuro-végétatif*—and the endocrine system transfer excitations of the psyche to the body. General medical practitioners are confounded when the patient cannot offer any details [hinting at the possible origins of the illness], so the mystery lies in the whole disease.[5]

3. See Jabbour, *Fī al-tawba*, 34.

4. See our introduction to *Qanūn yasū*ʿ [The Jesus canon], 8, and its footnote on page 10 (due to a printing error).

5. For example, my late friend, Doctor Iskandar Habīb, once made a mistake in a diagnosis because he ignored the trauma of the patient when he was a child. I drew his attention to the fact that the trauma had made him schizophrenic. The human is bewildering. Once I was tearing through books, but it wasn't my head that was affected but my liver via the intestines.

In psychoanalysis, it is known that the older the psychological factors in the child are, the deeper their effects. The problems of the first year are more troublesome than those of the second and are difficult to treat.

The series of bodily illnesses that psychosomatic medicine treats today is growing. It is rare for a disease to exist without psychological complications, and one must attend to both without fail.[6]

We can say with considerable moderation: if the physician diagnoses the illness correctly and comprehensively, and if the medication to treat it is available, then the cure is assured. And if healing is delayed beyond a reasonable time, then the patient is, to a great extent, responsible for what he brought to the scene in terms of psychological factors, such as fear, delusion, and the like. Psychological factors play their role in the head of the patient, and so he lives in delusion all his days, refusing to believe that he is not, in fact, ill.

The "aggression instinct"[7] has extensive foundations in the body. Both the child who forcefully seizes things with his hand from his earliest days and the child who bites his mother's breast are primed to explode in violence and aggression. We recall that it is their vehemence that moves them from what is lowest to what is highest, while obedience moves the human from what is highest to what is lowest.

The vehemence of anger which impels one to kill the other, or to injure and harm him, can be cooled if one controls the outburst of anger and is able to reduce the sharp excitation of his nerves and the paroxysms of his body; this halts the militant raging of his soul from enjoining evil, however tremendous one's malice.

6. Three years ago, this personal theory of mine caused me to prescribe a physical treatment for the healing of a sister. On January 4, 1992, I learned that Doctor Samir ʿAṭwi at the American University had diagnosed her. I treated her once with analysis only. Being in underdeveloped countries, I could not have known who discovered her illness before me or after me.

7. Freud began with the death instinct and "life instinct," then afterward ventured two more terms: "the aggression instinct" and "the sexual instinct." However, the human is far beyond being defined by the two aforementioned drives. We greatly underestimate his ability if we confine him to the concepts of instinct. Consequently, the thinking of Freud is dark, bereft of joyful expectation or a restorative sure-hope. The human is not an instinctual, animal creature, but a person in the image of God.

Conditioning the nerves and the body serves things of the spirit if done with the guidance of one experienced and learned;[8] it is useful for anyone to some degree, alleviating the pressure of the predator crouching within us and taming it to accord with a life of sociability and refinement.

We saw fit to dedicate this brief, simplified scientific analysis to specialists and the educated. In light of psychoanalysis, psycho-somatic medicine, and psychophysiology, one can analyze the matter as follows; precise scientific details fall outside our interest here, as they pertain to specialists.

Reclusive ascetics are blessed with a sense of great dread-awe in the presence of God. Falling down in worship [*sujūd*] was, still is, and will remain the gesture of humility.

All the states of our psyche leave an impression on the body. The heart, blood pressure, and heart rate play a very sensitive role in the states of our soul: joy, anger, sadness, grief, rapture, malice, and rancor . . . our breathing tightens in circumstances of distress and worry. Don't we say, "breathing a sigh of relief"?

If vehemence as well as elation, both the negative and positive, express themselves in the space of the chest, then how could our chests not be an important site for spiritual virginity?

The chest within us is a capaciousness;[9] in breathing it constricts and expands. By the mouth and the throat we express, in a bodily way, our desire for air, food, possessions, and even those whom we love, taking them into our chest and placing them in our hearts. The heart hungers for, and gazes upon, the beloved, but the whole chest, and even the mouth, throat, and hands, all have their roles in expression.

Anger and aggression utilize our nerves; hence, whoever controls his soul regulates his nerves and abstains from anger and aggression. Experienced monks have learned how to put to death, little by little, the vehemence of their anger by cooling the leaps of their bodies' nerves, since the different states of the body affect the psyche. It is always possible for the perceptive one to still the vehemence of his anger by conditioning the leaps of his

8. One experienced and learned [*'alīm*] is a great scientist [*'ālim*] of the psyche, not one who spreads claims of knowledge [*'ilm*] while not knowing. The imposters multiply, yet they are ignorant.

9. *Sa'a*, a term also meaning capacity, faculty, or power.—Trans.

nerves and cooling the movements of his body without a suppression that generates a counterreaction.

Humility is the ground from which no root of bitterness grows, and in which no arrogant thought or contention lives. Jesus said that He in His soul is "humble and meek";[10] how wonderful is this quality.

The hesychast monks realized through their bodily disposition in prayer a kind of fettering of the bodily orientations that serve transgression. They conform their bodies in such a way that the chest does not militate in anger or craving, the head is not raised in pride or infidelity, nor does the neck stiffen in an insolence and impertinence that kills submissiveness and piety.[11]

The monastic arranges his torso, head, and all they contain into a submissive, supplicatory, and humble state. Even when thinking, the thinker inclines his head and shuts his eyes until he finds the aim in his thought. In this state, one's nerves refrain from "nervousness," and thus they make the squandered energy of the nerves available. Each of us knows that states of discontentment, restlessness, and worry search within us for a means of discharge through restiveness, or through standing, sitting, and walking, with an at times excessive nervous feeling.[12]

The quiescent monk undertakes the work of controlling this normal nervous feeling into which we expend a daily portion of our energies, largely while we are unaware. With beautiful patience, the monastic makes them available for a pure prayer that wins over the plenitude of the Triple-Lights.[13]

10. Matthew 11:29.

11. In terms of timeless writings, Mount Athos has not always been consistent. It shone in the fourteenth and eighteenth centuries, and some of the fifteenth century. It brought forth mighty historical leaders, and it will know another flourishing in the twenty-first century.

12. *'Aṣabiyya*, a term central to Ibn Khaldūn's conceptualization of Bedouin group solidarity and his rendering of the dialectic of civilization in his *Muqaddimah*. This connection is clearly invoked here by Jabbour.—Trans.

13. *Fayaḍān al-anwār al-thālūthiyya*, a term that has resonances in Islam as well; *fayaḍān al-nūr*, the overflowing of light, is a concept used by Ibn Sīnā in his eleventh-century writing *al-Shifā'* (The book of healing) and al-Ghazālī's critical commentary on the latter in his *Tahāfut al-falāsifa* (The incoherence of the philosophers) and *Mishkāt al-anwār* (*The Niche of Lights*).—Trans.

Ordering the breath to cohere with prayer in silence and stillness pacifies the nervousness of our breath. When we recite the Jesus Prayer in total stillness, deliberately and measuredly, and make firm the connection between prayer and breathing, then prayer flows just as the breath and the blood do. Prayer has become itself the very blood and air of the spirit. This is a great gain.

Gradually, the body and its nerves become marionettes in the hands of the Spirit, ones that then use only a small amount of our energies. This eventuates with Jesus's presence in our chest, rather in all of our being. Thus, He expels all the furrows that malice and grudge have left in the heart such that it becomes diaphanous to the light of the Holy Trinity. The chest is the chief center through which our affects and emotions express themselves. Our praying intellect readily penetrates the affects, and our beautiful patience engraves prayer within us. Therefore, a favorable bodily posture, accompanied by endurance, patience, and purified prayer, leads to our transformation into the luminous temple of the Holy Spirit.

Gregory Palamas appointed himself a defender of the hesychast monks, who were in his day a troop of holy ones. One of them, Kallistos, would shine at times like Jesus on Mount Tabor. Truly, they tested the path and succeeded. Many experienced it after them. As long as the holy ones shine, the Fathers Jugie and Hausherr have overstepped.

This experience of the holy ones in the Holy Spirit is only appreciated in its true worth by one who has known its active effect. These two priests [that is, Jugie and Hausherr] grant rights to intellectual analysis that it does not possess. Where the Holy Spirit begins, the intellect comes to a standstill, prostrating flat, seized in stupor. Every renewal in the Orthodox world since Palamas has flowed from Mount Athos. How can we impute infidelity [*nukaffir*] to the new Tabor, which enveloped Horeb, and every holy place resembling the Horeb of Moses? Amiably, gently, moderately, and worshipfully!

The adversaries of the hesychasts rebuked them for fixing their gaze on the navel. In modern psychological sciences, it is now understood that this posture aids in dispelling distractions and in concentration. The hesychasts who fold their chests[14] are, to some extent, embracing the name of the

14. That is, taking the posture of hesychast prayer in which the chest is folded with the head downturned, and the gaze is centered on the navel (*omphaloskepsis*).—Trans.

Lord Jesus, enacting through bodily movements what the mother does when she embraces her child in affection and intimacy.[15]

Moreover, analysts know that pressure on both the incensive and appetitive powers leads to their searching out drainage canals and to their transference into unimportant things.

The transference of self-love into divine desire is no picnic. Indeed, it is a war with the serpent, who is undefeatable except through the ability of the Holy Spirit alone. Our being purified of self-love, in the view of Maximos the Confessor and others, is the work of the Holy Spirit and of a bellicose will that never retreats. Self-love defends itself by innumerable means. The devil nourishes it with his cunning; it infiltrates everything.

The spiritual war occurs in the scene of our daily existence; so, our nerves suffer what they suffer. Skill is needed to avoid nervous and psychological tensions going beyond spiritually reasonable bounds: excesses, radicalism, obscene extremism—these are demonic means of exhausting our energies, that we then fail and despair.

The spiritual militant hunts these two energies, the appetitive and the incensive, even into the drainage canals and margins, in order to be cleansed in his entirety. It is not the one who refrains from actual fornication and anger who is cleansed, but the one who has uprooted every impurity from the whole body and spirit, perfecting holiness in the fear of God: "Let us cleanse ourselves of every impurity of body and spirit, perfecting holiness in the fear of God"[16]—namely, all of our senses and sensibilities.[17]

In psychoanalysis, the body is entirely comprised of affective zones, and pleasure may shift to any one zone. Whoever finds pleasure in people's

15. The Russian ascetic Theophan the Recluse best understood the tradition of Mount Athos, rebutting the words of critics and freeing the people to pray the Jesus Prayer in the manner that suited them. What was crucial was to gather the scattered energies of the soul through watchfulness and discernment so that one might pray with the utmost fervor. Prayer is neither mutterings from the tip of the tongue nor "cold" intellectual-philosophical contemplation. It is a heart simmering and boiling with divine fervor in spiritual consciousness and watchfulness.

16. 2 Corinthians 7:1.

17. Maximos and John Climacus touch on this topic, anticipating Freud by an age. Freud was born on May 6, 1856, and died September 23, 1939. The difference between him and both Maximos and Climacus is around thirteen centuries.

acclaim takes an obscene satisfaction in his spirit and body. Did the Lord not call the hypocrite Pharisees ardent lovers of praise and vainglory: "Indeed one exalted before people is filth before God."[18]

Whoever takes delight in palaces, possessions, clothes, miters, and all the arrogant and empty appearances of might falls under this judgment. Whoever utters obscene speech or listens to it, or views it in wild films and the like, fornicates by their tongue, their ears, their eyes, and their touch . . . [19]

18. Luke 16:15.—Trans.

19. The question of evil and good occupied the mind of the famed Russian writer Dostoyevsky, as noted in Evdokimov, *Dostoïevsky et le problème du mal* and Zander, *Dostoïevsky*.

CHAPTER

9

REITERATION

We do not obliterate the body, its passions, wishes, and appetites. This would be repression (*refoulement*) if it occurs during childhood, and suppression (*répression*) if it occurs in adulthood.[1] In the first case, it hinders a full and sound development. In the second case, if reasonable limits are overstepped, it will produce counterreactions and become extremism, specifically, a blind extremism. But even suppression has some of its foundation in childhood.

The monastic's elders are vigilant in ensuring that the process of transference sits entirely between firmness and resolve on the one hand, and beautiful patience and moderation on the other. Indeed, it is crucial that life must be immersed in watchfulness, lucidity, and bravery, with a steadfastness that knows neither retreat nor hopelessness.

The monastic, in his absolute candor, fills the dark recesses of his life with a radiant light, and by this, he aids the elder in his leadership.[2]

1. This refers to the psychoanalytic distinction between repression in childhood (both primary and secondary repression—that is, *Unterdrückung* and *Verdrängung*, respectively) and to the conscious work of suppression. Whereas suppression is the conscious management of the undesirable within the unconscious, repression acts to form the subject without entering the field of consciousness, though it can be expressed in the form of the symptom. This primary form of resistance was first formulated by Freud in *Studies on Hysteria* (1892–1895), *SE* 2, and in "Repression" (1915), *SE* 14:141–158.—Trans.

2. We Orthodox do not differentiate between monastic spirituality and lay [*ʿalamānī*] spirituality; indeed, they are one. In Russia, the Optina Monastery

However, the elder does not absolve the monk of his sense of guilt. It remains alive and intensifies over time. It is an emergency alarm, sounding whenever a thought from those of the passions awakens in the mind. When it arises, one feels guilt and is called to fierce warfare.

The psychoanalyst concludes his patient's therapy once he has brought him to a certain state, whereby he becomes capable of reconciling with life and society; rarely does the analyst intervene in his level of character. The analyst is concerned with the elimination of conflicts and the restoration of harmony between the parts of the human's "I."

The elder is concerned with the monastic until he takes hold of the main passions and redirects their energies in service of the spirit. The ardent love of the body, wealth, the world, and its hollow pomp is transposed into an ardor for God.

The verve of aggression and the vehemence of anger are transformed into the durability of the person amid the war of passions and thoughts. The ascetic conscience is sharper than a fine sword. The true monastic is resolute, like the valiant martyrs. There are men who are unmatched in physical strength, but their upbringing has made them incapable of even cuffing their children. In contrast, there are men who foolishly clash and fight, but the Gospel changes them, and so they become incapable of anger. Religious education can transform the fiercest human into a creature of meek and pliable temperament.

Education has a pivotal role in tempering the ferocity of children. There may be genetic factors[3] that have made a child's constitution very strong,

---

was a leader in theological, philosophical, and pedagogical movements, with notable figures such as Dostoyevsky, Tolstoy, Gogol, and the holy elder Ambrosios. In Greece and Romania, people of the world also seek the counsel of monks, adopting them as confessors and spiritual fathers, as, in the view of Symeon the New Theologian, they are the most fit for the task.

3. Research in genetic science is ongoing, if relatively recent. From Adam and Eve until today, thousands of ancestors are behind each human. In our country, which has known every manner of conqueror, you may see faces of an exact resemblance to those of ancient conquerors. The field of genetics is very complex. I once asked an environmental specialist about the progress of environmental medicine in uncovering the influence of factors in the soil and the atmosphere on the human body, the nerves, skin, and senses. He was surprised by the question, so I then said before the physicians: We are still scientifically deficient and will not plumb the depths of the human for thousands of years; and so, let us confess,

and it is this strength of constitution that lies behind his being entirely fated for bullish verve and ferocity and the like. A sound upbringing takes hold early in the process of transforming this child into a human of refined character. This process of transference requires the family's flexibility, long-suffering, gentleness, and patience for success. I know two people possessing a courageous constitution, whose verve was cooled by education, and so they shy away from causing injury. Education restricted them.

Whither does the monastic arrive at the hands of his elder? He ends up implementing the words of Paul: for the monastic, food and its lack become equivalent, as do drink and its lack, possession and its lack, marriage and its lack. These are no longer positive and negative elements, but, more precisely, their being and nonbeing are equivalent, because the monastic lives as one who possesses and is not a possessor, as one who eats and is not an eater. Add to this the holiness of spirit and body, as well as a faith, love, and sure hope that are no longer deficient. That is, the monastic truly departs from his own being to become in God. His body becomes a husk that he bears for a time until he sheds it, just as the snake sheds its slough. His body becomes his companion up to the time of death; he humors it, but he does not do its will.

Psychoanalysis raises the matter of the objects of transference. Human instinctual drives [*gharā'iz*] are flexible, shifting their aims and vehicles. Love and hatred can shift to something other than the family. The ferocity of the child, for example, shifts into acts of breaking and smashing, and thus he shatters the doll in his hands. This ferocity may also shift toward animals or toward the self. The rebuke of a pathological, violent conscience (not a spiritual one) destroys his friendships and can lead him to suicide.

Love may shift from the family to other people; it may transpose onto animals, inorganic things, wealth, and possessions. Attachment is attachment, and attachment is ardor. The "fashion" of grooming dogs or cats in Europe or America is simply a process of transference, one that is dangerous in the long term because it is not a sound love. It conceals an unconscious hatred for humans and a transference toward animals. In this process, there is both love and aggression.

---

with Socrates, our ignorance. I raised this issue in *Sirr al-tadbīr al-ilāhī* [*The Mystery of the Divine Economy*] (1979), and perhaps even anticipated it in a 1973 research paper, but it was lost. No one comprehended the proposition because our thinking is stagnant and staid.

Sound love is one that inclines toward people as persons, such that one then shifts to a love of the perfect Persons—that is, the Holy Trinity. Love without intimate dialogue[4] is a contorted and distorted love. By what means do I intimately confide in the dog or the tomcat? Our affects are not reciprocal, and our existential communion[5] is missing. Even if the dog is loyal and the human treacherous, the human is still a person, capable of returning to God. As Father Lazarus Moore said: Every transgressor is a tomb for Christ, and we must prostrate ourselves before it, just as make prostrations before the tomb of Christ, until Christ rises therein.

We must be kind to animals, but not at the expense of being kind to people. I once said to a Frenchman: "Why are you all concerned with cats and dogs but not concerned with orphans and foundlings?" He replied: "Social assistance is responsible for them." What emotional coldness! The human is abandoned to the state, while the state is a thing, not a person. Dogs, which are also things, are creatures in the trust [*amāna*] of the human race. This is a counterfeit Christianity, the vapid and superficial imitate externally.

In psychotherapy, the patient's affects of love and aggression are transposed onto the psychoanalyst, aiding the patient in releasing them from the world of the repressed, absolving and dissolving them in safe forms.

The monastic inheritance hit upon this therapy centuries ago. The monks anticipated the psychoanalysts in discovering this method. Psychoanalysts work to restore the past, filling in its gaps so that the patient can reconstitute his character according to his age, rather than remaining impeded by the obstructions of childhood. The monastic elders do not encourage the monk to live out his ethically impure past, as that pollutes his present.

The psychologically ill patient is not his own age. The restoration of the elements of his life history to the scene of his consciousness leads to the vanishing of childhood symptoms and to the liberation of the sources of

4. *Munājāt*, a word that can mean "litany" or one's intimate supplication to God, is commonly used to refer to a genre of writing or discourse that is often associated with Sufism (for example, the *Munājāt Namah* of Abdullah Ansari, or the *Munājāt* of Suhrawardi). As Ibn al-ʿArabī writes in *Fuṣūṣ al-ḥikam*, "prayer is a *munājāt*, as it is a remembrance [*dhikr*]" (223).—Trans.

5. *Al-mushārika al-wijdāniyya*. The latter term, *wijdān*, implies not only experience and affect but that from which these two are derived—that is, that which stands out in existence (*wujūd*).—Trans.

squandered power, which come to serve the structure of his character, and to perfect its parts and elements in harmony, cooperation, and a sound inner unity.

The monastic strives to purify his mind from the thoughts of the passions and thus he immobilizes the movements of the passions so that the thought of Christ may dwell in his mind. He expels thought by thought.[6] He discards the thoughts of the passions to replace them with the remembrance of the name of the Lord Jesus and what it bequeaths within the heart—profound worship, awesome reverence, and rapturous ardor for God to the heights possible by His blessing.[7]

The spiritual guide does not listen to his disciple as a man confessing his guilt, but as a human telling a story of lamentation and weeping while fully maintaining his conscious oversight; this practice requires oversight,[8] whereas the [psychologically ill] patient needs to be freed from it.

The sense of guilt [*dhanb*] is overwhelming for some patients because the applied (psychoanalytic) process is not centered on confessing faults

6. From the observations of the monastic Fathers: a demonic thought expels another demonic thought. The miser, for example, may fear losing people, and so he is generous. A man generously bestows love by appearing as virtuous, and so he expels miserliness. A woman makes a habit of being overly concerned with her reputation and dignity, and thus she intensifies her bodily abstinence even though she has not become a spiritual stalwart; there are many examples of this.

7. The Jesus Prayer itself was composed piece by piece, and then it became the most important spiritual activity for the monks of Mount Athos in the fourteenth century; do we discount it because it is modern? The church is not a rigid institution, but a living, creative body. We cannot say to the mystical and theological geniuses: I require immobility as well as a strict and rigid rule. The divine blessing dwelling within them is a luminous, innovative plenitude [*fayḍ*].

8. *Riqāba*, a term meaning censorship or conscience, works across the two practices of spiritual guidance and psychoanalytic therapy that Jabbour describes. The term shares the same root as *murāqaba*, a central term in Sufism, which is an analogue of *yaqaẓa* (in Greek, *nēpsis*), denoting a constant watchfulness that facilitates a life in God. In psychoanalysis, *riqāba* denotes what Freud theorized as a force of self-supervision in dream-thoughts, which he later theorized as the *Über-Ich* or superego. Jabbour, as in this and previous chapters, is keen to distinguish between the psychoanalytic patient and the monastic novice on this point—that is, in the need to either lessen or heighten the force of this censorship, which is related to both conscience and the sense of guilt.—Trans.

[*dhunūb*]. These patients become obsessed with rebuking themselves, bemoaning themselves, and unconsciously pleading for punishment. They find in the analyst an image of the punishing father or mother and anticipate punishment from them. Some of them relish narrating a never-ending list of sins, and so this punishing, unconscious brutality is evident.

The patient remains a patient, and the monastic remains a man of sound energies, striving for greater acts of bravery through the transference of his being from one of appetites and cravings to an earthly angel who has been liberated from the noose of the body. Watchfulness is a vital object for the monastics, while, for the patient, the reduction of oversight is a precondition for bettering the course of his nature.

The analyst remains a physician of the soul, while the elder is a physician of the spirit. The spiritual procedure is immeasurably more advanced than the psychological one, and both processes are beset by dangers. Psychotherapy is not successful for all patients, and not all monastics reach the level of successful spiritual practice. The vicissitudes are numerous, and God knows the fate of people, their states, and the alternations of their disposition.

Confession for churches in the world

Without a doubt, confession as it is practiced in cities and villages is an object of considerable ridicule; Father Alexander Schmemann mocked it at the end of his book, *Great Lent*, translated by Father Ibrahīm Sarrūj.[9]

We have no men fully trained in confession at the monasteries of Mount Athos. Conditions will not be spiritually suitable until priests are trained on Mount Athos and they meet with the approval of the monastics, something superior to a million doctorates in theology. Degrees in theology without practice carry no weight on Mount Athos. The priesthood will remain a profession for us, like any other, until the fragrance of Athos comes to us. We are indebted to the Fathers of our age like Isḥāq ʿAtāllāh, Ephraim Kyriakos, and Yūḥanna Yazigi,[10] for opening the path of Athos for our

9. See *al-Ṣawm al-kabīr*, the Arabic translation of Schmemann's *Great Lent.*—Trans.

10. Isḥāq ʿAtāllāh (d. 1998) was a Lebanese Athonite and a disciple of Elder Paisios (1924–1994) who wrote an Arabic version of his life. Among other works of translation (including editions of the Septuagint and Psalter), Isḥāq translated

revivalist youth in the See of Antioch. Physicians and lawyers are trained before practicing their work in earnest and independently; likewise, those holding theology degrees need longer training, as the profession of the priesthood is more difficult than those of medicine or law. A psychiatric patient spends months and years frequently returning to the psychoanalyst, who likewise submits himself to therapy sessions periodically so that he remains in good order.

Spiritual care is at least as important as this; rather, it is even more so. One may not succeed at the monasteries of Mouth Athos for four or ten years. Likewise, one may not be fit to practice guidance for ten or fifteen years, and only if he has the qualities that enable him to be a guide. The priesthood is not a robe and a headdress, in which one roams from house to house making one's living; rather, it is the profession of the guardian angel. The spiritual father, too, is a guardian angel.

Those selected to be priests must at least be subjected to psychological examination by the heads of the monasteries. And if one of them appears to need more than this, he is obliged to present himself to a truly faithful psychiatric physician. Theological colleges must transform into centers of exacting spiritual training; otherwise, religious leaders will continue to be actors and jesters.

The West began to show an interest in this subject, but an interest in research remains the near-complete master of the scene. Surveying their writings spiritually, one is shocked to find that religion has yielded studies and research, but not a spiritual life in the depth of union with the Holy Trinity.

Once Patriarch Elias IV said to the professors of theology in Athens (when he was Metropolitan of Aleppo) something to the effect of:

"You all study theology, whereas we wring it out by divine blessing."

So, then: there is no righteousness or reform save by the monastic communities advancing intellectually and spiritually in the manner of the

---

the work of Isaac the Syrian from the Greek text (*Nusukīyyāt*). Ephraim Kyriakos is the current Metropolitan of Tripoli and Koura and a prolific writer. He was taken to Athos by Isḥāq during Lebanon's war and became a monastic at St. Paul's Monastery. He returned to Lebanon and began the monastic community of the Holy Archangel Michael in Biqʿātā. Yūḥanna Yazigi is now the Patriarch of the Antiochian Orthodox Church (John X). Before this, he also worked to reestablish monastic life at the Patriarchal Monastery of St. George (Dayr Mār Jirjis) al-Ḥumayrāʾ, Syria.—Trans.

Optina monastery of old Russia. The monastic is a brave spiritual hero, while the priest is an apostle. One cannot be permitted to follow the path of these two vocations unless we are persuaded by truth, and not by delusion, to make him a companion of the most honorable professions, the most holy, the most vital, and the most dangerous. Otherwise, we will cause the total ruination of his flock, as if we were to hand a plane over to someone who does not know how to fly.

Evagrios considered the one who prays to be a theologian and the theologian to be the one who prays. So then, what can studies without prayer be except so much noise?

Confession and repentance

Repentance is the foundation of which confession is a part. Father Schmemann's criticism was apt for exposing the manner of a confession isolated from repentance. As we have seen, candor is the means of healing for psychiatric patients and for the progression of monastics; therefore, candor is useful for all people. Every person breathes easier when he relates his troubles to others and "vents." Freud's first patient called the method of his therapy "the talking cure."[11] No one is ignorant of the benefits of speaking to refresh the soul and to reconsider things in order to put them in their true place and redress much of what has passed.

Confession and communion

The Lord Jesus delivered to the church, through the apostles, the authority to loose and bind transgressions.[12]

Communion is a blessed occasion for taking account of oneself, and to receive Jesus's body and blood in a good spiritual state.

Some people startle you, writing what they write. Father Irénée Hausherr racked his brain going against the hesychast monks of Mount Athos, publishing a monograph that insisted that the Jesus Prayer was not ancient

11. A reference to Anna O., a patient who suffered from hysterical paralysis and was treated by Josef Breuer. Along with Freud, Breuer would go on to write *Studies on Hysteria*, about the therapeutic treatment of Anna O. and other so-called hysterics.—Trans.

12. John 20:22–23.

and scoffing at the book by Father Lev Gillet. However, Guillaumont discovered the Jesus Prayer on the wall of an Egyptian monastery, and thus Hausherr's argument collapsed, as did the attack of his colleague, Father Jugie, on Palamas.

Some resemble Hausherr and try, in the name of scholarship, to demolish a crucial spiritual institution. We do not accept this, as scholarly research can be demolished with the discovery of a single scrap of paper.

On the other hand, undertaking something beautiful in the church is of very great benefit. Confession is a very venerable monastic institution. If it extends to the lives of the people in the world, we increase their spiritual depth and piety.

The job of priests is to preach and provide guidance. If they lead the flock spiritually to commune in the Eucharist[13] with remorse, repentance, and the beating of one's breast, they would, by this, render a righteous service to God. Even if they fall below this standard today, the disgrace is borne by the whole of the people, who sees its church as an orphaned foundling, and which care nothing for her fate but rather criticize her and dissect her without any willingness to sacrifice so as to raise a new generation of apostolic workers. Everyone holds others responsible in order to avoid bearing their share. We are Orthodox in talk only, when it is to our advantage.

The prayer of absolution

Without a doubt, the true penitent obtains release from his transgressions through the priest's prayer, while the unrepentant does not. The priest grants absolution[14] through the authority granted to him; that is, by the action of the Holy Spirit who forgives the transgression of the penitent. He who does not repent does not receive forgiveness, and the prayer of absolution does not benefit him.

"Truly, truly, I say to you: you will surely weep and lament while the world rejoices, and you will grieve, but your grief will turn into joy . . . and you are now grieved, yet I will see you again, and you will rejoice in your hearts, and no one will take your joy from you."[15]

13. *Al-qurbān*, the Oblation.—Trans.

14. *Ḥilla*, but from the same root as *taḥlīl*, which can also be used to connote the release from transgressions.—Trans.

15. John 16:20–22.

The subject of joy is repeatedly discussed in the New Testament and by the Fathers.[16] Spiritual joy is tied to repentance. The penitent buries his transgressions through his tears and lamentation, and he washes them through the blood of Christ. Repentance is the renewal of baptism and the continuation of its blessing. By sincere repentance, we are washed clean by the blood of Christ of the transgressions that we have committed after baptism. By repentance, baptism continues to yield all of its fruit within us. Through it, the Holy Spirit remains blazing within us, burning up—thanks to the blood of Christ shed for us—every transgression and illumining our hearts by His holy fire.

Repentance is also resurrection. We bury our transgressions in the sure hope of the resurrection with Christ. Therefore, repentance is the mystery of Golgotha and the tomb.[17] In it, we crucify ourselves with Christ, entomb ourselves with Christ, and resurrect with Christ. In repentance, we are transferred with the entombed Christ from death to the resurrection, and seated at the right hand of God.

The true Christian is the true penitent. Without repentance, faith, baptism, confession, and the Eucharist are of no use; rather, the Christian receives judgment, because he has neglected the mercy through which God is merciful to us. The life of a Christian is with Christ and in Christ. It is a continuous and constant renewal in the fire of repentance that purifies us, just as metals are purified in the crucible of fire.

If we willed, we could be like Paul, who said in his letter to the Galatians: "For I by the law have died to the law in order to live for God. With Christ I was crucified, so it is not I who live, but rather Christ lives in me, and if I am now in the body, then my life is in faith in the Son of God who loved me and gave Himself for me."[18]

16. The conversation of the holy Seraphim of Sarov with his disciple Motovilov is clear.

17. After this book, I produced *Yā yasūʿāhu!* [My Jesus!] It is a book of interpretation [*tafsīr*] of the period from Great and Holy Friday to Pentecost, but in the form of prayer and contemplation. In it is an exposition of the relationship of the Transfiguration [*al-tajallī*] to Golgotha and the tomb, etc., for Jesus on the cross defeats transgression, death, and Hell, and opens paradise to us. The cross is the sign of victory, not of humiliation and degradation; it is glory and light. [This book was published by Manshūrāt al-Nūr in Beirut.—Trans.]

18. Galatians 2:19–20.

If we will this, we must repent in the manner figured above, seeing that we, alongside John the Evangelist, diminish so that Christ increases within us: "It is necessary for Him to increase and for me to diminish."[19] This is the ultimate aim of the Christian life, that I am emptied of my own being to be filled with Jesus, to make perfect what is diminished in my body with the sufferings of Christ. "Indeed, I rejoice now in my sufferings, for by my sufferings for your sake I make complete what was lacking of Christ's hardships in my body, for the sake of His body, which is the church."[20]

I must drink up His brimming cup to the full;[21] otherwise, it is counterfeiting, playacting, and buffoonery, which we touched on in the book *The Counterfeits*;[22] it concluded with the journey of Tūmā to Mount Athos in order to be trained, after baptism, according to life in God, under obedience to the masters of spiritual practice. Orthodox spirituality is monastic, and our spiritual life will not be successful unless we enliven the inheritance of Mount Athos among us. The rest is foolish buffoonery and trading in religion at the bazaar, haggling over Christ who is ever-crucified by our iniquitous hands.

Objection

Some deludedly think that they are devout, continuing in their prayers and fasting, carrying out some pious motions. Some wonder why their sudden enthusiasm for the faith did not bring them to the transfiguration with Christ on Mount Tabor. Some object to the truth so that they may return, after confessing and communing, to transgressions and yesterday's filth.

The holy Dimitri of Rostov gave the following answer to this: God chose to save the thief crucified with Him after only a few minutes, and He Himself chooses to save others by means of continual struggles, spanning over years and, at times, decades. One of the righteous Fathers, John Kolobos,[23] led a young woman, Paisia, to repentance after she had fallen from her piety into licentiousness. It didn't take long; she quickly repented and soon

19. John 3:30.
20. Colossians 1:24.
21. A reference to Psalm 74 and Matthew 20:22.—Trans.
22. See Jabbour, *al-Muzayyafūn*.—Trans.
23. For more on this desert father, see Stephen J. Davis's translation of, and introduction to, *The Arabic Life of St. John the Little*.—Trans.

passed away. Her repentance was fervent and fiery, and so it bore fruit more quickly than the repentance of those who spend a lifetime in repentance without her fervor. Kolobos saw "a luminous path stretching from heaven to her, and he saw the angels of God leading away her soul. . . . He knew that a single hour of her repentance was more pleasing to God than the drawn-out repentance that many others (carry out), who do not show the zeal of her exemplary repentance."[24]

There are fantastic figurations of the human condition in the sayings of John Kolobos. The soul is an adulterer in the city. Christ married her,[25] robbing her many ardent lovers of her. The assault of the lovers and the demons continues after the marriage, even if the soul takes refuge near the Lord at all times.[26] This is the state of the psyche that wants to change and repent.

There is no perfect holiness on the earth, only a striving toward perfection. Throughout the long march, we fall many times and return to God, promising to change. We violate that promise and keep breaking promise after promise, until we breathe our last breath, devoted to Him according to the measure of our struggle and the effusive rains of His mercy and blessing.

The monastic may spend three or four years or perhaps more at the monastery, or in reclusion at his hermitage, relapsing and returning to God. We repent and fall because we are humans, but God has mercy on us.

No one should imagine that the spiritual struggle is a walk in the park, an opportunity to take the air in a lush meadow. Truly, it is an unyielding war with the evil powers that continues until one's last breath. In every war, there are losses and victories. We often fall and stumble, but God will raise us up hereafter.

Those who are for Christ, and those who break themselves for Christ, forfeit themselves, piece by piece, to return to the saving dominion of Jesus. They lose their will in order to loose,[27] as ascending rungs on a ladder,

24. *Apothegmata Patrum*, Saying 40 in *PG* 95, 217; Regnault, *Les Sentences des Pères du désert* and Guy, *Recherches sur la tradition grecque des Apophthegmata Patrum*, 134.

25. As in the Greek equivalent *psychē*, the grammatical gender of the term *nafs* is feminine.—Trans.

26. *Apothegmata Patrum*, Saying 16 in *PG* 95; Regnault, *Les Sentences des Pères du désert*, 127. In *al-Tajalliyāt fī dustūr al-īmān* [*Disclosures in the Constitution of Faith*], we presented a similar view as Origen and Ambrose on the church and the self.

27. *Taḥull*, the same word used for the loosening of transgressions in confessor and related to the word for analysis (*taḥlīl*) (cf. ftn 14 in this chapter).—Trans.

the will of Christ within them. Everything within them transfers to Christ; even their bodies are transferred. Their members that were instruments of iniquity become instruments of righteousness and holiness. The Holy Spirit shines in the body; their eyes and tongues are changed, until Christ comes to be in them, all in all.

The Fathers speak of the transference of the senses. Everything is inspirited—that is, becomes spiritual. An identity card[28] does not make a person Orthodox; a fruitless baptism does not produce the fruit of repentance, which appears through sincere works of righteousness. The prophet Ezekiel said:

> The Lord Master says: I am not pleased with the death of the hypocrite, but that the hypocrite repent from his way and live. So repent. Repent of your evil ways. . . . Indeed, the righteousness of the righteous does not save him on the day of his disobedience, and the hypocrisy of the hypocrite does not bring ruin to him on the day he repents of his hypocrisy, nor is the righteous able to live in righteousness on the day of his transgression. If I said to the righteous, you truly live, and he takes confidence in his righteousness and does iniquity, truly all of his righteousness is forgotten, and he dies by the iniquity that he wrought. And if I say to the hypocrite, Indeed you die utterly, and then he repents of his transgression, and performs judgment and justice—if that hypocrite returned the offering, discharged what he misappropriated, and proceeded through the paths of life without doing iniquity—then he truly lives and does not die. . . . If the righteous forsakes his righteousness and does iniquity, then he dies by it, and if the hypocrite repents of his hypocrisy and performs judgment and justice, then he lives by it.[29]

Confession at the Monastery of the Holy Spirit

I confessed to the head of the Monastery of the Holy Spirit in Greece. The monastery head was sitting in his office, and I sat beside him. The confes-

28. *Huwiyya*, an identity card used in Syria and Lebanon that contains one's religious identity (in Lebanon, the practice of denoting one's religion on the identity card was ended in 2009).—Trans.

29. Ezekiel 33:11–19, Yāzigī translation.

sion was a conversation; this form is more beneficial for one in need of spiritual guidance and relief from what weighs on his heart. The spiritual battle presses upon the chest of the faithful; he needs a spiritual guide to save him from its entanglements. This is impossible for us until we have a generation of brilliant young men trained on Mount Athos. The Optina Monastery in Russia played a role that the cohort of Russian clergy did not play; it was the lighthouse of Russia and a magnet attracting men of thought. Russian monastic literature reached far and wide, becoming the inheritance of the immortal Russian writer Dostoyevsky. Did this magnificent inheritance push the great French Catholic writer François Mauriac, a man of deep faith, to say: "If from one place light will shine, this place must be Russia."[30]

Who is the true penitent who obtains forgiveness and the loosing of his transgressions? Let us hear our great teacher Gregory the Theologian:

> However, you tell me that Novatus did not accept the repentance of those who rejected their faith in the midst of oppression. What does that mean? If they did not appear at all remorseful, then he did well—I, too, do not remit the transgressions of those who have not lamented their iniquities, or those who have not been sufficiently regretful over them, or likewise those who have not sufficiently put into practice a change of life in compensation for their crimes. For those whom I accept in repentance, I appoint for them a suitable place—but, if they have bathed in tears, then see, this is behavior [i.e., Novatus's] that I cannot follow. . . . Novatus set no punishment for greed, this other type of idol-worship, yet he condemned sexual immorality forcefully, to such an extent that one may suppose that this man has entirely escaped the tyranny of the body and flesh.[31]

30. Quoted by Dmitrii Dudko. See Mitrī Kūtiā's translation of his writing *al-Rajā' alladhī finā* [The hope that is in us], 99. [See also an English translation, *Our Hope*]. The Russian people enjoy, thanks to their upbringing: *ṣūfī*-ascetic inclinations, a high spiritual level, and fervent religious feeling, despite the cold climate. The German Kant called for a strict ethics. Russian spiritually oversteps this limit.

31. Homily 39, paragraph 19. [The original Greek text can be found in Moreschini (ed.), *Grégoire de Nazianze: Discours 38–41*, *SC* 358, while an English translation has appeared in Daley, *Gregory of Nazianzus*.—Trans.]

So that some may better understand, it should be noted that the long clause falling between the two dashes is a parenthetical clause. We should read the rest in this way: "then he did well; but, if they have bathed in tears . . ." The aforementioned suitable place in the parenthetical clause is the rule of repentance that was, from ancient times, undertaken in the church.

Shortly before this, Gregory discussed the baptism of martyrdom and the baptism of repentance. He noted that

> there also exists a fourth type of baptism. The baptism of martyrdom and blood, which exceeds the other kinds in value, in that it cannot be thereafter sullied by any stain. I know also of a fifth baptism, the baptism of tears. Indeed, it is more toilsome than the preceding baptisms, because it floods one's couch or bed with tears every night. With it, the sores of iniquity exude their loathsome odor,[32] and one proceeds in mourning and grief, resembling the repentance of Manasseh[33] and the humility of the people of Nineveh, who were forgiven.[34] One speaks the language of the publican in the temple and finds himself justified, unlike the haughty Pharisee.[35] One kneels to the ground like the Canaanite woman,[36] seeking mercy, and, being famished, asks and begs for crumbs of bread, the food of the starving dogs.[37]

Palamas expands on the thoughts of his namesake Gregory the Theologian and those of John Climacus. Thus, he said:

> Owing to fear of God,[38] the appetitive part of the psyche, instead of being mortified, remains affective (*passif*), and is transformed into an energy pleasing to God, producing salvific humility and lamentation, obtaining the wealth of forgiveness and bringing to remembrance the divine prophethood, that is, tears of repentance. These

32. The text by Yāzigī: "I sobbed in my sighing, for every night I flood my bed with tears and spread them upon my couch. My eyes have wasted away from anguish and grown old" (Psalm 6:7–8).
33. 2 Chronicles 33:11–23.
34. Jonah 3:5.
35. Luke 18:13.
36. Matthew 15:22 and Mark 7:25.
37. Homily 39:17.
38. Proverbs 1:7 and 9:10.

tears, pleasing to God and purifying, give wing to prayer, as the Fathers say.[39] Thus, joined to prayer, they illumine the eyes of the spirit, according to Gregory the Theologian,[40] they safeguard the blessing of divine ablution. When this blessing is present they call attention to it, and when it vanishes they compose it. For this reason, being washed again is a second sanctified birth[41] and a second divine baptism. Gregory named them as such. They demand greater toil, yet they are not lesser than the first baptism; they (that is, tears) are even higher than it, as one of the Fathers declared: "The spring of tears after baptism is higher than baptism."[42] These tears purify us and save us from earthly things, they elevate us and join us to the blessing of divine adoption that, through them (tears), edifies the one who possesses them. Is it not so that these tears are an activity common to the body and to the passible part of the soul?

And he said also, transmitting Isaac the Syrian: "The holy ones say that there exists a common activity amidst the body and the soul. . . . It is said: 'For whoever wishes to be saved from vices is saved through weeping, and whoever wishes to acquire the virtues likewise acquires them by weeping.' "[43]

This is one thing; another that we see is the holy Gregory Palamas, in the fourteenth century, insisting on the importance of communing[44] and discussing communion almost constantly.[45]

We know that Palamas lived as a monastic on Mount Athos and that he is the culmination of thirteen centuries of Christian history in spiritual depth and spiritual and theological breadth. In Cassian's writing, confession occupies an important place for the fourth-century monastics. Our church, moreover, does not distinguish between monastics and people of

39. John Climacus, *The Ladder of Divine Ascent*, Rung 28 in *PG* 88, 1140.

40. Homily 4.31, *PG* 404 A.

41. Titus 3:5.

42. John Climacus, *The Ladder of Divine Ascent* Rung 7 in *PG* 88, 804 B A.

43. Palamas, *Défense*, 356–358. The holy Symeon the Theologian speaks along these lines. See Darrouzès and Neyrand (eds.), *Syméon le Nouveau Théologien* (*SC* 51), especially page 50.

44. Homily 37.

45. Homily 56 and the sermons in the book edited by Dr. Oikonomos [that is, Gergory Palamas, *Tou en hagiois patros hemōn Grēgoriou.*—Trans].

the world regarding the obligations of the spiritual life; negligence and abeyance in a given time do not affect the importance of this decisive point.

On the other hand, what is the benefit of encouraging people to commune without first encouraging them to prepare and repent? Palamas, and before him Chrysostom and the monastics, stressed confession. Did not the Apostle Paul warn us in his letter to the people of Corinth[46] of the danger of approaching the Lord's body and blood unworthily?

> For whoever eats the bread of the Lord and drinks of His cup unworthily is guilty with respect to the body and blood of the Lord. Let a person test himself and thus let him eat of this bread and drink from this cup. For whoever eats and drinks unworthily rather eats and drinks judgment to himself, for he does not distinguish the body of the Lord. Therefore, many of you are ill and sickly, and many of you have died. If we condemned ourselves, we would not be condemned. In our judgment we are rather instructed by the Lord, in order that He not condemn us along with the world.

Reform will not happen through more chaos. Orthodoxy cares about quality without neglecting quantity. If we desire to reform the worn-out and forlorn conditions of the Orthodox, we must offer valuable sermons, provide lucid guidance, and disseminate worthy publications. The reform of their condition is accomplished through apostolic work, not through arbitrariness and superficiality. Apostolic work needs apostles, not classical priests, for services without fiery exhortation, redolent with the fervor of the Holy Spirit.

Spiritual guidance is the most difficult kind of guidance. If not for the blessing of the Holy Spirit, neither the guide nor the guided would succeed; and if we abolish confession, we essentially abolish guidance.[47]

Guidance in our ancient Christian East has a glorious history, the lineaments of which are traced through many attestations, such as Father Hausherr's massive volume (322 pages of medium print): *La direction spirituelle en Orient autrefois* [Spiritual direction in the erstwhile East].

46. 1 Corinthians 11:27–33.

47. I am irritated by the hasty scrutinization of guidance and writings without maturity, oversight, or practice. Without maturity, pride mixes with jealousy. Valor is the result of an enduring and deep practice.

CHAPTER

10

Repentance and Joy

It seems from this book that confession, repentance, and monasticism is a regime of melancholia and mourning. Does Christianity instruct lamentation and nothing else?

Indeed, the Apostle Paul taught us in his letter to the Philippians to rejoice, and he repeatedly calls on us to rejoice, as he said:

> "By this I will rejoice; but furthermore, I will rejoice."[1]
>
> "Complete my joy."[2]
>
> "I rejoiced and was made glad with you all, so by this you likewise rejoice and be glad with me."[3]
>
> "All of you rejoice . . . accept him in all joy."[4]
>
> "Rejoice in the Lord."[5]
>
> "O my beloved brethren, for whom is my yearning, you who are my delight and my crown."[6]
>
> "Rejoice in the Lord always, and I say again, rejoice."[7]
>
> "Indeed, I have rejoiced in the Lord with awesome joy."[8]

1. Philippians 1:18.
2. Philippians 2:2.
3. Philippians 2:18.
4. Philippians 2:29.
5. Philippians 3:1. See also Isaiah 21:10.
6. Philippians 4:1.
7. Philippians 4:4.
8. Philippians 4:10.

And he said in the second letter to the Corinthians:

> "As if we are mourning but ever rejoicing."[9]
> "I overflow with joy in all our distress."[10]

And there is something even more important than this, Paul said that joy is the fruit of the Holy Spirit.[11]

The existence of joy is one of the fruits of the Holy Spirit (such as love, peace, abstinence, meekness, compassion, and the like).[12] This means a great deal. It naturally falls within the array of the Holy Spirit's effects in our lives. So, whoever attains the Holy Spirit with power has attained the eternal source of delight and joy, and the attainment of both is the reward for the bitter struggle against transgressions.

Orthodoxy became known in the Christian world for emphasizing the resurrection of the Lord Jesus. In its prayers, it focuses on the resurrection and its joy; one of them says: "We have seen the resurrection of Christ. Let us fall down in worship of the holy Lord Jesus . . . Before Your cross, O Christ our God, we fall down in worship, and we praise and glorify Your holy resurrection, for behold, through the cross, joy has come to all the world. . . ."[13]

Even the cross is a fount of joy and a victory, as Christ prevailed over the devil, Hell, and transgression by His cross. Jesus, according to the interpretation of the church Fathers, considered the cross His glory. Golgotha is a mount upon which the glory of the Lord is disclosed,[14] with victory proclaimed over the enemies of Jesus.

Repentance establishes joy. The holy Symeon the New Theologian was a great lamenter, but his tears were of two types: tears of repentance and tears of joy.

9. 2 Corinthians 6:10.

10. 2 Corinthians 7:4.

11. Galatians 5:22.

12. Galatians 5:22.

13. A resurrection hymn that is prayed at the conclusion of the Divine Liturgy and chanted throughout the forty-day celebration of Pascha. It also follows the reading of the Gospel at the predawn prayer (*sahr*) on Sundays.—Trans.

14. *Tajalla,* a reference to the disclosure of Christ's divine glory on Mount Tabor (*al-tajallī*).—Trans.

So, theologically, repentance convenes the sufferings of the Lord, His burial, and His resurrection. By it, I bury my transgression, and in Jesus I rise from spiritual death.

The penitent crucifies his psyche in sorrow with Christ, being regretful, remorseful, mournful and melancholic, lamenting and weeping; yet his sadness turns into joy.

A state of continual repentance is crucial. Every day we transgress, and whenever we transgress, we repent, and God laments our weakness and pulls us up out of the abyss of our iniquities. The greatest of those who have gone astray is he who thinks that he has attained perfection or a portion of it; there is no perfection save what Jesus resurrects within us. All virtues, goods, and pieties are relative unless they are ripened fruits of the Holy Spirit.[15]

We need only cast ourselves—without appraisal, precaution, or fear, without remorse or regret—into the hands of God, and God will order our affairs. For when we become His, He leads us according to the righteous intentions that He has toward us. Our fate[16] is entrusted to His hands. There is a plan, inscribed for each one of His cross-bearing beloved ones within His divine knowledge, to lead them to the perfection of His love, to union with Him, and to the enjoyment of His eternal light. We need only supplicate Him that this be disclosed within us completely.[17]

Excursus

Among spiritually important topics at the level of psychoanalysis and its science of characterology,[18] there is the study of Christian types.

The *ṣūfī* type possesses fresh desire, yielding and pliant toward God, and does not accept being confined to the common types.

15. Galatians 5:22.

16. *Qadr*, the divine decree.—Trans.

17. Of course, I do not mean that my divine fate is my assurance, or stems from the collaboration of divine grace and human volition. Human struggle brings forth the rains of grace.

18. *'Ilm al-ṭibā'* (the science of innate nature), here referring to the early twentieth-century discipline of characterology used in both psychoanalysis and German critical theory.—Trans.

The German Kant cast the human within a strict ethical mold and did not leave any outlet for the flame of desire. The Kantian human is an anthropological machine given good morals.

The average person is suited for this normal type, one that is compatible with social life and correct social behavior; the human is predisposed to order the soul according to the image of the body, which performs its functions systematically and precisely.

The first type is excepted from this common rule. Evildoers are exceptions in society; they are men of war. The mystics are also men of war. The Sufis make war on evil and soar toward God, while evildoers become the enemies of the human, the human race, and the universe. However, if a great criminal turns into a great penitent, the heavens are torn open, and he comes to occupy them.

This topic is very useful if studied in depth, as not all the inhabitants of the monasteries are fiery torches.

Of course, education in the home plays its part in the survival of this flame that refuses to be cast into a limited and strict mold of good order.

Supplication

O Jesus,

What do I say now? My tongue is impotent.

What do I ask of you? I have no desiderata to fashion; I do not know my true need, as my erring imaginings show me the good wherever snares of iniquity lie in wait for me.

But You who know all, know my need better than me. Permit me, after what I have imagined in this book, to beseech You:

Make each of my wants, my wishes, and my desires to wither, to remove me from my self; take exclusive possession of me in my entirety. For any portion that remains of my self becomes a powder keg; no one knows, save You, when it will detonate. The whole of my imagined spiritual edifice is built on a minefield. I have no sense of when my imaginary tower will collapse; neither do I possess righteousness, only dissimulation and the manifestations of hypocrisy.

I have not once striven for righteousness, but my iniquity preceded me, to corrupt my path and taint my inclinations with its poison, coating my piety with its malignancy, deception, and beguilements.

O my divine Jesus, send Your Holy Spirit to rip me out of my self and to completely and perfectly join me to You. For You alone are the hope of my salvation; there is no hope in my self, nor in others, for we all are under the heavy burden of transgression, slumbering in the minefields. My defenses are useless, regardless of the extent to which I have advanced, progressed, or improved.

You alone are my defense, my healing cure, the panacea that preserves me from relapse, decay, and decline.

O my Savior!! Tear me out of my own self by Your Holy Spirit, bring me near to Your heavenly Father as a sacrifice, sprinkled with Your pure and blameless blood, and do not allow my heart to incline to any but You. You indeed are the compassionate benefactor, and to You is due praise with the Father and the Holy Spirit, always and unto the ages of ages.

Amen.

CHAPTER

11

A Historical-Geographical Fragment

In this book, one notes the citation of several names from the Holy Fathers. What are their native countries?

Anthony and the ancient **Desert Fathers** were Egyptians, men who belonged to the fourth and fifth centuries.

Evagrios was a disciple of Gregory the Theologian from the land of Pontus (the Black Sea). He came to Palestine and became an ascetic in Egypt, but in the wilderness of Egypt he joined the brethren of Ammonas—those corrupted by the teachings of Origen the Egyptian (third century), who was, in turn, corrupted by Plato and the Greek philosophy condemned by the Fifth Ecumenical Council. If we discount their heresies, these two [Evagrios and Origen] were among the most brilliant church writers.

Evagrios died in the year 399. He was the author of ascetic writings that became immortalized through their subsequent influence—from John Climacus, the great ascetic writer (who died around 650), to Maximos the Confessor[1] (died 662), a Palestinian who is the capstone of the sciences of

1. A Syriac manuscript of a contemporary writer says that Maximos is from Khasfīn in the province of the Syrian Golan. The story of his being from Constantinople has fallen apart. Tūmā, Metropolitan of the Maronites at Kafr Tab (Khān Shaykhūn), supports this in 1089. No one heeded this before (see Rustum, *Kanīsa madīna allāh anṭākiyya al-ʿuẓmā* [The church of the great city of God, Antioch], 2: 75). As for Sinai, it followed the state of the Nabataeans,

the ancients, theologically, spiritually, and mystically, to Isaac the Syrian, the bishop of Nineveh, who is a brilliant ascetic-*ṣūfī* writer (seventh century). And how many have been influenced by them up to our day, and how numerous they are.

John Climacus, the Syrian, was head of the Monastery of Sinai, where he left an eternal legacy.

Maximos the Confessor was from the Golan.

Isaac the Syrian, born in Qatar, became bishop of Nineveh. He resigned after six months and became an ascetic in Ahvaz, and, praise be to God, he then vacated the bishopric, which provided him reclusion and sufism [*taṣawwuf*], and so he enriched us with his legacy.

Sophronios, a Damascene, became Patriarch of al-Quds [Jerusalem] in the year 634 and died in 638. He was a hero of the resistance against the heretical innovation of the one will [Monothelitism], and it is he who forged the path of struggle for Maximos. Their connection to Sinai was unshakable. Moreover, Sinai itself had an unshakable connection to the writer Diadochos, whom Johannes Quasten (one of the most famous modern specialists on the Church Fathers) gathered together with the cohort of Syriac writers.[2] Sophronios died sometime after 457/458. He left a significant impact on Maximos as well.

There is a school of Gazan monasticism that had an influence on Sinai. Its eremitic leaders were the marvelous Barsanuphius and John, as well as Dorotheos the Antiochian physician (sixth century).

Symeon the Stylite was from the mountains of Amanus.[3] He lived atop the well-known pillar in the region of Mount Symeon, in the province of

---

which included Damascus in the days of Paul. It belonged to the Arab states, as mentioned in the Galatian letter. Paul flees from Damascus to "Arabia," that is, to the Hawran.

2. Dayr al-Harf published his composition in 1992.

3. I published his *Life* in Aleppo in 1992. [See Jabbour, *al-Qaddīs samaʿān al-ʿamūdī.*]

Aleppo in the fifth century. He began the movement of Stylites, until they became a great cohort in the north and east of Syria, in addition to the army of hermits and monks.

As for the general currents, there are two, which are described in the next section.

1—The Current of Pseudo-Dionysius

People had long been under the false impression that **Dionysius the Areopagite** was a disciple of the Apostle Paul, but it is now confirmed that he was Syrian.

Symeon the New Theologian may be the greatest Christian *ṣūfi*, according to some.[4] He died in the year 1022, leaving behind a unique theological-ascetic-*ṣūfī* legacy. He was influenced by those previously mentioned and improved on things in the most innovative way.[5]

Gregory Palamas, Archbishop of Thessaloniki and previously a monastic of the monasteries of Mount Athos, is a shining star in the fourteenth century alongside the luminaries that are the holy Athonites. The fourteenth century was the century of Mount Athos.

Gregory of Sinai was from the region of Izmir. He fell into captivity and spent years in prison at Latakia. Its inhabitants ransomed him; then he traveled to Cyprus and from there to Sinai, where he studied its inheritance. He brought the fragrances of Sinai and the Jesus prayer, which he learned on the island of Crete from the monk Arsenios, with him to Mount Athos. Gregory fell asleep in the year 1346 and was a contemporary of Palamas, who died in the year 1359.

4. He was a contentious figure in Constantinople.

5. *Tajwīd*, means to "beautify" or "make better" and refers almost exclusively to the art of reciting the Qur'ān. Symeon was a renowned and prolific poet. See the English translation of his hymns by Griggs, *Divine Eros*, as well as Greenfield's translation of Niketas Stethatos's Greek account of his life *The Life of Saint Symeon the New Theologian*.—Trans.

Cassian was from Romania. He changed much and became a disciple of Chrysostom after residing with the Fathers of Egypt. He completed his life in France, where he left behind his wonderful books written in Latin.

Benedict the Latin [of Nursia] was influenced by Basil the Great, Cassian, and others.

Nikiphoros, a monastic in the thirteenth century, innovated on the method of the hesychasts. Discourse about stillness and those practicing it is very ancient, even if Nikiphoros forged a way for it. Palamas was entrusted with the defense of the hesychast Athonites. Palamas was a great example of one who even-handedly drew from the inheritance as a whole: the Cappadocians, Pseudo-Makarios, Maximos the Confessor, Isaac of Nineveh, John of Damascus, and Symeon the New Theologian, whose thought and theology were influenced by Maximos the Confessor.

Pseudo-Dionysius was a late writer, a Syrian; his extant writings appeared around the years 500/510. If we subtract from him the influence of Neoplatonism and some other deviations, he was a *ṣūfī* and theological writer of the highest caliber. Vladimir Lossky defended him at length, then confessed—influenced by Gandillac's critique[6]—that he was indeed influenced by Platonism; still, he defended him once more, arguing that he exploded Neoplatonism from within. Dionysius left an influence on Maximos and others, and even on Palamas, who corrected some of his errors.[7] In my book *God Is with Us, Submit Yourselves*,[8] I stated that he put the teachings of the Cappadocian Fathers in order. Afterward, Lossky's essay appeared, which argued likewise.[9] This means that the author was not a follower of Neoplatonism.

6. Maurice de Gandillac was the translator of Pseudo-Dionysius's writings and a scholar of Neoplatonism.—Trans.

7. His influence on the West is very broad. See Lossky's dissertation in French. ["Théologie négative et connaissance de Dieu chez Maître Eckhart"—Trans.]

8. See Jabbour, *Maʿanā huwa allāh fa-inhazamū*.—Trans.

9. A reference to Lossky, *Essai sur la théologie mystique de l'Église d'Orient.* See also Lossky "La notion des 'analogies'"—Trans.

2—The Current of Makarios

It was long thought that **Makarios** was Makarios the Egyptian. However, today's consensus refutes this and is inclined to consider him a Syrian. The latest research discusses the current of Makarios. My friend, the French Father Placide Deseille, does not rule out the possibility that he may have been a Syrian who became a disciple of Makarios the Great of Egypt.

John Chrysostom was an Antiochian. He was the bishop of Constantinople. He fell asleep in the year 407.

Gregorios bin al-ʿIbrī [Bar ʿEbroyo] was a Syriac bishop of Aleppo. He was the preeminent scholar of his day in the thirteenth century. He fell asleep in the year 1287. He was influenced by Evagrios and Isaac of Nineveh. He believed in the unity of Christians.

We see in this summary, and in the volume *The Mystery of the Divine Economy*,[10] that our Mashriq gave the Christian world its theological structure and its ascetic-*ṣūfī* structure.

What remains in our lives of this inheritance? Ignorance that we are of this inheritance remains.

No one from Homs has seen the compositions of Romanos the Psalmist, whom the Frenchman Paul Lemerle called the greatest poet in the history of the Byzantine Empire.

Likewise, who from Damascus has obtained the Canon of Repentance, which the holy Andrew of Damascus composed (it was published at the end of the book *On Repentance*)[11] since he is counted as a Damascene? The number is nonexistent, or certainly negligible.

We have not yet rid ourselves of the sterility, absurdity, and backwardness inherited from the Ottoman era and what preceded it, such that we can connect to our authentic inheritance. We have won successes since 1942,[12] but the true success will be in the coming centuries. It remains for us to enliven this inheritance, even if only by publishing it in print, to make way for a comprehensive revival.

10. See Jabbour, *Sirr al-tadbīr al-ilāhī*.—Trans.
11. See Jabbour, *Fī al-tawba*.—Trans.
12. A reference to the founding of the Orthodox Youth Movement.—Trans.

The holy Gregory the Theologian calls for the benefit brought about by any advancement of the good, however simple. Concerning the tongue of God, Isaiah the prophet said: Indeed, the Word of God does not return to Him empty.[13]

Do we despair? No. The question is one of the maturity of the soul, of civilization, and of history. Our land, which gave us this great inheritance and then became barren and desolate, will one day be washed clean by torrents of abundant and heavenly rain from God our Savior. We only need to prepare for this with love, desire for God, and pure prayer.

If feuds have torn it apart piece by piece, then nothing remains but love, gentleness, patience, and forbearance, to mend what has been broken and to restore God to our hearts, hollowed out by the worm of hatred and its ilk.

13. Isaiah 55:11.

GLOSSARY

akhlāq—Ethical formation or character.
ʿālam—The world, creation, cosmos.
al-ākhar—The other.
al-ākhira—The hereafter; the afterlife.
ʿamaliyya—A method or procedure; a way of proceeding practically.
al-anā—The I; the ego.
ʿaql—The intellect; the intelligible faculty; the seat of the heart and organ of divine knowledge; a translation of the Greek term *nous*.
athara—Selfishness; Jabbour's translation of Maximos's Greek term *philautia*.
bāṭin—The hidden, inner, related to one's insides (the heart, the chest, the intestines).
batula—Bravery; the courage required for confession and ascetic struggle.
ḍamīr—Conscience, one's innermost self and ethical intuition.
dhanb—A misdeed or transgression; the sense of guilt (*shuʿūr bi-l-dhanb*).
dhāt—The self, one's own being or facticity.
dhikr—Remembrance, anamnesis; the perpetual remembrance of God or the continuous invocation of the name of Jesus (cf. ***ṣalāt yasūʿ***) in monastic practice.
dhihn—The mind, the rational faculty, and a translation of the Greek *dianoia*.
dunyā—The lower world, the world of the passions.
fawq al-anā—What is above the "I"; the superego.
gharīza—Instinct, impulse; in Freud, *Instinkt.*
ḥāl—Condition or the state of the soul.
hawā, pl. *ahwāʾ*—The passions or passion as the capacity for affect; conceptualized both as exterior forces and the root force of the soul.

hudūʾiyya—Quiescence, the Arabic translation of the Greek ascetic term *hesychia*, meaning stillness. It refers to the ascetic practice of "hesychasm" codified by the monks of Mount Athos in the fourteenth century.
al-huwa—He or it; the id.
ʿilm—Science, knowledge, a method of knowing.
irshād—Spiritual guidance; the relation of spiritual guidance between a guide (*murshid*) and a disciple (*murīd* or *tilmīdh*) of which confession (cf. ***iʿtirāf***) is a defining part.
ʿishq—Ardor, passionate love.
iʿtirāf—Acknowledgement or recognition; the practice of confession in a relationship of spiritual guidance between an elder and disciple or between a priest and his community members.
ittiḥād—Union, specifically, in Islam and Christianity, union with God; a term connected to debates on the manifestation of Christ and the subsequent union of human and divine natures.
jawf—A hollow, used by Jabbour and Islamic commentaries to characterize the human, which, as a creature, lacks the divine quality of solidity (cf. ***ṣamad***).
jasad—The physical body, as opposed to *jism*, which denotes the ensouled body.
jihād—Struggle; ascetic effort or spiritual combat.
maʿrifa—Inner knowledge.
maʿqūl—Pertaining to the intellect (*ʿaql*), the highest part of the soul; Jabbour's translation of Maximos' use of the term *logikos* and so relating to the intellect's ability to discern the *logoi*, the divine causes, of things.
mayl—Inclination, tendency, drive; in Freud, *Trieb*.
murāqaba—Watchfulness; self-observation; oversight (cf. ***yaqaẓa***).
mutaṣawwif—A practitioner of Sufism (cf. ***taṣawwuf***); used by Jabbour to refer to both Christians and Muslims.
nafs—Soul, psyche, self, the limn between spirit and body.
qalb—The heart; seated in the intellect or *nous* in Orthodox ascetic writing.
al-qism al-ghaḍabiyya—The incensive and wrathful part of the soul/psyche (cf. ***nafs***); a translation of the Greek term *thymos*.
al-qism al-shahwāniyya—The appetite or desirous part of the soul/psyche (cf. ***nafs***); a translation of the Greek term *to epithymētikon*.
al-qurbān—The Oblation; the Eucharistic offering.
rāhib—A monastic (used for both men and women); one who holds God in fear and awe.
rūḥ—Spirit, referring to the aspect of the human that can participate in God through His Holy Spirit (*al-rūḥ al-qudus*).
ṣalāt yasūʿ—The Jesus Prayer or the Prayer of the Heart.
ṣamad—Solid and uncomposed (a divine characteristic).

shahāda—martyrdom and attestation, describing the act of one who bears witness through being subjected to trials.
shaykh—An elder, a monastic leader or spiritual guide.
shawq—Divine longing.
shayṭān—The devil; Satan; a demon or evil jinn.
ṣūfī—Ascetic or mystic, used as an adjective; cf. ***mutaṣawwif.***
shuʿūr—Consciousness; the sensible; the expressible; that of which one has awareness.
al-lā-shuʿūr—The unconscious; the insensible and that of which one is unaware.
taʾalluh—To become like God, uniting with His divine energies or characteristics; a translation of the Greek word *theōsis.*
taḍādd—Ambivalence; contradiction; polarity; the actual and simultaneous existence of contrary forces.
tadbīr—Ordering, the divine mercy of God; a translation of the equivalent Greek term, *oikonomia.*
taḥlīl—Analysis, as in psychoanalysis (*al-taḥlīl al-nafsī*) and the unfettering of the psyche in confession.
taḥwīl—Transference; transformation; a change of state (*ḥāl*), from Freud's term *Übertragung.* Jabbour reads this process in Maximos the Confessor and Gregory Palamas as well, as the process by which the passible aspects of the soul, in being directed toward God, become dispassionate.
al-tajallī—Divine disclosure, often referring to the feast of Transfiguration and, more specifically, the disclosure of Christ's divinity to his disciples on Mount Tabor; it also describes witnessing of the divine light, the practice around which hesychasm is oriented (cf. ***hudūʾiyya***).
tarbiya—Pedagogy, child-rearing, and upbringing.
taṣawwuf—Practices of Islamic asceticism or reclusion; a reference to Islamic mysticism.
yaqaẓa—Spiritual watchfulness, guarding the heart; a translation of the Greek *nēpsis.*
ẓāhir—The manifest, apparent, related to what is outward.
zuhd—Asceticism, renunciation, reclusion.

WORKS CITED

ʿAbd al-Raḥīm, Yāsīn. *Mawsūʿat al-ʿāmmiyya al-sūriyya*. Ministry of Culture, Damascus: Manshūrāt al-Hay'aa al-ʿĀma al-Sūriyya li-l-Kitāb, 2012.

Abrahamov, Binyamin. "World." In *Encyclopaedia of the Qurʾān Online*, edited by Johanna Pink, University of Freiburg. Leiden: Brill. Accessed online February 9, 2023.

Abu-Manneh, Butrus. "The Christians between Ottomanism and Syrian Nationalism: The Ideas of Butrus Al-Bustani." *International Journal of Middle East Studies* 11, no. 3 (1980): 287–304.

Andrew of Damascus [Andrew of Crete]. *Qānūn al-tawba*. Translated by Spiro Jabbour. 2nd ed. Latakia: Muṭrāniyyat al-Lādhiqīya, 1996.

Arida, Robert. "Hearing, Receiving, and Entering TO ΜΥΣΤΗΡΙΟΝ/TA ΜΥΣΤΗΡΙΑ: Patristic Insights Unveiling the Crux Interpretum (Isaiah 6:9–10) of the Sower Parable." *St. Vladamir's Theological Quarterly* 38, no. 2 (1994).

Arnaldez, R. "Lāhūt, and Nāsūt." In *Encyclopaedia of Islam*. 2nd ed., edited by P. Bearman, Th. Bianquis, C. E. Bosworth et al. http://dx.doi.org/10.1163/1573-3912_islam_COM_0561.

Asad, Talal. *Formations of the Secular: Christianity, Islam, Modernity*. Stanford, California: Stanford University Press, 2003.

———. *Genealogies of Religion: Discipline and Reasons of Power in Christianity and Islam*. Baltimore: Johns Hopkins University Press, 1993.

———. "Thinking about Religion through Wittgenstein." *Critical Times* 3, no. 3 (2020): 403–442. https://doi.org/10.1215/26410478-8662304.

Athanasios, *Sīrat al-qiddīs anṭūniyūs al-kabīr*. Translated by Michel Najim. Qalḥāt: Manshūrāt Maʿhad al-Qaddīs Yuḥanna al-Dimashqī, 1979.

Balthasar, Hans Urs von. *Cosmic Liturgy: The Universe According to Maximus the Confessor*. San Francisco: Ignatius Press, 2003.

———. *Liturgie cosmique: Maxime le Confesseur*. Paris: Aubier, 1947.

Bardawil, Fadi A. *Revolution and Disenchantment: Arab Marxism and the Binds of Emancipation*. Durham, NC: Duke University Press, 2020

Batatu, Hanna. 1999. *Syria's Peasantry, the Descendants of Its Lesser Rural Notables, and Their Politics*. Princeton, NJ: Princeton University Press.

Baun, Dylan. "Fighting the Punks: The Routine Practices and Sectarian Outcomes of the 1958 War." In *Winning Lebanon: Youth Politics, Populism, and the Production of Sectarian Violence, 1920–1958*, 155–185. Cambridge Middle East Studies. Cambridge: Cambridge University Press, 2020.

Beck, Edmund, ed. *Des heiligen Ephraem des Syrers Sermones*. Louvain: Secrétariat du Corpus SCO, 1970.

Bendaly, Costi. *Images parentales et attitudes religieuses: Dialogue avec Freud*. vol. 3. Beyrouth: An-Nour Coop, 2007.

Benevich, Grigory. "Maximus Confessor's Interpretation of Abraham's Hospitality in Genesis 18 and the Preceding Orthodox Tradition." *Scrinium* 13, 1 (2017): 43-52, doi: https://doi.org/10.1163/18177565-00131p06.

Benjamin, Walter. "Die Aufgabe des Übersetzers." In *textlog.de*. Accessed August 2024 [1923]. https://www.textlog.de/benjamin/baudelaire/tableaux-parisiens/aufgabe-des-uebersetzers

———. "The Task of the Translator." Translated by Steven Rendall. *TTR: traduction, terminologie, rédaction* 10, no. 2 (1997): 151–165.

Benslama, Fethi. *La psychanalyse à l'épreuve de l'islam*. Paris: Aubier, 2002.

———. *Psychoanalysis and the Challenge of Islam*. Translated by Robert Bononno. Minneapolis: University of Minnesota Press, 2009.

Bettelheim, Bruno. *Freud and Man's Soul*. New York: Knopf, 1982.

Bowman, Bradley. *Christian Monastic Life in Early Islam*. Edinburgh, Scotland: Edinburgh University Press, 2021. https://doi.org/10.1515/9781474479707.

———. "Refuge in the Bosoms of the Mountains: A Ninth-Century Muslim Appraisal of Monastic Piety." *Islam and Christian-Muslim Relations* 30, no. 4 (2019): 459–482.

Bradshaw, David. *Aristotle East and West: Metaphysics and the Division of Christendom*. Cambridge: Cambridge University Press, 2004.

Breuer, Josef, and Sigmund Freud. *Studies on Hysteria*. Translated by James Strachey. New York: Basic Books, 1987 [1895].

Brockelmann, C. "al-Anbāri, Abū Bakr". In P. Bearman (ed.), *Encyclopaedia of Islam New Edition Online* (*EI-2 English*). Brill, 2012. doi:http://dx.doi.org/10.1163/1573-3912_islam_SIM_0660.

Bustān al-ruhbān: *Li-ābā' al-kanīsa al-qibṭiyya*. Beni Suef: Muṭrāniyya Banī Suwayf wa al-Bahnsā, 1977.

Chabbi, Jacqueline. "Whisper." In *Encyclopaedia of the Qur'ān*, edited by Johanna Pink, University of Freiburg. Leiden: Brill. Accessed online on December 29, 2022

Charnay, Jean-Paul, Jacques Berque, and Pierre Alexandre. *L'ambivalence dans la culture arabe*. Paris: Éditions Anthropos, 1967.

Chryssavgis, John, and Pachomios (Robert) Penkett. *Abba Isaiah of Scetis Ascetic Discourses*. Kalamazoo, Michigan: Cistercian Publications, 2002.

Colliander, Tito. *Ṭarīq al-nussāk*. Translated by Spiro Jabbour. Tripoli, Lebanon: al-Manshūrāt al-Urthūdhuksiyya, 1981.

———. *Way of the Ascetics: The Ancient Tradition of Discipline and Inner Growth*. Translated by Katharine Ferré. Crestwood, NY: St. Vladimir's Seminary Press, 1985.

Corbin, Henri. *Alone with the Alone: Creative Imagination in the Ṣūfism of Ibn 'Arabī*. Translated by Ralph Manheim. Princeton, NJ: Princeton University Press, 1998.

———. *L'ímagination créatrice dans le soufisme d'Ibn 'Arabi*. 2nd ed. Paris: Flammarion, 1977.

Dalbiez, Roland. *La méthod psychanalytique et la doctrine freudienne*. 2 vols. Paris: Descell de Brouwer, 1936.

Daley, Brian E. *Gregory of Nazianzus*. London: Routledge, 2006.

Darrouzès, Jean, and Louis Neyrand, eds. *Syméon le Nouveau Théologien: Chapitres théologiques, gnostiques et pratiques*. Sources Chrétiennes 51. Paris: Cerf, 1996.

Davis, Stephen J. *The Arabic Life of St. John the Little by Zacharias of Sakhā. Coptica* 7. Los Angeles: St. Mark Foundation and St. Shenouda the Archimandrite Coptic Society, 2008.

de Certeau, Michel. *The Mystic Fable: The Sixteenth and Seventeenth Centuries*. Translated by Michael B. Smith. 2 vols. Chicago: University of Chicago Press, 1992–2015.

Delli, Eudoxia, and Vasileios Thermos, eds. *Soul and Psyche as a Surprise: Psychoanalysis and Orthodox Theology in Dialogue*. Alhambra, California: Sebastian Press, 2021.

Diadochos of Photiki. *On Spiritual Knowledge and Discrimination: One Hundred Texts*. In Palmer et al. (eds.) *The Philokalia*, vol. 1. London: Faber & Faber, 1979.

Dubilet, Alex. *The Self-Emptying Subject: Kenosis and Immanence, Medieval to Modern*. New York: Fordham University Press, 2018.

Dudko, Dimitrii. *Our Hope*. Crestwood, NY: St. Vladimir's Seminary Press, 1977.

———. *al-Rajā' alladhī fīnā*. Translated by Mitrī Kūtiā. Tripoli, Lebanon: Dār al-Inshā' li-l-Ṭibā'a wa al-Nashr, 1978.

Eldridge, Aaron Frederick, and Basit Kareem Iqbal. "A Tropics of Estrangement: *Ghurba* in Four Scenes." *Diacritics* 50, no. 1 (2022): 112–140. https://doi.org/10.1353/dia.2022.0004.

El Shakry, Omnia. *The Arabic Freud: Psychoanalysis and Islam in Modern Egypt*. Princeton, NJ: Princeton University Press, 2017. https://doi.org/10.1515/9781400888030.

———. "The Work of Illness in the Aftermath of a 'Surpassing Disaster': Medical Humanities in the Middle East and North Africa." *Culture, Medicine, and Psychiatry*. March 13, 2023. https://doi.org/10.1007/s11013-023-09818-4.

El Shakry, Omnia, Sara Pursley, and Caroline McKusick, eds. "Psychoanalysis and the Middle East: Discourses and Encounters." Special issue, *Psychoanalysis and History* 20, no. 3 (2018).

Ephraim the Syrian. *Spiritual Psalter or, Reflections on God*. Translated by Antonina Janda. Liberty, TN: St. John of Kronstadt Press, 1997.

Evdokimov, Paul. *Dostoïevsky et le problème du mal*. Lyon: Ondes, Éd. du Livre Français, 1942.

Ewing, Katherine Pratt. *Arguing Sainthood: Modernity, Psychoanalysis, and Islam*. Durham, NC: Duke University Press, 1997. https://doi.org/10.1515/9780822379126.

al-Fayrūzabādī. *al-Qāmūs al-muḥīṭ*. http://arabiclexicon.hawramani.com/firuzabadi-al-qamus-al-muhit/.

Fenichel, Otto. *The Psychoanalytic Theory of Neurosis*. 2nd ed. London: Routledge, 1996. https://doi.org/10.4324/9780203754436.

Freud, Sigmund. *Civilization and Its Discontents*. Translated by James Strachey. New York: W. W. Norton, 1961 [1930].

———. *Essais de psychanalyse*. Translated by Samuel Jankélévitch. Paris: Payot, 1927.

———. *Essais de psychanalyse appliquée*. Translated by Marie Bonaparte. Paris: Gallimard, 1952.

———. *al-Ḥuzn wa al-ikti'āb*. Edited by Olaf Nicolai. Translated by Mohammad Abu-Zaid. Leipzig: Self-published, 2009.

———. *Mā fawq mabda' al-ladhdha* [Beyond the Pleasure Principle]. Translated by Isḥāq Ramzī. Cairo: Dār al-Ma'ārif, 1998.

———. *Psychoanalysis and Faith: the Letters of Sigmund Freud and Oskar Pfister*. Edited by Ernst L. Freud and Heinrich Meng. Translated by Eric Mosbacher. New York: Basic Books, 1963.

———. 2014. *Sigmund Freud, Oskar Pfister: Briefwechsel 1909-1939*. Edited by Isabelle Noth. Zürich: Theologischer Verlag Zürich, 2014.

———. *The Standard Edition of the Complete Psychological Works of Sigmund Freud*, vols. 1–24. Translated and edited by James Strachey, in collaboration with Anna Freud, assisted by Alix Strachey and Alan Tyson. London: Hogarth Press, 1981.
———. *Tafsīr al-aḥlām*. Translated by Mustafa Safwan and reviewed by Mustafa Ziywar. Cairo: Dar al-Maʿārif, 2004.
Garrigues, Jean-Miguel. *Maxime le Confesseur: La charité, avenir divin de l'homme*. Paris: Beauchesne, 1976.
al-Ghazālī, Abū Ḥāmid. *Kitāb dhikr al-mawt wa ma baʿdahu*. Book 40 of *Iḥyāʾ ʿulūm al-dīn*. Beirut: Dār al-Kutub al-ʿIlmiyya, n.d.
———. *The Niche of Lights* [*Mishkāt al-anwār*]. Translated by David Buchman. Provo, Utah: Brigham Young University Press, 1998.
———. *The Remembrance of Death and the Afterlife*. Translated by T. J. Winter. Cambridge: Islamic Texts Society, 1989.
———. *Tahāfut al-falāsifa*. Cairo: Dār al-Maʿārifa, 1966.
———. *On Vigilance and Self Examination. Kitāb al-murāqaba wa'l-muḥāsaba, Book 38 of The Revival of the Religious Sciences, Iḥyā ʿulūm al-dīn*. Translated with notes by Anthony F. Shaker. Cambridge: Islamic Texts Society, 2015.
Glover, Edward. *Freud or Jung*. London: George Allen, 1950.
———. *Technique de la psychanalyse*. Translated by Camille Laurin. Paris: Presses Universitaires de France, 1958.
———. *The Technique of Psychoanalysis*. New York: International Universities Press, 1955.
Grafton, David. *The Contested Origins of the 1865 Arabic Bible*. Leiden: Brill, 2015.
"St. Greogory Palamas," Special Issue Series in *Analogia: The Pemptousia Journal for Theological Studies*, vols. 3–6, 2017–2019.
Gregory Palamas. *Défense des saints hésychastes*. Translated by John Meyendorff. Leuven: Spicilegium sacrum lovaniense, 1973.
———. "Homélie sur la Présentation de la Vierge." Translated by John Meyendorff. *Contacts: revue française de l'orthodoxie* 25 (1959): 22–23.
———. *Saint Gregory Palamas: The Homilies*. 3rd ed. Edited and translated by Christopher Veniamin. Essex: Mount Thabor Publishing, 2022.
———. "al-Ṣūra al-ilāhiyya fī al-insān ladā ghrīghūrīus bālāmās." Translated by Patriarch Ilyās Muʿawaad. *al-Nashra al-baṭrīarkiyya* (December 1973): n.p.
———. *Tou en hagiois patros hemōn Grēgoriou, archiepiskopou Thessalonikēs, tou Palama Homiliai XXII*. Edited by Sophoklēs Oikonomos. Athens: Typois Ph. Karampinē and K. Vapha, 1861.

Grehan, James. *Twilight of the Saints: Everyday Religion in Ottoman Syria and Palestine.* New York: Oxford University Press, 2014. https://doi.org/10.1093/acprof:oso/9780199373031.001.0001.

Guy, Jean-Claudes. *Paroles des anciens: Apophtegmes des Pères du désert.* Paris: Éditions du Seuil, 1976.

———. *Recherches sur la tradition grecque des Apophthegmata Patrum.* Bruxelles: Société des Bollandistes, 1962.

Haddad, Gibril Fouad. "Beautiful Names of Allah (al-Asmāʾ al-Ḥusnā)." In *Integrated Encyclopedia of the Qurʾān.* Accessed December 28, 2022. https://online.iequran.com/articles/B/49.

Hamori, A. "Al-Mutanabbī." In *Abbasid Belles Lettres.* Edited by Julia Ashtiany, 300–314. Cambridge: Cambridge University Press, 1990. https://doi.org/10.1017/CHOL9780521240161.019.

Hanna, Loay. "The Famous Smith-Van Dyck Bible of 1860: Nothing Else but a Polished Re-Edition of the Orthodox Gospels?" *Parole de l'Orient* 42 (2016): 255–270.

Hausherr, Irénée. *Direction spirituelle en Orient autrefois.* Rome: Pont. Institutum Orientalium Studiorum, 1955.

———. *La méthode d'oraison hésychaste*, Orientalia christiana 9, 2, no. 36. Rome: Pontificium Institutum Orientalium Studiorum, 1927.

———. *Noms du Christ et voies d'oraison.* Rome: Pont. Institutum Orientalium Studiorum, 1960.

Hausherr, Irénée, ed. *Les leçons d'un contemplatif: Le traité de l'oraison d'Évagre le Pontique.* Paris: Beauchesne, 1960.

Hauter, Ashwak. "Reconstructing the Community, Reconstructing the Image: Refuge in Islam in Yemen and Lacan After Islam." *European Journal of Psychoanalysis* 10, no. 1 (2023).

Ḥaydar, Shafīq. *Tarjamāt qiyāmiyya.* Beirut: Taʿāwuniyya al-Nūr al-Urthūdhuksiyya, 2017.

Heidegger, Martin. *Plato's Sophist.* Translated by Richard Rojcewicz and André Schuwer. Bloomington: Indiana University Press, 2003.

Hesychios the Priest. *On Watchfulness and Holiness.* In Palmer et al. (eds.) *The Philokalia*, vol. 1. London: Faber & Faber, 1979.

Ibn Abī al-Dunyā, *al-Muntaqā min kitāb al-ruhbān.* Maktaba al-Shāmila. https://shamela.org.

Ibn al-Anbārī, Abu Bakr. *Kitāb al-aḍādd.* Edited by Muhammad Abū al-Faḍal Ibrāhīm. Beirut: al-Maktaba al-ʿAṣriyya, 1987.

Ibn al-ʿArabī. *Fuṣūṣ al-ḥikam.* Beirut: *Dār al-Kitāb al-ʿArabī*, n.d.

Ibn Kathīr. *Tafsīr al-qurʾān al-ʿaẓīm.* Accessed December 2022. https://www.altafsir.com.

Ibn Khaldun. *The Muqaddimah: An Introduction to History*. 3 vols. Translated by Franz Rosenthal. Princeton, NJ: Bollingen Series, 1956.
Ibn al-Muqaffaʿ. *Kitāb Kalīlah wa-Dimnah*. Beirut: Dār al-Āfāq al-Jadīdah, 1978.
Ibn Sīnā. *al-Shifāʾ*. Cairo: Al-Maṭba'ah al-Amīrīyah, 1952.
Ilyās (Muʿawwad). *al-Ābāʾ al-rusūliyyūn*. Tripoli, Lebanon: Manshūrāt al-Nūr, 1982.
Isaac the Syrian. *Ascetical Homilies of Saint Isaac the Syrian*. 2nd ed. Boston: Holy Transfiguration Monastery, 2011.
———. *Nusukīyyāt*. Translated by Isḥaq ʿAṭāllāh. Tripoli, Lebanon: Manshūrāt al-Nūr, 1983.
Isṭfān, Gregorios, *Aʿmidat al-īmān al-urthūdhuksī*. Tripoli, Lebanon: Saint Gregory Palamas Publications, 2018.
Jabbour, Spiro. "Classification et Explication des *ad'dad*: d'après le *Kitâb al-Ad'dâd d'*Al-Anbârî." In *L'ambivalence dans la culture arabe*, edited by Jean-Paul Charnay and Jacques Berque, 65–80. Paris: Éditions Anthropos, 1967.
———. "L'interprétation psychanalytique des *ad'dad*." In *L'ambivalence dans la culture arabe*, edited by Jean-Paul Charnay and Jacques Berque, 296–302. Paris: Éditions Anthropos, 1967.
———. *Maʿnā huwa allāh fa-inhazamū*. Beirut: n.p., 1996.
———. "Munāqashāt ʿan fiqh al-lugha wa-l-taḍādd fī al-lugha." *al-Maʿrifa* (November 1981): 184–189.
———. *al-Muzayyafūn*, Tripoli, Lebanon: Maktaba al-Sāi'ḥ, 1983.
———. *al-Qaddīs samaʿān al-ʿamūdī*. Aleppo: Muṭrāniyya Ḥalab, 1992.
———. *Qānūn yasūʿ*. Latakia: Muṭrāniyya al-Lādhiqīya, 1995.
———. *Qird am insān?* Tripoli, Lebanon: al-Manshūrāt al-Jāmiʿah, 1983.
———. *Rūḥāniyyat al-kanīsa al-urthūdhuksiyya*, [original publication date 2004?]. Accessed online: https://www.alsiraj.org/blog/archives/1464.
———. *Sirr al-tadbīr al-ilāhī: al-tajassud*. Tripoli, Lebanon: al-Manshūrāt al-Urthūdhuksiyya, 1980.
———. *al-Tajalliyāt fī dustūr al-īmān*. Latakia: Muṭrāniyyat al-Lādhiqīya, 1995.
———. *Fī al-tawba*. Tripoli, Lebanon: Maktabat al-Sāi'ḥ, 1997.
———. "Yasūʿ al-masīḥ ʿand al-ābāʾ." *Majlat al-Nūr* (May 1978): 17–18.
———. *Yasūʿ am yhwh?*. Tripoli, Lebanon: al-Manshūrāt al-Urthūdhuksiyya, 1997.
Jameson, Fredric. "The Vanishing Mediator: Narrative Structure in Max Weber." *New German Critique* 1, no. 1 (1973): 52–89. https://doi.org/10.2307/487630.

al-Jawharī, Abū Naṣr Ismā'īl ibn Ḥammād, and Muḥammad ibn Abī Bakr Rāzī. *Mukhtār al-ṣiḥāḥ*. Bayrūt: Maktabah Lubnān, 1985.
John Climacus. *The Ladder of Divine Ascent*. Translated by Lazarus Moore. Boston: Holy Transfiguration Monastery, 2012.
———. *al-Sullam ilā allāh*. Dayr al-Ḥarf: Monastery of Mār Jirjis, 1989.
John of Damascus. *Three Treatises on the Divine Images*. Translated by Andrew Louth. Crestwood, NY: St. Vladimir's Seminary Press, 2003.
Jones, Ernest. "The Early Development of Female Sexuality [1927]." In *Female Sexuality: The Early Psychoanalytic Controversies*, edited by Russell Grigg, Dominique Hecq, and Craig Smith, 133–145. London: Routledge, 1999.
Jugie, Martin. "'Palamas, Grégoire' and 'Palamite (controverse).'" In *Dictionnaire de théologie catholique*, vol. 11, part 2, 1735–1818. Paris.
———. *Theologia dogmatica Christianorum Orientalium ab Ecclesia catholica dissidentium*. Paris: Letouzey et Ané, 1926–1935.
Kallistos and Ignatios Xanthopoulos, "Mi'awiyya al-rūḥiyya." In *Fīlūkāliyā: al-ābā' al-zāhidīn*, vol 1. Translated by Ḥabīb Bāshā. Faraya, Lebanon: al-Manshūrāt al-Qiyāma, 1992.
Kamāl, Ribḥī. *al-Taḍādd fī daw' al-lughat al-sāmīyya: dirāsat muqārina*. Beirut: Dār al-Nahḍa al-'Arabiyya, 1975.
Kapila, Shruti. "The 'Godless' Freud and His Indian Friends: An Indian Agenda for Psychoanalysis." In *Psychiatry and Empire*, edited by Sloan Mahone and Megan Vaughan. Basingstoke, UK: Palgrave Macmillan, 2007.
al-Kāshānī, 'Abd al-Razzāq. *Iṣṭilāḥāt al-ṣūfiyya*. Edited by 'Abd al-'Āl Shāhīn. Cario: Dār al-Fanān, 1992.
———. *Sharḥ al-qashānī 'alā fuṣūṣ al-ḥikam*. Beirut: Dār al-Kutub al-'Ilmiyya, 2007.
Kassatly, Houda. *La communauté monastique de Deir el Harf*. Balamand, Lebanon: Université de Balamand, 1996.
Kesel, Marc De. *Eros and Ethics: Reading Jacques Lacan's Seminar VII*. Translated by Sigi Jottkandt. Albany: State University of New York Press, 2009.
Khanna, Ranjana. *Dark Continents: Psychoanalysis and Colonialism*. Durham, NC: Duke University Press, 2003.
Khodr, Georges. *Law ḥakaytu masrā al-ṭufūla*. Beirut: Ta'āwuniyya al-Nūr al-Urthūdhuksiyya, 1989.
———. *al-Quds*. Beirut: Ta'āwuniyya al-Nūr al-Urthūdhuksiyya, 2003.
———. *The Ways of Childhood*. Translated by Nuha Jurayj. Crestwood, NY: St. Vladimir's Seminary Press, 2016.
Kirchmeyer, Jean "Grecque (Église)." In *Dictionnaire de spiritualité ascétique et mystique*, edited by Marcel Viller, Ferdinand Cavallera, and Joseph de Guibert. Paris: G. Beauchesne, 1932.

al-Kitāb al-muqaddas: al-ʿahd al-jadīd. n.p.: Orthodox Archdiocese of Baghdad, Kuwait and Dependencies, 2002.

Koder, Johannes, ed. *Syméon Le Nouveau Théologien, Hymnes,* vol. 2. Translated by Louis Neyrand. Sources Chrétiennes 174. Paris: Cerf, 1971.

Kyriakos, Ephraim. "Visite de Mgr Ephrem de Tripoli à l'Institut Saint-Serge 1ère partie." *Institut de théologie orthodoxe Saint-Serge*. May 17, 2011. Video, 33:51. https://vimeo.com/23987936.

Lacan, Jacques. *The Four Fundamental Concepts of Psychoanalysis*. Translated by Alan Sheridan. New York: W. W. Norton, 1977.

———. "Kant with Sade." Translated by James B. Swenson. *October* 51 (1989): 55–75. https://doi.org/10.2307/778891.

———. "In Memory of Ernest Jones: On His Theory of Symbolism." In *Écrits*. Translated by Bruce Fink. New York: W. W. Norton, 2006.

———. "Presentation on Psychical Causality." In *Écrits*. Translated by Bruce Fink. New York: W. W. Norton, 2006.

———. *The Seminar of Jacques Lacan, Book II: The Ego in Freud's Theory and in the Techniques of Psychoanalysis, 1954–1955*. Edited by Jacques-Alain Miller. Translated by Sylvana Tomaselli. New York: W. W. Norton, 1991.

———. *The Seminar of Jacques Lacan, Book VII: The Ethics of Psychoanalysis, 1959–1960*. Edited by Jacques-Alain Miller. Translated by Dennis Porter. New York: W. W. Norton, 1992.

———. *The Seminar of Jacques Lacan, Book VIII: Transference, 1960–1961*. Edited by Jacques-Alain Miller. Translated by Bruce Fink. Cambridge: Polity, 2015.

———. *The Seminar of Jacques Lacan, Book XX: On Feminine Sexuality: The Limits of Love and Knowledge, 1972–1973*. Edited by Jacques-Alain Miller. Translated by Bruce Fink. New York: W. W. Norton, 1999.

Lamy, Thomas Joseph, ed. *Sancti Ephraem Syri: Hymni et sermones*. 4 vols. Piscataway, NJ: Gorgias Press, 2011.

Lane, Edward William. "خل." In *Arabic–English Lexicon* [1867]. Accessed August 31, 2023. http://arabiclexicon.hawramani.com.

———."نفس." In *Arabic–English Lexicon* [1867]. Accessed February 21, 2023. http://arabiclexicon.hawramani.com.

———. "نفر." In *Arabic–English Lexicon* [1867]. Accessed February 21, 2023. http://arabiclexicon.hawramani.com.

Laplanche, Jean, and Jean-Bertrand Pontalis. *The Language of Psycho-analysis*. Translated by Donald Nicholson-Smith. New York: W. W. Norton, 1973 [1967].

Leirvik, Oddbjørn. "Conscience in Arabic and the Semantic History of 'Ḍamīr.'" *Journal of Arabic and Islamic Studies* 9 (March 2017): 18–36. https://doi.org/10.5617/jais.4595.

Lossky, Vladimir. *Eckhart's Apophatic Theology: Knowing the Unknowable God.* Translated by Sophrony and Jonathan Sutton. Cambridge, UK : James Clarke, 2024.

———. *Essai sur la théologie mystique de l'Église d'Orient.* Paris: Aubier, 1944.

———. *The Mystical Theology of the Eastern Church.* Crestwood, NY: St. Vladimir's Seminary Press, 1976.

———. "La notion des 'analogies' chez Denys le pseudo-Areopagite." *Recherches des sciences philosophiques et religeuses* 28 (1939): 204–221.

———. "Théologie négative et connaissance de Dieu chez Maître Eckhart." PhD diss. Paris: Vrin, 1960.

———. *The Vision of God.* Translated by Asheleigh Moorhouse. London: Faith Press, 1963.

Loudovikos, Nikolaos. *Psykanalysē kai Orthodoxē theologia.* Athens: Harmos, 2003.

Louth, Andrew. *The Origins of the Christian Mystical Tradition: From Plato to Denys.* 2nd ed. Oxford: Oxford University Press, 2007.

MacDonald, D. B., "Ilhām." In Various Authors & Editors (ed.), *Encyclopaedia of Islam First Edition Online.* Brill, 2012. doi: https://doi.org/10.1163/2214-871X_ei1_SIM_3158.

Maximos the Confessor. *The Ascetic Life: The Four Centuries on Charity.* Translated by P. Sherwood. New York: Newman Press, 1955.

———. *Centuries sur la charité.* Translated by Joseph Pegon. Paris: Éditions du Cerf, 1945.

———. *On Difficulties in the Church Fathers: The Ambigua.* 2 vols. Edited and translated by Maximos Constas. Cambridge, MA: Harvard University Press. 2014.

———. *On Difficulties in Sacred Scripture: The Responses to Thalassios.* Translated by Maximos Constas. Washington, D.C.: The Catholic University of America Press, 2018.

———. *Four Hundred Texts on Love.* In Palmer et al. (eds.) *The Philokalia*, vol. 2. London: Faber & Faber, 1981.

Meyendorff, John. *Introduction à l'étude de Grégoire Palamas.* Paris: Éditions du Seuil, 1959.

Mian, Ali Altaf. "Genres of Desire: The Erotic in Deobandī Islam." *History of Religions* 59, no. 2 (2019): 108–145.

Migne, Jacques-Paul, ed. *Patrologiae Cursus Completus, Series Latina.* 221 vols. Paris: Imprimerie Catholique, 1844–1855.

Migne, Jacques-Paul, ed. *Patrologiae Cursus Completus, Series Graeca.* 162 vols. Paris: Imprimerie Catholique, 1857–1866.

Mikhail, Arsenius (ed.). *Guides to the Eucharist in Medieval Egypt: Three Arabic commentaries on the Coptic Liturgy*. New York: Fordham University Press, 2022.

Moreschini, Claudio, ed. *Grégoire de Nazianze Discours*, 38–41. Translated by Paul Gallay. Sources Chrétiennes 358. Paris: Cerf, 1990.

Mutanabbī, Abū al-Ṭayyib, 'Alī ibn Aḥmad Wāḥidī, and Friedrich Heinrich Dieterici. *Dīwān Abī al-Ṭayyib al-Mutanabbī*. Berlīn: Baghdād, Maktabat al-Muthannā, 1967.

Nicholson, R., and G. C. Anawati. "Ittiḥād". In P. Bearman (ed.), *Encyclopaedia of Islam New Edition Online* (*EI-2 English*), Brill, 2012. doi:http://dx.doi.org/10.1163/1573-3912_islam_COM_0398.

Nikodimos and Makarios, eds. *The Philokalia: The Complete Text*. 5 vols. Translated and edited by G. E. H. Palmer, Philip Sherrard, and Kallistos Ware. London: Faber & Faber, 1979–2023.

———. *Philokalia tōn hierōn neptikōn*. 5 vols. Edited by Archimandrite Epiphanios Theodōropoulos. Athens: Astir/Papadimitriou. 1957–1963.

Odabaei, Milad. "Modernity from Elsewhere: Psychoanalysis, Ethnography, and Speculative Horizons of Self-Assertion." *Comparative Studies of South Asia, Africa and the Middle East* 42, no. 1 (2022): 270–277. https://doi.org/10.1215/1089201X-9698320.

The Orthodox Youth Movement. *Anṭākiyya tatajaddad: shahādāt wa nuṣūṣ* (1943–1992). Tripoli: Manshūrāt al-Nūr, 1950.

Pandolfo, Stefania. *Impasse of the Angels: Scenes from a Moroccan Space of Memory*. Chicago: University of Chicago Press, 1997.

———. *Knot of the Soul: Madness, Psychoanalysis, Islam*. Chicago: University of Chicago Press, 2018.

Pentovsky, Aleksei, ed. *The Pilgrim's Tale*. Translated by T. Allan Smith. New York: Paulist Press, 1999.

Pfister, Oskar. *Christianity and Fear*. Translated by W. H. Johnston. London: G. Allen & Unwin, 1948.

———. *Das Christentum und die Angst: Eine religionspsychologische, historische und religionshygienische Untersuchung*. Zürich: Artemis, 1944.

———. *Die psychanalytische Methode: Eine erfahrungswissenschaftlich-systematische Darstellung*. Leipzig: J. Klinkhardt, 1913.

———. *The Psychoanalytic Method*. Translated by Charles Rockwell Payne. Abingdon, England: Routledge, 1999.

Places, Édouard des. *Diadoque de Photicé: Œuvres spirituelles*. Sources Chrétiennes 5. Paris: Cerf, 1953.

Plautus. *Amphitryon. The Comedy of Asses. The Pot of Gold. The Two Bacchises. The Captives*. Edited and translated by Wolfgang De Melo. Cambridge, MA: Harvard University Press, 2011.

Qayṣar, Ibn Kātib, *Commentary on the Apocalypse of John.* In Stephen J. Davis, T. C. Schmidt, and Shawqi Talia (eds.), *Revelation 1–3 in Christian Arabic Commentary: John's First Vision and the Letters to the Seven Churches.* New York: Fordham University Press, 2019.

Rafīq, ʿAjam. *Mūsūʿat musṭalaḥāt al-taṣawwuf al-islāmī.* Beirut: Maktaba Lubnān Nāshirūn, 1999.

Rank, Otto. "Die Don Juan-Gestalt: Ein Beitrag zum Verständnis der sozialen Funktion der Dichtkunst." *Imago* 8 (1922): 142–196.

Regnault, Lucien. *Les Pères du désert: à travers leurs apophtegmes.* Sablé-sur-Sarthe: Abbaye Saint-Pierre de Solesmes, 1987.

———. *Les Sentences des Pères du désert: collection alphabétique.* Solesmes: Abbaye Saint-Pierre de Solesmes, 1981.

Renard, John. "Images of Abraham in the Writings of Jalāl Ad-Dīn Rūmī." *Journal of the American Oriental Society* 106, no. 4 (1986): 633–640. https://doi.org/10.2307/603527.

Riou, Alain. *Le monde et l'Église selon Maxime le Confesseur.* Paris: Beauchesne, 1973.

Rippin, Andrew. "Waswas." In *The Qurʾan: An Encyclopedia*, edited by Oliver Leaman. London: Routledge, 2006.

Rosso, Corrado. *Procès à La Rochefoucauld et à la maxime.* Pisa: Editrice Libreria Goliardica, 1986.

Russell, Norman. *Gregory Palamas and the Making of Palamism in the Modern Age.* Oxford: Oxford University Press, 2019.

———. *Gregory Palamas: The Hesychast Controversy and the Debate with Islam.* Liverpool: Liverpool University Press, 2022.

Rustum, Asad. *Kanīsa madīna allāh anṭākiyya al-ʿuẓmā.* 3 vols. Damascus: Batrīarkiyya Anṭākiyya wa-sā'ir al-Mashriq li-l-Rūm al-Urthūdhuks, 2022.

Safouan Moustapha. *Pourquoi le monde arabe n'est pas libre: Politique de l'écriture et terrorisme religieux.* Paris: Denoel, 2008.

———. *Why Are the Arabs Not Free? The Politics of Writing.* London: Wiley-Blackwell, 2007.

Schmemann, Alexander. *Great Lent: Journey to Pascha.* Crestwood, New York: St. Vladimir's Seminary Press, 1974.

———. *al-Ṣawm al-kabīr.* Translated by Ibrahīm Sarrūj. Tripoli, Lebanon: al-Manshūrāt al-Urthūdhuksiyya, 1999.

Seyed-Gohrab, A. A. (Ali Asghar). *Laylī and Majnūn: Love, Madness, and Mystic Longing in Niẓāmī's Epic Romance.* Leiden: Brill, 2003.

al-Shābushtī. *The Book of Monasteries.* Translated and edited by Hilary Kilpatrick. New York: New York University Press, 2023

Shah, Mustafa. "Iḥsān." In K. Fleet, G. Krämer, D. Matringe, J. Nawas and D. J. Stewart (eds.), *Encyclopaedia of Islam Three Online*. Brill, 2020. doi: https://doi.org/10.1163/1573-3912_ei3_COM_32381.

al-Shidyāq, Aḥmad Fāris. *al-Kutub al-muqaddasa wa-hiya kutub al-ʿahd al-ʿatīq wa-l-ʿahd al-jadīd li-rabbinā yasūʿ al-masīḥ*. Tripoli, Lebanon: Maktabat al-Sā'iḥ, 1983 [1857].

Smith, Michael B. Translator's Note to *The Mystic Fable*, vol. 1, by Michel de Certeau. Translated by Michael B. Smith. Chicago: University of Chicago Press, 1992.

Sophrony (Sakharov). *Muʿāyana allāh kamā huwa*. Translated by Hudā Fu'ād Zakkā. Manshūrāt al-Nūr, 1989.

———. *We Shall See Him as He Is*. Essex: Stavropegic Monastery of St. John the Baptist, 1988.

Soyubol, Kutluğhan. "Turkey Psychoanalyzed, Psychoanalysis Turkified: The Case of İzzettin Şadan." *Comparative Studies of South Asia, Africa, and the Middle East* 38, no. 1 (2018): 57–72. https://doi.org/10.1215/1089201x-4389979.

Stethatos, Niketas. *The Life of Saint Symeon the New Theologian*. Translated by Richard P. H. Greenfield. Cambridge, MA: Harvard University Press, 2013.

Stetkevych, Suzanne Pinckney. *The Poetics of Islamic Legitimacy: Myth, Gender, and Ceremony in the Classical Arabic Ode*. Bloomington: Indiana University Press, 2002.

Swanson, Mark. "Ibn Sabbā'." *Christian-Muslim Relations: A Bibliographical History*. Edited by David Thomas et al., 4:918–923. Leiden: Brill, 2009–2016.

Symeon the New Theologian, *Divine Eros: Hymns of Saint Symeon the New Theologian*. Translated by Daniel K. Griggs. Crestwood, NY: St. Vladimir's Seminary Press, 2010.

Tannous, Jack. *The Making of the Medieval Middle East: Religion, Society, and Simple Believers*. Princeton, NJ: Princeton University Press, 2018.

Thomas, David, ed. *Christian-Muslim Relations: A Bibliographical History*. 52 vols. Leiden: Brill, 2009–2025.

Toscano, Alberto. *Fanaticism: On the Uses of an Idea*. London: Verso, 2010.

Treiger, Alexander. "Al-Ghazālī's 'Mirror Christology' and Its Possible East-Syriac Sources." *The Muslim World* 101, no. 4 (2011): 698–713. https://doi.org/10.1111/j.1478-1913.2011.01370.x.

———. *Inspired Knowledge in Islamic Thought: Al-Ghazālī's Theory of Mystical Cognition and Its Avicennian Foundation*. London: Routledge, 2011.

———. "Mutual Influences and Borrowings." In *Routledge Handbook on Christian–Muslim Relations*, edited by David Thomas, 194–206. London: Routledge, 2018. https://doi.org/10.4324/9781315745077-22.

al-Tunisī, Muhammad Khalīfa. "Al-anāniyya wa al-athara." *al-ʿarabiyya* 291 (February 1983): 162–163.

Vasiliĭ [Basile Krivochéine]. *Dans la lumière du Christ: Saint Syméon le Nouveau Théologien 949–1022: Vie, spiritualité, doctrine.* Chevetogne, Belgique: Editions de Chevetogne, 1980.

Verhovskoy, Sergei. *Бог и человек: Учение о Боге и Богопознанил в свете православииа.* New York: Chekhov Publishing House, 1956.

Vlachos, Hierotheos. *Orthodox Psychotherapy: The Science of the Fathers.* Translated by Esther Williams. Levadhia, Greece: Birth of the Theotokos Monastery, 1994.

Waitz, Carl, and Theresa Clement Tisdale. *Lacanian Psychoanalysis and Eastern Orthodox Christian Anthropology in Dialogue.* New York: Routledge, 2022.

Ward, Benedicta. *The Sayings of the Desert Fathers: The Alphabetical Collection.* London: Mowbrays, 1975.

Wedeen, Lisa. *Ambiguities of Domination: Politics, Rhetoric, and Symbols in Contemporary Syria.* Chicago: University of Chicago Press, 2015.

Weiss, Max. "Genealogies of Baʿthism: Michel ʿAflaq Between Personalism and Arabic Nationalism." *Modern Intellectual History* 17, no. 4 (2020): 1193–1224. https://doi.org/10.1017/S1479244319000088.

Wensinck, A. J., "Niyya." In P. Bearman (ed.), *Encyclopaedia of Islam New Edition Online (EI-2 English)*. Brill, 2012. doi: https://doi.org/10.1163/1573-3912_islam_SIM_5935.

Wittgenstein, Ludwig. *The Blue and Brown Books.* Oxford: Blackwell, 1958.

———. *Philosophical Investigations.* 4th ed. Translated by G. E. M. Anscombe, P. M. S. Hacker, and Joachim Schulte. Chichester: Wiley-Blackwell, 2009.

Zander, Louis. *Dostoïevsky: Le problème du bien.* Paris: Correa, 1946.

Zecher, Jonathan L. *The Role of Death in the Ladder of Divine Ascent and the Greek Ascetic Tradition.* Oxford: Oxford University Press, 2015.

INDEX

ʿAbdullah, Youssef, xvi
Abel, Karl, xxiii
Abraham: as beloved of God (*khalīl allāh*), xxxiv–xxxvii, 44n71; at Christ's descent into hell, 15; and life in the spirit, 68
absolution, xxx, 138
Adam: at Christ's descent into hell, 15; Fall of, 56, 113–114; as first human, 40, 114; human corruption through Adamic error, 40–41, 46, 56, 106, 114, 118; human as son of, 38; Jesus Christ as other, 40; as prophet, xxxiii. *See also* Adam and Eve; paradise
Adam and Eve: creation of, 8–9; Fall from paradise, 8–9, 26, 29, 44–45, 63, 118; as progenitors of the human race, 131n3. *See also* Adam; paradise
affective communion, 81–82
affects, xxviii, xxxviii, 5–6, 82: affective drives of the psyche, xli; affective instinct, 111; analysis and, 111, 128, 133; animals and, 133; the chest and, 127; children and, 12; counterfeit, 92; fetal, 32; love as strongest of the, 77–78; monastics and, 82; passions as capacity for, 159; prayer and, 127; psychosomatic medicine and, 122; repression in marriage and, 122–123; susceptibility to, 11; transference and, 112, 133; victory over evil, 123
ambivalence (*taḍādd*), 161: Bedouins and, 1n17; children and, 32–34, 36–37; contronyms and, 54–55; of the drive, xxv–xxvi; guilt and, xxv–xxvi; the heart and, 39n31; instinctual drives and, xxvii; in Jung and Freud, xlviin8; language as manifestation of, xxv, 54–55; overdetermination as, 110n66; social relation and, 33–34, 36, 50; between spiritual elder and monastic, 76; spiritual struggle as, xxvi; spiritual tepidity as, 69n8, 76
Ambrose (of Optina), 131n2, 141n26
analysis. *See* psychoanalytic therapy
Anawati, G.C., xlixn13
Andrew of Crete, 68
Andrew of Damascus, 74, 156
Anthony the Great, 76, 85–87, 152
anthropology, xxix, xxxin51, xlvin6
Antiochian Orthodox Church. *See* Patriarchate of Antioch
anxiety, 11n2
aphanisis (*shuʿūr bi-l-talāshī*), 24, 25n13
apostasy, 17, 143
apostles: apostolic work, 146; authority to loose and bind transgressions, 137; baptism of, 10. *See also individual apostles*
appetitive part of the psyche (Ar., *al-qism al-shahwāniyya*; Gr., *to thymikon*), 160: in affective life, 122; in conflict with the mind, 43; evil and, 43; intelligibility and, 107; subduing the, 100; transference into divine love, 101, 108–110, 121, 128, 144; union between incensive and, 123, 128
Aquinas, Thomas, 6n11
Arabic literature, 52–53, 77, 80
Arida, Robert, xxxvii
Aristotle, xxiii, xlvii, 6n11, 102
Arnaldez, R., 47n83
Arsenius the Great, 95
Asad, Talal, xi, xxxin49

asceticism (*zuhd*), 159, 161: abstinence and, 85n46; confessors and, 18; consciousness and the unconscious in, 96; controlling the passions and, 2–3; in the Eastern Mediterranean, xxix; food and, 95; higher and lower powers and, 84–85; martyrdom and, 86–87, 91–92; martyrdom of the conscience and, 87n52; Maximos the Confessor and, 112–113; monastics and, 66, 72–73, 80–81; mysticism, sufism, and, xlixn12; participation in God's energies and, 41n46; pleasure principle and, 113; purification of the conscience and, 105; restriction of the body and, 95–96, 118; sense of guilt and, 25; sleep and, 95; transference and, 96; tears of repentance and, 75; watchfulness and, 89n59
al-Assad, Hafez, xv–xvi, 53n102
ʿAtāllāh, Isḥāq, 135
Athanasius the Great, 86–87
atomic bomb, xxiv, 4–5
attachment: and ardor, 95, 132; children's, to milk and warmth, 31; to food, 118; to the good, 106; of mother to son, 79n34; monastics and, 95; non-preponderance of, 50; religious, xxxi; to worldly things, 72, 103
Attalus (martyr), 85

Balamand Monastery (Lebanon), xvii
Balthasar, Hans Urs von, 41–43
baptism: as birth, 47, 105; of blood (martyrdom), 87, 144–145; confession and, 10, 13; Holy Spirit and, 47; joy as, 139; of martyrdom, 87, 144–145; and Pentecost, xlv, 10, 15; and repentance, 139, 142; of repentance, 10, 144–145; of tears of repentance, 87, 144–145
Bardawil, Fadi A., xviiin8
Basil the Great, 9n3, 37, 86, 155
Batatu, Hanna, xvin2
Beatitudes, 68, 75
beauty, 25, 123
Bedouins, ln17
Benedict the Latin, 155
Benevich, Grigory, 44
Benjamin, Walter, xi–xii
Benslama, Fethi, xxxiin52
Berdyaev, Nicholas, 6n11
Berque, Jacques, 54
Bitimios (Desert Father), 87
body (*jism, jasad*), 160: affectivity and the, 122–123; chastity and the, 123; children and the, 9; control of the, 62, 95, 123; deterioration and the, 29; image of the human and the, 12n6; as living sacrifice, 102–103; participation in transfiguration, 123; passions and the, 30, 42, 56, 62–63, 65, 68, 72, 83–84, 88, 95, 97, 108, 112–114, 118; perversion of the, 122; resurrection of the, 39; self-love and the, 62; spiritual struggle and the, 58; the unconscious and the, 11. *See also* body and psyche; body and soul; body and spirit
body and psyche: interrelation between the, xlix; the senses and the formation of the psyche, 5; unity of the, 121–122. *See also* body; psyche
body and soul: interrelation of the, 118, 122, 125, 145, 150; participation in the coming age, 99; theosis and the, xxxviii. *See also* body; soul
body and spirit: conflict between the, 57, 62, 65–66, 72, 103; connection through the passible part of the psyche, 103, 121–122; creation of the, 26, 31; death and the, 4, 6, 8, 29; development of the, 56; interrelation of the, 5, 6n11, 122–123; purification of the, 128; theosis and the, xxxviii; unity of the, 6, 119. *See also* body; spirit
Bosch, Hieronymus, xxxixn77
Bowman, Bradley, xxxviiin75
Bradshaw, David, xxin15, 101n21
bravery: asceticism and, 95, 159; confession and, xxiv–xxv, 23–25, 135; Jesus Christ and, 23; monastics and, 83–85, 130, 137, 159; steadfastness (*ṣumūd*) and, xxiv. *See also* courageous speech
breastfeeding, 31–32, 37, 124
Breuer, Josef, 137n11
Brianchaninov, Ignatius, 21
bribery, 52
Brockelmann, C., xxvin31
Byzantine Empire, xvn1, xxv, 18, 156

Caiaphas, 23
Cain and Abel, 49
Canaanite woman, 144
canon to Jesus Christ, 67
canon of Andrew of Crete (or Damascus), 68, 156
capital, 9n3, 70
Cappadocian Fathers, 155
castration, 24n12
cats, 132–133
Certeau, Michel de, xxxviiin74, xxxix
Chabbi, Jacqeline, 11n2
characterology, xlvii, 149–150
Charnay, Jean-Paul, 54
chest, 159: affects and emotions situated in the, 127; as capaciousness, 83n40, 125; Jesus

Christ's presence in the, 127; spiritual life situated in the, 125
childbearing, 31–32, 43, 45–47, 75, 88n56, 117
childhood: addiction and, 117; ambivalence and, 36; compassion and, 52; psychoanalysis and, xlviii; repression and, 117, 133
childrearing (*tarbiya*), 31, 54, 131–132, 161; coddling and, 116; control and, 78; deprivation and, 117; egoism and, 79; errors in, 49; excessive affection and, 78; freedom and, 78; self-love and, 115–116; sense of guilt and, 56–60; respect in, 78; spiritual development and, 56–57; virtues and, 132. *See also* family; fathers; mothers
children: affectivity and, 12; aggression instinct and, 58, 74, 117, 124; ambivalence and, 32, 34; cheating their parents, 33; coddling and pampering of, 31–32, 34, 116–117; conscience and, 54, 58; cultivation of virtue in, 116–117; destruction and violence by, 31, 49, 132; discontentment and, 3; ego, formation of, xxi, 34n10, 56, 114n79, 115–117; egoism in, 32, 114n79, 115–116; envy in, 116; existential questions and, 1; fearing hunger, 56; ferocity in, 131–132; genetics and, 131; gluttony and, 32; greed and, 32; hypersensitivity in, 60; indulgence of, 37, 58; infatuation with one's, 31; inferiority in, 31–32; ingratitude and, 58; jealousy and, 32, 58, 116; malice and, 32; neurosis and, 60; personality formation and, 12, 54; poor upbringing of, 60; psychological development of, xlvi, 5, 9, 12, 22, 24, 28, 31–32, 36, 54–55, 57, 59, 114–117, 130, 132; repression and, 94, 117–118, 122, 130; restriction of, 3, 31–32, 58; sadism and, 60; self-love and, 115–116; self-punishment and, 60; sense of guilt and, 58–60, 63; sexual instincts and, 74, 110; sexual repression and, 122; spiritual development and, 8–9, 54, 56–57, 59; sublimation and, 110; temperament and, 12, 58, 131; transference and, 132; trauma and, 123–124; vanity and, 32
collective unconscious (*inconscient collectif*), 8
Colliander, Tito, 57
colonialism in the Middle East, xxxi–xxxii
communion. *See* Eucharist
confession (of transgressions), xxiv–xiv, 147, 159–161: absolution and, 138; baptism and, 10, 13; bravery and, xxiv; Catholic, 22; confessors, 18, 131n2; as conversation, 143; martyrdom and, xxiv, 23, 87; monastics and, 87, 94–96, 130–131, 133–135, 138, 145; as object of ridicule, 135; Eucharist and, 146; Jabbour and, xxiv, 142–143; psychoanalytic therapy compared with, 17, 22, 28, 71–72, 94, 130–131; repentance and, 13, 134–135, 137, 139, 143; sense of guilt and, 71, 134; spiritual guidance and, 146; steadfastness and, xxiv; Symeon the New Theologian limiting, 17n23; training for, 135–136, 143; transference and, 146; witnessing to truth and, xxiv. *See also* courageous speech; spiritual elder; spiritual guidance
conscience (*ḍamīr*), 159: across psychoanalysis and spiritual guidance, 134; ambivalence and, 36; ascetic, 131; children and the development of the, 54, 58, 60; confession and the, 24; desire for God and the, 83–84; instincts in conflict with the, 59, 74, 132; martyrdom of, 85; monasticism and, 74; psychoanalysis and the, 22–23; purification of the, 105; repression and the, 28; shame and the, 51; Sufism, 35n11; transference and the, 132; watchfulness and the, xxviii; weakness of the, 30n2; wealth and, 70
consciousness (Ar., *shuʿūr*; Fr., *conscience*), 161: children and, 12, 60, 63; fetal, 5; Freud and, 27n17; hesychastic prayer and, 128n15; repression and, 72, 130, 133; sense of guilt and, xxvn29, 13n11, 60, 63; spiritual guidance and, 94
Constantinople, 18–19, 20n29, 152n1, 154, 156
contronyms (*aḍdād*), xxvi, 54–55, 73n20
Corbin, Henri, xxiii
corruption: the body and, 39–40, 56; capital and, 9; human nature and, 26, 29, 38–48, 106–107; love and, 77; the passions and, 44, 47, 108, 150; speech and, 63; unconscious drives, 114. *See also* incorruption; death
counterfeit, the, xix–xxi, xxvi, xxxvii: capaciousness of the heart, 61n120; Christianity and, xix, xxxii, 70–71, 133; Islam and, 51n99; resemblance and, 12n7; scientists and, 5; social relations and, 33; spiritual struggle and, xix, 71, 140; virtue and, 61, 134
courageous speech, xxvi–xxv, 23–25, 135, 159
creation, 25: of the human, 26, 29
Crete, 154
cure, xxxiv, 74, 110n66, 111, 124, 151
Cyprus, 154

Dalbiez, Roland, xxii
Davis, Stephen J., 96n4, 140n23

death: Adamic error and, 26, 41, 45; asceticism and, 3; as blessing or triumph, 3–4, 74; bodily, 1–2, 8, 29, 45, 63, 113, 141; body as companion until, 132; of Christ, xxix; fear of, 56; Freud and, xxiv; of the hypocrite, 142; martyrs' desire for, 86; for others, 115–116; putting the passions to, 25, 103, 125; spiritual, 29, 45, 64, 149; spiritual struggle continuing until, xxxix, 4; sundering of the body and psyche/spirit in, 6, 121. *See also* martyrdom
death, remembrance of (*dhikr al-mawt*), xxiii, xxiv, 1–7, 92n67, 101, 159
death drive (Ger., *Todestrieb*), 28n22, 62–63, 124n7. *See also* drives
Deseille, Placide (friend of author), 156
Desert Fathers, xlviii, 87–88, 95, 117, 140–141, 152–154. *See also individual names*
Diadochos of Photiki, 80, 81n36, 153: ascetic practice and, 105–106; divine light and, xlv–xlvi; Jesus prayer and, 101n23, 119; martyrdom and, 87; perfect confession and, 87; pleasure principle and, 112; remembrance of God and, 65n2, 101n23; remembrance of Jesus, 101n23
Dimitri of Rostov, 140
discernment (Ar. *tamyīz*; Gr. *diakrisis*), 101, 128n15: martyrdom and, 87n52; in monastic elders, 17, 61, 76, 95; in monastics, 72; as spiritual insight, 1n1, 51n99
disclosure. *See* divine disclosure
dispassion, xlviiin10: asceticism and, xxix; Maximos the Confessor and, 109; passible part of the psyche and, 100, 111n68; spiritual struggle and, 102; transference and, 111n68, 123, 161; watchfulness and, xli
divine disclosure (*tajallī*), xxxviin74, 161: the body and, xxxviii–xxxix; Mount Tabor and, 9n4, 10n1, 100n20, 148n14; spiritual struggle and, xxxviii; transference and, xxviii, 101n21. *See also* transfiguration
divine economy (Ar., *tadbīr ilahī*; Gr., *oikonomia*;), 4, 72, 161
divine energies, participation in the, 41n46, 97
divine fate, 2, 13, 52, 149
divine image: the human and, 8–9, 26, 73, 124n7; Jesus Christ as, 100n20; and likeness, 26; monastics and, 73; lay people and, 73
divine light: disclosure of, 9, 11, 100n20; God as, xlv, lvi, 96–97, 126–127, 149, 161; hesychasm and, xx, xxix, 161; illumination by, xxvii, xlvi, lv–lvi, 15, 87n52, 96–97, 109, 111, 139, 149; witnessing, xx, xxix, 100n20. *See also* transfiguration
Divine Liturgy, 96n3, 148n13
divine names, 7n13, 40n38, 44n68, 59n116
divine Truth (*al-ḥaqq*): xxv, xxxv–xxxvi, 48n91, 107n50
divine witnessing. *See* God, witnessing to
dogs, 132–133
Don Juanism, 70n11, 111
Dorotheos of Gaza, 80
Dostoevsky, Fyodor, 129n19, 131n2, 143
dreams: analysis of, xlvii, 89–90; childhood and, 96; condensation and displacement, xxvi, 90, 96, 110–111; dream-work (Ar., *ʿamal al-aḥlām*; Ger., *Traumarbeit*), xli, 89–90; pleasure and, 89; transference and, xxvii; the unconscious and, 96
drinking, 30
drive (Ar., *gharīza*, *mayl*; Ger., *Trieb*), 114, 116, 160: affective drives, xli; ambivalence and the, xxv, xxvii; death drive (Ger., *Todestrieb*), 28n22, 62–63, 124n7; Freud and the, xxiv; incensive drive (*thymos*), 100–101n21, 110n65, 124n7; instinct and, 117n88; Lacan and, xxiii, 117n88; repression and the, xxxix, 74, 111; sense of guilt and the, xxvi; sexual drive, 69n9, 124n7; sublimation and the, xxvii, 110n21, 111; transference and the, xxvii, xxxviii, 63, 132
Druze, 17n22
Dubilet, Alex, 7n12

East, the, l, 34–35, 50n94, 75, 146
eating, 30, 36–37, 62, 95, 117–118, 132
Eckhart, Meister, 7n12
ecumenical councils, 20, 152
ego (Ar., *al-ana*; Ger., *Ich*), 159, 22–23, 159: ambivalence and the, 34n10; analysis and the, 131; fetal development and the, 5; Freud and the, xxi, 22n4, 27–28, 78n33; libido and the, xxixn42; regression and the, 28; repression and the, 27, 72; self-love and the, xix; spirit and, 11; transcendental, 7n12
Egypt: Desert Fathers of, 95, 117n86, 152, 155–156; Jesus Prayer and, 80–81, 138; translation of Freud in, xxxiii
El Shakry, Omnia, xxn11, xxvin35, xxxi–xxxiv, xxxviiin75, 24n10
elders. *See* spiritual elders
Eldridge, Aaron, xviiin7
Elias, Patriarch, 136
Ephrem the Syrian, 74–75, 80, 88, 90–91: prayer of, 67
Epiphanios (saint), 15
eremitic monasticism, 76
error. *See* transgressions
eternal life, 40–41, 48

ethics, 159: ascetic literature and, xlviii; capital and, 70; child development and, 54–60; conscience and, 22, 28; counterfeit, 61, 99n18, 100, 114; Kant and, 143n31, 150; monastics and, 133; psychoanalytic, xxiii; psychological development and, 54–62; reality principle and, 113n75; repression and, 99–100; social relations and, xxxiii, 30n2, 70; spiritual struggle and, 63; sublimation and, 110; *ṣūfī* nature of, xl, 100; unconscious and, xli, 114
etiquette (*adab*), 33
Eucharist (*al-qurbān*), 160: confession and, 146; confession as eucharistic offering, 23n8; Gregory Palamas and the, 145; Pentecost and, 15; preparation for, 146; repentance and, 91n64, 138–139; 146
Europe, xxiii, xxxii–xxxiii, 49n93, 99n18, 132: inability of Gospels to educate, 4
Eusebius, 85n48
Evagrios Ponticus, xlviii, 152–153: divine witnessing and, 14nn13–14; influence on Gregorios bin al-ʿIbrī, 156; passion and, 49n92; repression and, 99n18, 109; theologians as those who pray, 137; thoughts as evil spirits and, 66
Evdokimov, Paul, 129n19
Ewing, Katherine Pratt, xxxiin51
exile, xxv, 19, 24, 89n60

family: betrayal of, 52–53, 70; child development and, 1, 5, 12, 24, 31–32, 34, 37, 56–62, 80, 115–116, 132; familiarity and, 66–67; marriage and, 79–80n34; monastics and, 84; prodigal son and, 16n19; transference and, 132. *See also* childrearing; fathers; mothers
fasting, xxvi, 66, 80–81, 95, 117–118, 140
fate. *See* divine fate
fathers, 5, 31, 53, 135. *See also* childrearing; family; mothers
Fénichel, Otto, xxii
fetal development: xxiv, xlvi, 5–6, 8–9, 31–32, 38–39, 55–57. *See also* childbearing
films, 49, 129
forgetting, 23, 92n67
forgiveness, 36, 99, 138, 143–144
form of life, xx, xxix, xxxix, 17
formation (*akhlāq*), 12, 77, 159
fornication, 122, 128: by the senses, 129
France, xv, xxiii, xlvin6, li, 85, 155
free association, 22, 27
free will, 41, 45, 48, 60, 71, 105. *See also* gnomic will
Freud, Sigmund, 52n97, 94n1: aggression drive and, 124n7; ambivalence and, xxvii; Anna O. and, 137n11; ascetic literature and, xlviii; Asad and, xxxin49; castration and, 24n12; Catholic confession and, 21–22, 99; Climacus and 128n17; consciousness and, 27n18, 112; death drive and, 28n22, 124n7; dispassion and, xxix; dream analysis and, 89–90, 96n4, 110, 134n8; drive and, 160; ego and, 27nn18–19, 78n33; instinct and, 159; gendered passion and, 77n30; Jung and, xlvii; libido, 112; life instinct and, 124n7; Maximos the Confessor and, 109–114, 128n17; Middle East and, xxxiii; mind and soul and, xxx; narcissism and, 32, 44n70, 114; Palamas and, xxvii; Pfister and, xlvii; pleasure principle and, 34, 112; psychical systems and, 109n63; reaction formations and, xl, 10; religion and, 99; regression and, 28n21; repression and, 130n1; sadism and masochism and, 69n9; sexual instinct and, 124n7; sublimation and, 77n30, 110; superego and, 134n8; suppression and, 130n1; talking cure and, 137; topography of the psyche and, 22–23n4; transference and, xxvii, 96, 111–112, 161; translation of, into Arabic, xxxiii xxxviii; sense of guilt and, 13n11; unconscious and, xxxv, xxxix, xl, 27n17, 112; watchfulness and, xl–xli
Freud, Sigmund, works by: "The Antithetical Meaning of Primary Words", xxiin21, xxiii; *Beyond the Pleasure Principle*, xxi–xxii, xxiv, xxvii, 109n63, 113; *Civilization and Its Discontents*, 51n97; "Dream-work", xxiii; "The Ego and the Id", xxi–xxii, 77n30; *Future of an Illusion*, 99n18; "Group Psychology and the Analysis of the Ego", xxii; *Interpretation of Dreams*, xxiii, 96, 110n66; *Jokes and their Relation to the Unconscious*, xxi; "Mourning and Melancholia", 75n25; "On Narcissism", 32n4; "A Note Upon the 'Mystic Writing-Pad'", 11n5; "Notes Upon a Case of Obsessional Neurosis", 11n2; "Obsessive Actions and Religious Practices", xxvn29; "An Outline of Psychoanalysis", xxviin36; "Some character-types met with in psycho-analytic work", 61n119; *Studies on Hysteria*, 130n1, 137n11; "Thoughts for the Times on War and Death", xxii, xxiv; "Three Essays on the Theory of Sexuality", 69n9, 100n19; "Totem and Taboo", xxiin21; "The Uncanny", xx, 11n2; "The Unconscious", xxi
friendship: betrayal and, 36, 52–53; deference and, 66; loyalty and, 34–35

gambling, 117
Gandhi, Indira, 53
Gandillac, Maurice de, 155
Garrigues, Jean-Miguel, 47n86, 106n45
Gehenna, 4
genetics, 131
Germany, 149n18
al-Ghazālī, xxiv, xxviiin38, xxxiv, xli, 2, 14, 51n99, 86n49, 126n13
Gillet, Lev, 81n37, 138
Glover, Edward, xxii, xlviin9, 94n1
gnomic will (*thelēma gnōmikon*), 45, 48: opposed to natural and divine will, 45n72
gnosis. *See* God, knowledge of
God: ardor for, in Orthodoxy, xlix, 134; ardor for, in Sufism, 122; children of, 46; as creator, 44; desire for, 48–49, 83–84, 108; devotion of the senses to, 90; disclosure of, 149; estrangement from, 4, 44, 89n60; the Father, 9; fear of, 128, 144; fleeing from, 68; knowledge of (Ar., *maʿrifa*; Gr., *gnōsis*), 14, 14n13, 51n99, 103–105; as light, 97; love of, 98, 102–104, 109, 121, 123; participation in (Ar., *taʾalluh*; Gr., *theosis*), xxxvi, xxxviii, 46, 105, 109; passible part of the psyche as sacrifice to, 102; presence of, 68; remembrance of, 65, 92; as scientist, 60n116; striving towards, 57, 141; transference of the passions towards, xxvi–xxviii, xlixn14, 93, 98–99, 101, 103–109, 111n68, 112, 118, 121, 128, 130–132, 135, 142, 144; union with (*ittiḥād*), xxiv, xli, xlix, 4, 14, 123, 151, 160; witnessing to (*mushāhada*), xxiv–xxv, 14, 14n13, 85; worship of, 103, 125, 134
Gogol, Nikolai, 131n2
Gospels. *See under* Scriptural references, Gospels
Great Fast, 15n17, 16, 67n4, 68n5, 95, 139n17
Gregorios bin al-ʿIbrī, 156
Gregory Dialogos, 86n51
Gregory of Nyssa, 46, 80: on transference, 97, 99n16
Gregory Palamas, 154–155: aggression instinct, 117; asceticism and, xx–xi; baptism of repentance and, 91n64; beauty and, 25–26; body as living sacrifice and, 102; confession and, 146; death of, 99n16; dispassion and, xxix, 102; divine light and, 97, 100n20, 111; Eucharist and, 145–146; evil and, 123; Freudian psychoanalysis and, xlviii; Hausherr and Jugie's critique of, 119, 138; hesychasm and, xx–xi, 127; interconnectedness of body and psyche and, 99, 121–123; Jabbour's citation of, ix, 161; John Meyendorff and, 119; passible part of the psyche and, 121–122; passions and, 49n92; Pentecost and, 15n16; *Philokalia* and, xx–xi; repression and, 117; reproduction and, 46–47; tears of repentance and, 144; transference and, 99–100, 121, 161; transferring the passions to God and, xvii, xxxviii, 100–105, 121–123, 144; Transfiguration and, 10, 123; translation of, ix; unity of the human and, 123
Gregory the Theologian: advancement of the good and, 157; baptism by tears (repentance) and blood (martyrdom) and, 87, 143–145; creation of the human and, 26; death and, 3n5; death of, 99; Evagrios and, 153; Gregory Palamas and, 99, 144; the Nativity and, 43; purification of the psyche and, 104; repentance and, 143–145; transference toward God and, 144
Grehan, James, xxxviiin75
Guillaumont, Antoine, 138
guilt, sense of (Ar., *shuʿūr bi-l-dhanb*; Ger., *Schuldbewusstein*), 159: aggression instinct and the, 28, 33; children and the, 58–61; confession and the, 71, 134; conscience and the, 134; Jabbour and the, xxv–xxvi; liberal classes and the, 59; monastics and the, 72, 74–75, 96, 131, 134; repentance and the, 13; repression and the, 61; spiritual life and the, 62–64, 68; shame and the, 25, 32–33, 96

Habīb, Iskandar (friend of the author), 123n5
Haddad, Gibril Fouad, 7n13
halal, 33, 51
haram, 33n9
Hausherr, Irénée, xx, xlvi, xlix, 81, 119, 127, 137, 146
Hauter, Ashwak, xxxiin51
heart (*qalb*), 159–161: ambivalence and the, xl; blood pressure and heart rate, 125; capaciousness of the, xxviii, 61n120; conscience and the, 35; evil and the, 37; hardness of, 112n71, 114–115; Ibn al-ʿArabī and the, xxxvn62; illumination of the, by divine light, 97, 127, 139; Jesus Prayer and the, 128, 134; joy and the, 138; *khalīlī* and the, xxxv; love and the, 125; melancholy and the, xli; monastic and the, 72, 134; openness of, 81; passions and the, 41; Pentecost and the, 15; psyche and the, 117; purification of the, 38, 97; restoration of God to the, 157; as site of transference of self-love into divine

desire, xxviii; spirit and the, 39n34; turning of the, 33n8, 39n31, 58n115; 61n120, 92n68
Heidegger, Martin, 102n28
hesychasm (Ar., *hudū'iyya*; Gr., *hesychia*), xx, xxin15, 155, 160: divine light and, xxix, 100, 161; the heart and, xxviii; Mary's bearing of Christ as, 47n81; Mount Athos and, 119–120; *nafs* and xxvii; participation in God and, 41; prayer and, xxvii, 126–128, 137; stillness and, xlviin10, 27n20, 160. *See also* Gregory Palamas; Jesus prayer
Hesychius of Sinai, 81
higher powers, xxvii–xxviii, 84–85, 100n21
Hobbes, Thomas, 51n97
hollow (*jawf*), 55, 160
homelessness, 49n93
Hume, David, 7n12

Ibn Abī al-Dunyā, xxxviiin75
Ibn al-'Arabī, xxiii, xxxiii, xxxv, 10n1, 44n71, 51n99, 133n4
Ibn al-'Ibrī, Gregorios, xxiv, 14, 156
Ibn Kathīr, 92n67
Ibn Kātib Qayṣar, 96n4
Ibn Khaldun, ln17, 50n94, 96n4, 126n12
Ibn al-Muqaffa', 53
Ibn Sīnā, 126n13
icon, 56n112, 72
id (Ar., *huwa*; Ger., *Das Es*), xxi, xxixn42, 22, 27, 160
idolatry, 18, 70, 103, 115
Ignatius of Antioch, 85
Ignatios Xanthopolous, 15n16
illness, psychological: ambivalence and, 36n14; the body and, 95, 117, 123–124, 126; diagnosis of, xlviii, 123–124; childhood and the development of, xlviii, 122; nervousness and nervous disorders: 25, 62, 95, 126–128; psychological trauma and, 84–85; religious education and, 99; sadism and masochism as, 69; self-infliction of, 62; sense of guilt and, 63; sexual instinct and, 111; spirituality as, 57; whisperings and, 11
illness, physical: 3, 29, 62, 95
illumination. *See* divine illumination
image. *See* divine image
imaginal, xxxiv
imagination, xxxiii, 107
immortality. *See* eternal life
incensive part of the psyche (Ar., *al-qism al-ghaḍabiyya*; Gr., *to epithymitikon*), 100–101, 128, 160: appetitive and, 123; the body and, 122; repression of, 122; transformed into love, 108–110, 122; transformed into patience, 101; transference of, toward God, 101, 107–109, 122
incorruption, 26, 39, 48, 106
individual (*shakhṣ*). *See* personhood
instinct (Ar., *gharīza*; Ger., *Instinkt*), xl, 4, 62, 109, 117, 124n7, 159: aggression, 28, 117, 124n7; conscience and, 59; death, 124n7; life, 124n7; repression and, 74, 100, 111; sexual, 74, 124n7
instinctual drive (*gharā'iz*), xxvii, 111, 132, 159
Institute of Psychosomatic Medicine (Paris), li
intellect (*'aql*), 5, 9, 12–13, 41n46, 159; evil thoughts polluting the, 66, 72, 74; dignity of the, 106
intelligible world, 39n34, 102, 107, 109
internet, 49
Iqbal, Basit, xviiin7
Isaac of Ninevah. *See* Isaac the Syrian
Isaac the Syrian, xlviii, 153: citation by Jabbour, xvi, xxiv; influence on Gregorios Ibn al-'Ibrī, 156; influence on Gregory Palamas, 155; lamentation by, 74; pure prayer and, 14–15; translation of works by, 136n10; tears of repentance and, 145
Isaiah (prophet), 68, 157
Islam: created world and, 73n19; discernment and, 51n99; divine disclosure and, 10; divine light and, 126; divine names and, 7n13, 40n38, 44n68, 59n116; divine truth (*al-ḥaqq*) and, 48; Eid al-Adha, 52n100; God's relationship to humans and, xlixn13; inundation by the Uncreated and, 41n46; Jabbour's invocation of, xxiv, xxxiii; Jacques Lacan and, xxiii; knowledge of God and, 26; martyrdom and, 86; psyche, soul, and spirit in, 39; Orthodox Christianity and, xxxiii, xxxviiin75; psychoanalysis and, xxvin35, xxxiii; remembrance of God and death and, 92n67; as secular clinic, xxxii; righteous action (*iḥsān*) and, 70n10; spiritual discipline in, 2; transference in, xxvin35; unconscious and, xlin1. *See also* Qur'ān, *ṣūfī* (mystic, *khalīlī*), Sufism
isolation, 70n11
Israel: occupation of Palestine by, xviii, 20n29
Isṭfān, Gregorios, xxin15, 101n21

Jabbour, Spiro: confession by, 142; eulogy for, xliii; madness for Christ and, xli, xliv; Orthodox Youth Movement and, xliii; spiritual struggle of, xliv; translations of the Scriptures by, xvi
Jabbour, Spiro, works by: "Ambivalence", 54; *Ape or Human?*, xlvi, 5n10; *The Counterfeits*, 46, 71, 140; *Disclosures in the Construction of Faith*, 3n5, 43; "Discussions on philology and ambivalence in language", 55; *God Is with Us, Submit Yourselves*, 155; *The Jesus Canon*, 123n4; *Jesus or Yahweh?*, 81n37; "L'homonymile des Addad", 54; *Monastic Confession*, liii; *The Mystery of the Divine Economy*, 3n5, 6n11, 46, 121, 132n3, 156; *On Repentance*, 17n23, 30n2, 123, 156; "The Psychoanalytic Interpretation of Contronyms", xxii, 112n72
James (apostle), 9–10, 65, 74–75. *See also* apostles
Jameson, Fredric, xxxiin54
Jerusalem, xvn1, xviin4, 18–19, 81n36, 153
Jesus Christ: as Adam, 40; baptism and, 15; bravery and, 23; crucifixion with, 139; death of, xxix, 48, 71, 113, 139, 140, 148–149; human nature of, 47, 113; incarnation of, 43, 45, 47–48, 71, 113; as life-giving spirit, 40; as Logos, 108; Monothelitism and, 18n24; obedience of, 113; passibility and, 113; passion for, 70n11; resurrection of, xxix, 139, 148–149; resurrection with, 139; transference to, 142. *See also* Jesus Prayer; *Logos, logos, legein*; transfiguration
Jesus Prayer (*ṣalāt yasū'*), 80, 119–120, 126–128, 160: ancient origins of, 80–81, 137–138; Gregory of Sinai and the, 154; remembrance and, 134; Russian additions to the, 80; transference and, xxvii. *See also* hesychast prayer
Job, 68
John the Baptist, 10, 15
John Cassian, xlvii–xlviii, 155: on confession, 145
John Chrysostom, 88–89, 91–93, 96n3, 146, 156
John Climacus, xlvii–xlviii, 153: appetitive and incensive parts of the psyche and, 128n17, 144; communal monastic life and, 76; dreams and, 89; icon of the *Ladder*, 56n112; influence of Evagrios on, 152; Jabbour's citation of, xxix; Jesus prayer and, 119; passions and, 49n92; prayer and, 9n5, 80–81, 119; remembrance of death and, 2n2; remembrance of God and, 101n23; tears of repentance and, 145. See also *Ladder of Divine Ascent, The*
John of Damascus, 12n6, 155
John the Evangelist (apostle), li, 9–10, 77, 101n24, 140. *See also* apostles
John Kolobos (Desert Father), 140–141
John of Scythopolis, 43
Jones, Ernest, xxii, 24n12, 112
joy, xli, xlvi, 147–151: as first fruit of the Holy Spirit, 148; grief turning into, 138; lamentation and, xxix; repentance and, 139, 147–151
Jugie, Martin, xx, xxin15, 119, 127, 138
Jung, Carl, xxviin36, xlvii, 8

Kallistos of Athos, 15n16
Kamāl, Ribḥī, 54–55
Kant, Immanuel, 7n12, 24n10, 99n18, 143, 150
Kāshānī, 'Abd al-Razzāq al-, xxxvi
Kassatly, Houda, xviiin5
kenosis, 140
Kesel, Marc De, xxiii
khalīlī, 44n71, 46n78, 47n84, 90n62, 105n44: Jabbour's usage of, xxxiv–xxxvii, xl, xlviiin11, xl
Khodr, Georges, xviin4
Kierkegaard, Søren, 6n11
kingdom of God, 40, 75, 98
Kirchmeyer, Jean, 85
knowledge of God. *See under* God
Krafft-Ebing, Richard von, 69n9
Kyriakos, Ephraim, xviii, xli, xliii–xliv, xlix, 135

La Rochefoucauld, François de, xixn9, 51, 79n34
labor, 78–79
Lacan, Jacques: ambivalence of language and, xxvn30; *aphanisis* and, 24n12; drive and instinct and, 117; ego and, 78n33; egoism and self-love and, xixn9; *faille* and, 71n14; Ibn al-'Arabī and, xxiii; Jabbour and, xxiii; La Rochefoucauld and, 51n98; sadism and masochism and, 69n9; sexuation and, 110n67; sublimation and, 110n65; transference and, xxxix, 24–25nn12–13
Ladder of Divine Ascent, The: childrearing and, 56; dreams and, 89, 96; Jabbour and, xlvii; Jesus Prayer and, 80–81; monastic obedience and, 83; remembrance of death and, 2n2; remembrance of God and, 101n23; tears of repentance and, xxix, 74–75, 144–145; transference and, 103, 101–142. *See also* John Climacus
lamentation. *See* tears of repentance
Laplanche, Jean, xxxix
Last Supper, xlv
law, xxxix, 139: of creation, 41, 44; of God, 23n4, 24n10, 42; moral, xxviii

Lazarus (of Bethany), 15
Lazarus and the rich man, 112n71, 114–115, 144
Lebanon, xvi, xlvin6: civil war in, xvi, xviii, 50, 136n8; construction and destruction of, 50; French occupation of, xvii; identity cards in, 142; monasticism in, 136n8; oath-taking in, 51n96; Orthodox and monastic revival in, xviii, xix
Leirvik, Oddbjørn, 35
Lemerle, Paul, 156
Lent. *See* Great Fast
libido, xxv, xxvii, xxixn42, 23n4, 112
light of Tabor. *See* divine light
likeness. *See under* divine image
liturgy, *See* Divine Liturgy
Logos, logos, legein (Ar., *nuṭq*), xi–xii, 102n28, 108–109
Longinos, 88
Lord's Prayer, 24n11
Lossky, Vladimir, xx–xxi, xxxviin71, 6n11, 7n12, 155
Louth, Andrew, xxxvi, xxxviiin74
love, 160: affectivity and, 13, 122; ambivalence and, xxvn27, xxvii, 32–33, 37; animals and, 132–133; anti-egoism as, 107; of the body, 112, 131; childrearing and, 79; divine disclosure and, 97; divine love, 43, 44, 77 108–109, 149; of eating, 30, 118; egoism and, 79; family and, 32, 62; of food, 95; of gambling, 95; gendered love, 77; God as, 13, 77; of God, xlixn14, 98, 101–105, 108–109, 121, 123, 131, 157; the heart and, 125; interlocution and, 133; Jesus Christ and, xxix, 139, 141; marriage and, 43, 78–80, 122; martyrdom and, 84; monastics and, 73; of one's neighbor, 102–105, 121; neurosis and, 25; psyche as sacrifice of, 122; pure prayer and, 9; repression and, 122; self-love (Ar., *athara*; Gr., *philautia*), xixn9, xli, 30, 41, 44–45, 51, 62–63, 83, 106, 113, 115, 128–129, 159; sense of guilt and, 60–61; senses and, 72; sex and, 77–78, 92, 122; spiritual guidance and, 76, 80; transference and, xl, 98, 100–101, 108, 110, 131–133; violence and, 49, 78. *See also under* virtues
lower powers, xxvii–xxviii, 84–85, 100n21, 109, 112

Macarius (the Syrian), 156
MacDonald, D.B., 11n2
madness, xxxiii, 60
madness for Christ, xli, xliv
Makarios the Egyptian, 87, 156
Manichaeanism, 42
Mark the Ascetic, 80
marriage: age and, 60n117; control and, 78; egoism and, 79–80n34, 116; excessive affection and, 78; freedom and, 78; mystery and, 43; repression and, 122; respect and, 66, 78; sex and love in, 49, 122; of the soul to Christ, 141; the unblemished and, 85n46; union with God and, 42n58; virtue and, 73; of women artists, 92
Martin (of Tours), Saint, 69n9
Marty, Pierre (friend of the author), li
martyrdom (*shahāda*), xxiv, 18, 84–86: 86–91, 131, 161: asceticism as, 87, 90–91; as baptism by blood, 87, 144; confession as, 23, 25; of conscience, 85, 87; Maximos and, 19–20; monasticism as, 84–87, 131; as murder, 87n52, 114; Palestinian oppression as, 91n65; rushing into, 87n52, 114; as self-love or egoism, 87n52, 114; spiritual struggle as, 86–91; truth and, 85, 87n52; unwillingness to die as martyr, 70; virginity as, 88
Mashriq, 150–157; as cradle of Christian theology, 156; ecclesiastic terms in the, 17n22; postcolonial revival in the, xvii, xx; religious fragmentation in the, 50; social struggle in, xx, xli, 92n69
masochism, 69n9
Matthew (apostle), 96n3. *See also* apostles
Mauriac, François, 143
Maximos the Confessor, 152–153: Abraham (*khalīl*) and, 44n71; appetitive and incensive powers, 43, 107–110, 123, 128; asceticism and, 105–109, 113; *athara* and, 159; baptism and, 105; as confessor, 18; corruption of the human and, 43, 46–48, 106; creation of the human and, 26n16; divine illumination and, 97, 109, 111, 123; divine love and, 109; free choice and, 44, 105; Freud and, 109–114, 128n17; gnomic will and, 45n72; influence on other ascetic writers, 152–155; intelligible and unintelligible and, 109, 112; knowledge of God and, 105; life and death of, 18–20, 23; *maʿqūl* and, 160; marriage and, 42; monastic obedience and, 83; participation in the divine and, 123; passions and, 14, 41–49, 83, 106–109, 111; pleasure principle and reality principle and, 112–113; psychoanalysis and, xxin48, 110–114; pure prayer and, 14; repression and, 111; self-love and, 30nn2–3, 41, 44, 107, 113n77, 114–115, 128; sexual act and pleasure and, 42–43, 56; sublimation and, 110–111; theosis and, 46n76, 105; transference and, 97, 99, 106–109, 111–115, 161; transgression and, 41, 45, 48, 56, 105–109, 114; as true penitent, 14; unity of the human and, 123; virtues and, 106–107

memory, 11, 23. *See also* forgetting
Meyendorff, John, xx, 25n14, 47n81, 97n7, 119
Mian, Ali Altaf, xxvin35
Migne, Jacques-Paul, 81n36
mind (*dhihn*), 2, 12, 13, 65, 97, 109, 159
Monastery of Mār Georgios (Dayr al-Ḥarf, Lebanon), xv–xvi, xviii, xliii, 57
Monastery of Mār Girgis (al-Mishtāya, Syria), xv, ln17
Monastery of Mār Ya'qūb (Lebanon), xviii
Monastery of Ruqād al-Sayyida (Bkiftīn, Lebanon), xvi
monastic elders. *See* spiritual elders
monastic (*rāhib*), 152–157, 159–161: asceticism and, xxvi, 66, 76, 80–81, 87, 92; body and, 66, 84, 132; confession and, 87, 94–96, 130–131, 133–135, 138, 145; as confessor, 17n23, 18, 131n2, 95n2; hesychasm and, 119–120; as image of Christ, 73; as living Gospel, 73; martyrdom and, 85–87; as non-possessor, 72, 132; obedience and, 23, 82–83, 120, 140; repentance and, 141; repression and, 94; Russia and, 21; sense of guilt and, 72, 74–75, 131; sexual feelings and, 90; social relations between, 76–77; spiritual struggle and, xxvi, 23, 72–77, 82–84, 107, 125, 132–133; stillness and, 28n20; tears of repentance and, 74–75, 147; virginity and, 73; withdrawal and, 17, 72–73; women artist as, 92. *See also under* confession; hesychasm; hesychast prayer; Mount Athos; spiritual elder; spiritual guidance
Monothelitism, 18n24, 19, 153
Moore, Lazarus, 133
mortality. *See* death
Moses, 11, 15
mothers: analysts as, 135; betrayal of, 33; childrearing and, 12, 31, 54, 56–57, 60, 78–79, 115–117, 124, 128; hesychast prayer as mother's embrace, 127–128; impurity of, 39; souls as, 88; spiritual elders as, 82. *See also* breastfeeding; childbearing; childrearing; family; fathers; Mother of God
Mother of God, 52: conception of, 46–47; psyche/soul as, 47
Mounier, Emmanuel, 6n11
Mount Athos: ascetic literature and, xlviii; Gregory of Sinai and, 154; hesychasm and, 99, 119–120, 126n11, 137, 160; Jabbour and, xlvi, xlix; monasticism on, 136; Orthodox asceticism on, xx; Palamas and, 145, 154; Jesus Prayer and, 81, 134n7, 137; as site of renewal in the Orthodox world, 127, 140; Theophan the Recluse and, 128n15; training of priests and elders on, 80, 135, 140, 143; transference and, 97; *Way of the Pilgrim* and, 21n1
Mount Tabor: Mount Athos as new, 127; Transfiguration on, 9–10, 100n20, 123, 127, 140, 148n14, 161
Murad, Yusuf, xxxiii, xxxv, xxxviiin75
murder; aggression instinct and, 124; Cain and Abel, 49; Ibn al-Muqaffa' and, 53; Indira Ghandi and, 53; martyrdom as, 87n52, 114; sex and, 78; as transgression, 16–17, 41, 52, 65
Murqus, Elias, xliii–xliv
al-Mutanabbī, 19n25, 52
mystics (*al-mutaṣawwifūn*). See *ṣūfī* (mystic, *khalīlī*); Sufism

nafs (psyche/soul), xxvi–xxvii, xxx, xlvi, 160: asceticism and the, 74n17; breath and the, 81n38; as living soul, 39n33, 40; *gnōmē* and the, 88n57, 105n43; grammatical gender of, 141n25; neurosis and the, 60n118; personhood and the 6n11; spirit and, 39n34
names of God: in Islam, xxxv, xlv, 7n13, 40n38, 44n68, 59n116
narcissism (*'āshiq li-nafsuhu*), xxv–xxvi, 32, 34n10, 44n70, 114
Neoplatonism, 155
neurosis (Ar. *al-'uṣāb al-nafsī*; Fr. *psychonévrose*), xxviii, 11n2, 22, 25n12, 60n118, 111
New Testament. *See* Scriptural references
Nicene Creed, 23n6
Nicholson, R., xlixn13
Nikiphoros (hesychast), 155
Nikodemos of Athos, 21
Noah, 15
noetic part of the psyche (*al-'aqiliyya*), 100n21, 109n64
North America, 49n93
Novatus, 143
nuclear warfare. *See* atomic bomb

Optina Monastery, 21, 130n2, 136–137, 143
Origen (of Alexandria), 85, 87n52, 114, 141n26, 152: not rushing into martyrdom, 87n52, 114
orphans, 133
Orthodox Christian clergy, 17n23, 73
Orthodox Christian doctrine, 18, 20
Orthodox Christian revival in the Mashriq, xvii–xviii, xix. *See also* Orthodox Youth Movement
Orthodox Christianity and Islam, xxxiii–xxxiv, xxxviiin75
Orthodox Christianity and psychoanalysis. *See* psychoanalysis and Orthodox Christianity

Orthodox Youth Movement (MJO), xv, xvii, xix, xxxin48, xliii, 135–136, 156n12
oversight. *See* superego

Palestine, xvii–xviii, xlviii, 20n29, 91n65, 152–153
pan-Arabism, xviii
Pandolfo, Stefania, xxvn28, xxxiii, xln81
paradise: counterfeit, 33; Fall from: 8–9, 29, 56; in or outside the body, 90; Jesus Christ opening, 139n17. *See also under* Adam; Adam and Eve
Pascha, 15n17, 148n13
passible part of the psyche (*to pathētikon*), 41: body and spirit joined by the, 103, 121–122; Jesus Christ and, 113; as living sacrifice, 121–122; as mediators, xxvii–xxviii; stilling of the, xxix; tears of repentance and, 145; transference of the, 99–103, 121, 122
passions (*ahwā'*), 159: abusiveness, 66; aggression, 28, 33, 36, 36n14, 76–77, 79, 82, 112n71, 124–125, 131; ambition, 112n71, 115; anger, 61, 67, 72, 76–77, 82, 100, 108, 124–125, 128, 131; appropriation, 51; ardor, 32, 72, 76, 95, 114, 132; arrogance, 16, 30, 61, 63, 82–83, 83n41, 126, 129; avarice, 51, 103, 115; betrayal, 33–34, 38, 51, 53; bitterness, 126; conceit, 72; contempt, 66; counterfeiting, 4, 12n7, 33, 51n99, 60–61, 70–71; covetousness, 30; cruelty, 62, 79; deception, 33, 51, 80, 115; defamation, 35; despair, 157; discontentment, 3, 35–36, 77, 79, 126; disdain, 67, 77; disgust, 77; disobedience, 38, 44, 142; disregard, 69n8; dissatisfaction, 83; dissemblance, 38, 51; dissimulation, 115, 150; egoism (*anāniyya*), 25, 30–31, 51, 61, 63, 66, 79, 83; ennui, 3, 77, 83; envy, 24, 30, 34, 62, 77; exasperation, 76; extremism, 84, 123, 128, 130; familiarity, 66–67; flattery, 35; gluttony, 62–63, 66; gossip, 35; greed, 51, 63; grief, 125; grudge, 127; harshness, 79; hate, 37, 73, 77; hopelessness, 130; hypocrisy, 142, 150; idleness, 79; impertinence, 126; impurity, 38, 103; indifference, 3n4, 66–67, 69n8, 115; infidelity, xxxiv, 126; iniquity, 38, 68, 70–71, 142, 144, 150; injustice, 52; insolence, 63, 126; jealousy, 31, 34, 62, 77–78, 79n34, 146; justification, 68, 144; laziness, 68n8; lying, 51; malice, 13, 36–37, 63, 103, 124–125, 127; melancholy, xxvi, xxix, xli, 34, 71n15, 74–75, 147, 149; mercilessness, 49–50, 82; miserliness, 18, 32, 114–115, 134n6; negligence, 69n8; nervousness, 126–127; perfidy, 51; pride, 3, 24–25; 30, 61, 63, 70–72, 126, 146; profligacy, 103; rancor, 125; resentment, 53, 61n120; restlessness, 79, 83, 126; rudeness, 66; sadness, 125; scorn, 77; self-admiration, 69–71; self-importance, 1, 63; self-interest, 63; self-love (Ar., *athara*; Gr., *philautia*), xixn9, xli, 30, 41, 44–45, 51, 62–63, 83, 106, 113, 115, 128; self–satisfaction, 64; slander, 33, 35, 36n14, 52–53; slowness, 69n8; stinginess, 114; suspicion, 51, 52, 108; tepidity, 69n8; torpor, 82; utilitarianism, 51, 79; vainglory, 89n60, 129; vehemence, 49, 124–125; viciousness, 50; violence, 79, 83n41, 124, 132; weariness, 77, 79, 83; worry, 79, 125–126; wrath, 61n120, 76–77
Patriarchate of Alexandria, 18
Patriarchate of Antioch, xv–xvii, xxxliii, 18, 20, 92, 136
Patriarchate of Constantinople, 18–19
Patriarchate of Jerusalem, xv, 18, 153
Patriarchate of Rome, 18
Paul (apostle), 26n16, 153–154: bodily corruption and, 39; bravery and, 23; confession and, 24; death and, 4; death of the passions and, 103; gendered passion and, 77; heaven and, 90; intelligible worship and, 102–103; joy and, 147–148; life in the Trinity and, xlv; monastic as non-possessor and, 132; presence of God and, 68; reproduction and, 45, 47; self-love and, 30nn2–3; as transgressor, 13, 16, 40–41, 68, 74; war between spirit and body and, 57, 62; tears of repentance and, 74
Pegon, Joseph, 109
Pentecost, xlv, 10, 15, 18, 139n17
perception, xx, 11n4
personalism, xlvin6, 6n11, 46n6
personhood (*shakhṣiyya*), 6, 8–9, 11–13, 22, 26, 28, 90
Peter (apostle), 9n4, 10, 19, 103. *See also* apostles
Peter of Damascus, 67
Pfister, Oskar, xxii, xlvii
Pharisees, 129, 144
Phillip (apostle), xlv, l–li
Philokalia, xx, xxviii, 21–22, 81n36
Pilate, Pontius, 23
Plato, 110n65, 152, 155
Plautus, 51n97
pleasure principle, xxix, 34n10, 112–113
Pontalis, Jean-Bertrand, xxxix

prayer: absolution and, xxx, 138; asceticism and, 92; as crucifixion of the body, 90; crucifixion of Jesus Christ and, 148; fasting, vigil, and, xxvi, 80–81; Great Fast and, 67, 139n17; the heart and, 128n15; hesychasm and, 80–81, 119–120, 126–128; illumination of the eyes of the spirit and, 145; labor and, 79–81; monastics and, 73, 75, 80; Mount Athos and, 80–81; overeating as enemy of, 118; *Philokalia* and, 21; prostration and, 68; pure prayer, xlix, 9, 14, 75, 104, 118, 126–127, 157; as remembrance, 133n4; repentance and, 140; theologians and, 137; transference toward God and, 79, 118. *See also names of individual prayers*

prayer of the heart. *See* Jesus prayer

prayers before communion, 67

preconscious, xxi

priests: confession to, 24–25, 95n2, 138, 160; priests as apostles, 137, 146; priests as guardian angels, 136; psychological examination of, 136; as rational sacrifices, 103; responsibilities of, 135–138; training of, 135–136

prodigal son, 16, 33n9

prostration, xxxix, 67–68, 125

Pseudo-Dionysius the Areopagite, 154–155

Pseudo-Makarios the Syrian: death and, 86; death of, 99n16; divine illumination and, 97n9; influence on Nikiphoros, 155; love for God and, 98; Pentecost and, 15n16

psyche, xxx–xxxi, 160, 161: abuse of the, 63; affectivity and the, 123; ambivalence and the, 54, 110n66; childhood and the, 24; confession and the, 25; control over the, 62; development of the, 5, 55–57; dispassion and the, xli, 100, 102; divine desire and the, 104; examination of the, 68; Freud and the, xxvii, 112; the heart and the, 117; Jesus Christ and the, 47; labor and the, 79; masochistic, 69; monastics and the, 17, 74, 82, 120; obedience and the, 120; passible parts of the, xxvii–xxviii, xxix, 99–103, 121–122; passions and the, 106; pleasures and the, 88; prayer and the, 81; psychoanalysis and the, xlviii; putting to death the, xxix, 72, 86, 100, 149; repentance and the, 13, 91n64; repression and the, 122; sexual function and traumas to the, 122; spiritual struggle and the, xxvi, 62, 67, 78, 90, 101; tears of repentance and the, xix; transference and the, 96n5, 98, 144; union with God and the, 123; virginity and the, 98; virtues and the, 106; watchfulness and the, xli. *See also* body and psyche; *nafs*; soul

psychiatric patients. *See* psychological illness; psychoanalytic therapy

psychoanalysis: Islam and, xxx–xxxviii; the Middle East and, xxx–xxxiv; religion and, xxxi–xxxiii. *See also* ambivalence; *aphanisis*; castration; characterology; collective unconscious; consciousness; cure; dreams; drives; ego; free association; Freud, Sigmund; Freud, Sigmund, works by; Glover, Edward; id; isolation; Jones, Ernest; Jung, Carl; Lacan, Jacques; libido; narcissism; neurosis; Pfister, Oskar; pleasure principle; preconscious; psychoanalysis and Orthodox Christianity; psychoanalytic therapy; reaction formations; Real; reality principle; regression; repression; sublimation; superego; sexuation; suppression; talking cure; transference; uncanny; unconscious

psychoanalysis and Orthodox Christianity: analysis and confession/spiritual guidance, xxvii, xxxix, 17, 22, 28n20, 71, 94, 131, 133, 135; analyst and spiritual elder, xxvii, 94, 135; the conscious and the intelligible, 112; Freud and Maximos, 109–113; narcissism and self-love, 114; openness during analysis and confession, 137; pleasure principle and reality principle, 112–113; psychological development in Freud and passibility in Maximos, 111; repression, 117, 120; resonances between, xviii–xli, xxxin48, xxxix, xlvi–xlvii; sexual repression and illnesses of the soul, 122; training of analysts and confessors, 136; transference, xxvi, xxviii, xxxviii–xxxix, xl, 9n5, 63, 100–101, 104–112, 115, 121, 128, 130–131; the unconscious and the unintelligible, 112; union with the Uncreated, xli

psychoanalytic therapy (*taḥlīl*), 59, 161: analyst as physician of the soul, 135; character of the patient and, 131; confession and, xxvii, xxxix, 17, 71, 94, 131, 133, 135; dreams and, 89–90, 96; relationship between analyst and analysand, 27–28, 59, 72; repression and, 27–28; as talking cure, xxi, xxx, xli, 137; transference between analyst and analysand, xxvi, 111, 133

psychosomatic medicine, xxvii, xlix, 121–129

psychotherapy, 133, 135

publican, 16, 144

Qatar, 153

Quasten, Johannes, 153

Qur'ān, 47n82: Abraham (*khalīl allāh*) in the, xxxv; divine names in the, 7n13; *jawf* in the, 55n111; Qur'ānic cure, xxxiii; recitation of the, 154n5; remembrance of God and death in the, 92n67; resemblance in the, 12n7; righteous action in the, 70n10; the world in the, 73n19

Rank, Otto, 111n69
reaction formations (*Reaktionsbildung*), xl, 100
reading, as addiction, 117–118
Real, the, xxvi, xxxv, 48n91
reality principle, 113
regression, 28n21, 94
Renard, John, xxxv
repentance (Ar., *tawba*; Gr., *metanoia*), 15: ambivalence and, 36; apostasy and, 143; asceticism and, 75, 91; baptism and, 13, 139, 142, 144; baptism of, 10, 139, 144; Catholicism and, 22; confession and, 13, 94, 137–138; death and, 7; Eucharist and, 146; Gospels and, 13; hypocrisy and, 142; Jabbour and, xxiv, liiin1; joy and, 139, 147–151; martyrdom and, 91; monasticism and, 94; as resurrection, 139; spiritual struggle and, xxxviii, 13, 75, 139–141, 149; true Christian as true penitent, 139; violence of, 13
repression: ambivalence and, 36; of the body, 84; childhood and, 22, 74, 94, 117–118, 122, 130; cultivation of character and, 33; ego and, 27; Ernest Jones and, 112n72; European Christianity and, 99–100; Evagrios and, 109; excessive labor and, 79; free association therapy and, 27; Freud and, xxv, xxxix; hypocrisy and, 61; incensive power and, 122; instinctual drives and, 100, 111; Jabbour and, xxv; monastics and, 94, 96, 120; psychiatric patients and, 72; psychotherapy and, 133; sense of guilt and, xxv; sexual, 122; transference and, xxviii, 111n68, 130; the unconscious and, xxi, xxxix, 27
revenge, 53–54
righteous action (*iḥsān*), 70n10, 73, 75
Rippin, Andrew, 11n2
Romania, 155
Romanos the Psalmist, 156
Roman Catholicism, xx, 8, 21, 22, 30n2. *See also* Western Christianity
Rome, 18, 19, 27n17
Russell, Norman, xxin15
Russia: hesychasm and, 119, 128n15; Jesus prayer and, 80, 119, 128; lay writings of, 130–131n2, 143; personalism and, 6n11; Philokalic revival in, 21–22; *Philosophical questions* journal, 54; monasticism and, 130–131n2, 137, 143; *ṣūfī*-ascetic character of Russian spirituality, 143n30. *See also* Dostoevsky, Fyodor; Gogol, Nikolai; Optina Monastery; Theophan the Recluse; Tolstoy, Leo; *Way of the Pilgrim*

sacrifice: Abraham and, xxxv; of animals by Jews, 102–103; apostles as, 85; body as living, 102–103; chastity and, 85; passible part of the psyche as, 102, 103, 121–122; self as, 87n52, 151
Sade, Marquis de, 69n9
sadism, 69
Safouan, Moustapha, xxxiin53
salvation, 19, 42, 46, 144, 151
Sarrūj, Ibrahīm, 135
Schmemann, Alexander, 135, 137
schizophrenia, 123n5
science (*ʿilm*), 4–6, 9, 57, 59, 131n3, 160
scientists. *See* science
Scriptural references, Acts of the Apostles, 41
Scriptural references, Epistles, 10–20, 75: Ephesians 77; Colossians, 103n34, 140n20; Corinthians, livn2, 23n5, 24, 26n16, 39, 40n39, 90n63, 101n22, 128n16, 146n46, 148, 148n9; Galatians, 45, 47n85, 62n121, 87n54, 139, 148nn11–12, 149n15, 153; 1 John, xlvi, 39; Peter, 9n4, 15; Philippians, 147; Romans, 38–39, 48n90, 68n6, 73n18, 102n27, 103; 2 Timothy, 30n2, 68n7; Titus, 145n41
Scriptural references, Gospels, ix, 10–20, 23, 75: of John, xlvn1, 19, 48n90, 114n81, 137n12, 138n15, 140; of Luke, 9n4, 16n20, 68n8, 114n82, 129n18, 144n35; of Matthew, 9n4, 19, 126n10, 140n21, 144n36; of Mark, 9n4, 87n54, 144n36
Scriptural references, Old Testament: Chronicles, 144; Ecclesiastes, 38; Genesis, 29, 37; Hosea, 103; Isaiah, xxxv, 38, 47; Job, 37–38; Jonah, 144; Kings, 37; Proverbs, 38, 144n38; Psalms, ix–x, 38, 71, 75, 115n83, 117, 140n21
secularism and psychoanalysis, xxxi–xxiii
self (*dhāt*), 2n2, 7n12, 68, 69n9
self-love. *See under* passions
senses: child development and the, 5, 9; fetal life and the, 5; God as excepted from the, 41n47; intuitive, 74; passions and the, 108; purification of the, 128; susceptibility and the, 11n4; transference of, toward God, 118
Seraphim of Sarov, 139n16
Sermon on the Mount, 68n8
sexual act: corruption and the, 46–47, 56, 78; marriage and the, 43, 78; violence and the, 78; sexual feelings versus the, 90
sexual function, effect of trauma on, 122
sexual immorality (*zinā*), 17, 103, 143
sexual impotence, 111
sexual instinct, 111, 124n7
sexual life, 62
sexual pleasure, 42–44, 46–47, 57, 78, 82
sexuation, 110n67
al-Shābushtī, xxxviii
Shah, Mustafa, 70n10
shame, 25, 32, 51, 96

Shawqi, Ahmed, 80
Sikhs, 53
Simon the Stylite, 85
Sinai, xlviii, 56n112, 152–154
Slavonic language, 21
sleep: passions and, 88, 90, 96; ascetics and, xli, 95
Smith, Michael B., xxxviiin74
smoking, 83, 117
social relations, xxv, xli, 33–34, 36, 52, 62, 82
Socrates, 132n3
Sophists, 59
Sophronios (saint), 153
soul, 159–160: as adulterer, 141; aggression instinct and the, 117; ambivalence and the, xlviin9; analyst as physician of the, 135; appetitive and incensive parts of the, 43, 122, 160; body as living, 39n33; body as lower, xxviii; body compared with the, 12n6; body of the (*sōma pneumatikon*), 39–40; bravery of the, 95; cure of the, xxxiv; Fall from paradise and the, 106; as feminine, 88; genealogy of the, 101n21; humility and the, 126; illnesses of the, 122; illumination of the, 15, 97, 109; infidelity of the, xxi; ingathering of the, 128n15; integration of body, spirit, and, xxxviii; interlocution and the, 137; labor and the, 79; lower energies of the, xxvi; martyrdom and the, 90; narcissism and the, 114; ordering of the, 120, 150; passible parts of the, 100–101, 103–104, 122, 145, 161; passions and the, 14, 24, 52, 62, 70, 88–89, 100–101, 103–104, 107, 116, 118, 124, 159; profligacy and the, 16; remembrance of death and the, 7; repentance and the, 14; science of the, xviii, xxi, xxxi, xxxix; *Seele* and, xxx; self-love and the, 114; sense of guilt and the, 33; spiritual guidance and the, 82; spiritual struggle and the, xxi, xxxix, xl, 51–52, 62, 70, 88–89, 118; tears of repentance and the, 145; theosis and the, xxxviii, xli; transference and the, xxxix, 109, 160; vigil and the, 90; as virgin mother, 88; watchfulness and the, xl, 128. *See also* body and soul; *nafs*; psyche; spirit
soul and body. *See* body and soul
Špidlík, Tomáš Josef, xlix
spirit (*rūḥ*), 160: body of the (*sōma psychikon*), 39–40; chastity of the, 123; development of the, 9; as distinguishing humans from animals, 5; ego and the, 11; integration of body, soul, and, xxxviii; Jesus Christ as, 40; life in the, 68–69; prayer and the, 127; pride and the, 3; purity of the, 66; transference and the, 96; worship of God in the, 103. *See also* body and spirit; *nafs*; psyche; soul
spiritual elder (*shaykh*), 161: psychoanalyst compared with, 94, 131; authority of, 76; characteristics of, 17, 94; as guardian angel, 136; Mount Athos and, 120, 140; obedience to, 23, 76–77, 82–83, 95, 140; openness between monastic and, 71, 82, 94, 96, 130; as physicians of the spirit, 135; relationship between monastic and, 76–77, 80, 82, 94–95, 130–131, 160; respect for, 77; sense of guilt and, 61, 131; spiritual struggle and, 84, 131–133; training of, 136–137; transference between disciple and, xxvi, 130. *See also* spiritual guidance
spiritual guidance (*irshād*), xxxiv, 76–77, 94–96, 119–120, 143, 146, 160–161: conditioning the body and nerves and, 125; confession and, 94, 146; conscience and, 134n8; priests and, 138; psychotherapy and monastic confession: 133–135; spiritual struggle and, xxvi, 23; strictness and leniency in, 4n8; training for, 136–137. *See also* confession; spiritual elders.
spiritual sight. *See* discernment
spiritual struggle (*jihād rūḥī*), 159–160: asceticism and, 86–87; academic theology and, xxi–xxii; afternoon as a time of, 83; controlling the tongue and, 65; counterfeit, xix, 71; dispassion and, 102; forfeiting one's, 17; Jabbour and, xxvi, xxix, xxx, xxxix, xli, xliv; joy and, 148; labor and, 78; martyrdom and, 86, 88–89; monastics and, 17, 107; night as a time of, 88–91, 107; sense of guilt and, 64; transference and, xxxviii; unrelenting nature of, 83, 141; virtues and, 71, 122; withdrawal and, xx
spiritual warfare. *See* spiritual struggle
Spyridon the Wonderworker, xv
St. Sergius Orthodox Theological Institute, xv
Stăniloae, Dumitru, 6n6
Strachey, James, xxvn29
sublimation (*taṣʿīd*): Freud and, 77n30, 110; illumination and, xxvii; transference and, xxvii, 110–111
ṣūfī (mystic, *khalīlī*), 161: acquisition of meekness, xl, 100; ascetics as, xxix, xlviii, xlixn12, 14, 90, 149–150; Christ's incarnation as, 47; inundation by the Uncreated, 41, 46, 90, 105; Isaac the Syrian as, 153; Jabbour's use of, xxiv, xxxvi–xxxvii, xlviiin11, 160–161; Orthodox ethics as, xl, 50, 100; Pseudo-Dionysius as, 155; Russian spirituality as, 143n30; Symeon the New Theologian as, 154; theological structure inherited from the ascetics in the Mashriq, 154; translation of, ix; waters of baptism, 105

Sufism, 160–161: Abraham (*khalīl allāh*) and, xxxv–xxxvi; divine union and, xlixn13, 4n6, 26; instinctual drive and, xxviin38; interlocution and, xxvi; inundation by the Uncreated and, 41n46; Jabbour and, xi, xxiv; *munājāt* and, 133n4; passion for God, 77n29, 123; righteous action and, 70; righteousness and, 14; *sarīra* and, 35; spiritual guidance and, xxxiv, 76; spiritual warfare and, 150; superego and, 134n8; transference and, xxxviiin75; unconscious and, xxxiii; watchfulness and, 134n8
suicide, 132
superego (Ar., *fawq al-ana*; Ger., *Über-Ich*), xxi, 22–23, 159: spiritual guidance and the, 134n8; guilt and the, xxv; repression and the, 27; spiritual watchfulness and the, xxviii
suppression, 130
Symeon the New Theologian, 154: confession and, 17n23, 95n2, 131n2; divine light and, 97, 111; incensive and appetitive powers and, 123; true penitence and, 14; weeping and, 75, 145n43, 148
Symeon the Stylite, 96, 153
Symeon the Translator, 15n16
Syria: ascetic writers from, 152–156; French occupation of, xvii; Hafez al-Assad and, xv–xvi, 53n102; identity cards in, 141; Jabbour and, xv–xviii; John Chrysostom and, 91; monasticism in, 136n8; Palestinian refugees in, 20n29; personalism in, 6n11; religious revival in, xviii, xix; swearing oaths in, 51n96; Syrian Stylites, 95

talking cure, xli, 137
Tannous, Jack, xxxviiin75
tears of repentance: asceticism and, 75; as baptism, 87, 144–145; confession and, 134; dispassion and, xxix; illumination of the eyes of the spirit and, 144–145; joy and, xxix, 74–75, 138–139, 147–149; sense of guilt and, 61n120, 134; transference and, 99; transgression and, 16–17, 143–144; virtue and, 145
television, 49
Thecla (martyr), 88–89
Theodoret of Cyrrhus, 36n14, 86n51
theologians, 137
theology, academic study of, xxi, 135–136
Theophan the Recluse, 21–22, 68n4, 128n15
Thomas, David, xxxviiin75
Tolstoy, Leo, 131n2
torture, 18, 23–24, 89, 91
Toscano, Alberto, xxxii
Toufic, Jalal, xix–xx
transcendental apperception, 7n12. *See also* Kant, Immanuel
transference (Ar., *taḥwīl*; Ger., *Übertragung*), 161: between analyst and analysand, xxxix, 111; from body to spirit, 57, 96; childrearing and, 132; divine light and, 100n20; dreams and, 110n66; ignorance and, 115; interlocution and, xxxix; Jacques Lacan and, 24n12, 25n13; of love to animals, 132–133; Maximos the Confessor and, 97, 99, 106–109, 111–115, 161; of passions toward God, xxviii, xxxviii–xxxix, xl, 9n5, 63, 100–101, 104, 108–109, 112, 121, 128, 130; senses and, 142; sublimation and, 110–111
transfiguration (*tajallī*), 161: the body and, 123; Christ's Transfiguration, 9n4, 10–11, 100n20, 123, 139n17, 140, 148n14; interlocution and, xxxix; spiritual struggle and, xl, 127, 140. *See also* divine disclosure; divine light
transgressions, 159: absolution and, 138–139, 143; Adamic error and, 8, 29, 30, 38, 41–42, 44, 56, 106, 117; apostles' authority to loose and bind, 137; the body and, 126; death and, 4, 42, 45; divine likeness and, 48; human being and, 6, 71, 151; Jesus Christ and, 45, 48, 113, 139, 148–149; Jesus Prayer and, 80, 119; Maximos the Confessor and, 107n50; monastics and, 83; Paul (apostle) and, 13, 41, 68; pride and, 63; remembrance of, 68, 68–69n8; repentance and, 13–14, 16, 22, 91n64, 139, 142–143, 149; return to, 140; saints as former transgressors, 93; sense of guilt and, 61; sexual act and, 42; spiritual struggle and, xlv, 17, 37–38, 64, 66, 74, 83, 148; as tombs for Christ, 133. *See also* confession (of transgressions)
translation into Arabic, 102, 135n10: of Alexander Schmemann, 135; of the canon of Andrew of Crete, 68; of the canon to Jesus Christ, 67n3; of psychoanalytic works, xxxiii, xxxv, xxxviiin75, 75; of the Scriptures, ix, xvi, 37n15, 38n25, 39n33, 40n39, 135n10
Trieger, Alexander, xxviin38, xxxviiin75
trust, 33–35, 52, 76

unblemished (*muḥṣinīn*), 85
uncanny, xx
unconscious (*al-lā-shuʿūr*), 5n9, 11, 161: across psychoanalysis and Orthodox Christianity, xxxi, xxxiv; ambivalence and, 33; analysis and the, 94; asceticism and the, 96; children and the, 12, 60–61; collective, 8; confession and, 96; conscience and the, 24n10; desire for punishment, 135; dreams and the, 96; drives, 114, 116; Freud and the, xxi, xxvii, xxxiii, xxxv, xxxix, xl, xlviii, 27n17, 112; heart, 35; Jabbour and the, xxi, xxxi, xxxiii,

unconscious (*al-lā-shu'ūr*) (*continued*) xxxv, xl–xli; lower energies of the soul as the, xxvii; monastics and the, 84, 96; repression and the, 22, 27, 96; as Rome/Eternal City, 27n17; sense of guilt and the, xxv–xxvi, 13n11, 60–61, 63, 96; sexual instinct and the, 111; Sufism and the, 35n11; suppression and the, 130; transference and the, 93, 96; translation into Arabic of the Freudian, xxxv
unconscious drives, 114, 116
unconscious heart (*sarīra*), 35
uncreated light. *See* divine light
unintelligible world, 109, 112
unity of the human, 134: as paradisal state, 123; psyche and body: 6, 119, 121; spiritual struggle and, 110n64; transference and, 109; as union with God, 123
unknowing (Ar., *'adam al-shu'ūr*; Fr., *inconscience*), 11

Velichkovskii, Paisii, 21
Verhovskoy, Sergei, 119
violence, 35, 78–79: against the passions, 2–3; arrogance and, 83; children and, 124; delight in, 49; Indira Ghandi and, 53; repentance and, 13; sex and, 78
Virgin Mary. *See* Mother of God
virginity, 73, 85: as martyrdom, 88; monastics and, 17; psyche and, 98; spiritual, 125; martyr Thecla and, 88
virtue: counterfeit, 24, 60–61, 70, 92, 100, 134n6; cultivation of: 36, 62, 71, 81, 83, 92, 101, 149; death and, 4; dispassion and, 100; lay people and, 73; monastics and, 80, 92; mothers and, 56; psyche and, 106; repentance and, 13, 16, 75; repression and, xxxix, 74; tears of repentance and, 17, 145
virtues: abstinence, 148; amiability, 52, 116; affection, 118; blessedness, 61; bravery, 1n17, 83–85, 95, 106, 110, 130, 135; chastity, 63, 85, 91, 95, 118, 121; compassion, 50–52, 61, 148; contentment, 36, 64; courage, 84, 98, 122; deference, 66; faith, 98; generosity, 116, 122, 134; gentleness, 9, 36, 52, 77–78, 82, 100, 116, 132; good judgment, 98, 101; graciousness, 17; honesty, 38, 61; humility, 9, 16–17, 25, 72, 74–75, 83, 83n41, 95, 99, 125–126, 144; implacability, 98; integrity, 52, 83n41; judiciousness, 112; justice, 63; kindness, 60, 77; long-suffering, 83, 98, 132; love, xxviii, xl, 16, 37, 61n120, 67, 77–78, 82, 100, 118, 132–133, 148, 157; lucidity, 106, 112; manliness (Ar., *rujūla*; Gr., *andreia*), 1n17, 82, 83n41; meekness, 17, 61, 77, 83, 100, 122, 126, 131, 148; munificence, 122; nobility, 84; obedience, 63, 72, 76–77, 124; patience, 61n120, 98, 101, 123, 127, 132; peace, 148; piety, 16, 122, 126, 138; pliancy, 37, 49, 81, 83, 93, 131, 149; purity, 37–39, 41, 66–67; righteousness, 14, 17, 24, 37, 70, 73, 75, 98, 142, 150; self-control, 78; sincerity, 34; steadfastness, 91, 98, 123, 130; submissiveness, 126; sympathy, 17, 49, 100, 116, 118; temperance, 36; tractability, 83; understanding, 98; wisdom, 72; zeal, 98
Vlachos, Hierotheos, 101n21
void (Ar., *'adam*; Fr., *faille*), xxvi, 13, 71

war with passions. *See* spiritual struggle
Ware, Kallistos, xlvi, 6n11
Ware, Timothy. *See* Ware, Kallistos
watchfulness (Ar., *yaqaẓa*; Gr., *nēpsis*), 134n8, 160–161: asceticism and, 95–96; as common to Islam and Orthodox Christianity, xxviii; dream-work and, xl–xli, 90; Jesus prayer and, 128n15; monastics and, 130, 135; pleasure and, 89; repression and, xl; sleep and, 96; sorrowful joy and, xli; superego and, xxviii; transference and, xxvii
Way of the Pilgrim, 21
wealth, 9n3, 33–34, 63, 70, 114–115, 131
Weber, Max, xxxiin54
Wedeen, Lisa, xvin2, 53n102
weeping. *See* tears of repentance
Weiss, Max, 6n11
West, the, xlvii, 6n11, 136
Western Christianity: Carl Jung and, 8n1; xxxii–xxxiii; intelligible contemplation of God in, 101; mysticism in, xxxviiin74; repressive ethics of, 99–100; as vanishing mediator between psychoanalysis and Islam. *See also* Roman Catholicism
will, 5, 109, 128, 141
Winter, Timothy, 2n2
Wittgenstein, Ludwig, x–xi

Yannaras, Christos, 6n11
Yazigi, Yūḥanna, 37–38, 135–136, 142n29, 144n32

Zā'id, Tawfīq, 54
Zander, Louis, 129n19
Zecher, Jonathan L., 2n2
Zizioulas, John, 6n11

Spiro Jabbour was a scholar and hierodeacon in the Rūm Antiochian Orthodox Church. He was born in the Syrian town of Muzayraa in 1923 and died in 2018 at the Monastery of St. George in Deir al-Harf.

Aaron F. Eldridge is a Postdoctoral Fellow in the Department of Anthropology at the University of Toronto.

Christian Arabic Texts in Translation

Stephen J. Davis, T. C. Schmidt, and Shawqi Talia (eds.), *Revelation 1–3 in Christian Arabic Commentary: John's First Vision and the Letters to the Seven Churches*

Arsenius Mikhail (ed.), *Guides to the Eucharist in Medieval Egypt: Three Arabic Commentaries on the Coptic Liturgy*

Spiro Jabbour, *Confession and Psychoanalysis*. Translated by Aaron Frederick Eldridge

www.ingramcontent.com/pod-product-compliance
Lightning Source LLC
Chambersburg PA
CBHW020403080526
44584CB00014B/1155
9781531512736